Human Killing Machines

Human Killing Machines

Systematic Indoctrination in Iran, Nazi Germany, Al Qaeda, and Abu Ghraib

ADAM LANKFORD

LEXINGTON BOOKS

A division of
ROWMAN & LITTLEFIELD PUBLISHERS, INC.
Lanham • Boulder • New York • Toronto • Plymouth, UK

LEXINGTON BOOKS

A division of Rowman & Littlefield Publishers, Inc.
A wholly owned subsidiary of The Rowman & Littlefield Publishing Group, Inc.
4501 Forbes Boulevard, Suite 200
Lanham, MD 20706

Estover Road
Plymouth PL6 7PY
United Kingdom

British Library Cataloguing in Publication Information Available

Library of Congress Cataloging-in-Publication Data

Lankford, Adam, 1979-
   Human killing machines : systematic indoctrination in Iran, Nazi Germany, al
Qaeda, and Abu Ghraib / Adam Lankford.
       p. cm.
   Includes bibliographical references and index.

   ISBN: 978-0-7391-3416-0

   1. Terrorism--Psychological aspects--Case studies. 2. Brainwashing--Case
studies. 3. Psychological warfare--Case studies. I. Title.
   HV6431.L34625 2009
   363.325--dc22   2008050204

Printed in the United States of America

♾™ The paper used in this publication meets the minimum requirements of American
National Standard for Information Sciences—Permanence of Paper for Printed Library
Materials, ANSI/NISO Z39.48–1992.

To those who taught me to question authority
and then put up with my relentless rebellious streak—
thank you for the one true inoculation against "just following orders,"
for which I'm forever grateful

Contents

Figures and Tables

Preface

People who kill and abuse others have often been characterized as inherently abnormal. This description can be comforting—it implies a fundamental distinction between good and evil, between us and them. Sometimes it's accurate: lone serial killers, for instance, often have severe mental problems rarely found in the general population. But when it comes to organized atrocities like torture, terrorism, and genocide, the evidence indicates that perpetrators of such evil are often relatively ordinary people. They do not become killers due to psychological disorders or early life traumas. They turn to violence because they are compelled to do so by a powerful system with clear goals that can be achieved through violent means.

This book shows how systems use specific strategies of recruitment, training, authorization, bureaucracy, isolation, and dehumanization to condition and indoctrinate their members. Once properly programmed, the systems' new "machines" commit acts of violence without typical moral reflection or hesitation—they dutifully perform violence on command, even when it means killing or torturing people.

By applying the framework for systematic indoctrination to the famous Milgram and Zimbardo experiments, as well as to case studies of real-world brutality in Nazi Germany, Al Qaeda, modern day Iran, and Abu Ghraib, we discover just how dangerously effective such methods can be. At the same time, the key similarities and differences between these cases reveal some of the most critical threats to global security today. Based on these findings, recommendations are made for how we can begin to reform the U.S. military and increase its accountability, shake Al Qaeda terrorists' commitment to their missions, and reverse course on Iran to bring the oppressive regime down from the inside.

Acknowledgments

Perhaps it stems from some deep-seated need for control: I've always found it easier to offer help than to seek it. I'm happy to do a favor for someone else, but asking for one—especially without offering anything tangible in return—has always felt uncomfortable. And yet, throughout the process of writing this book, I have benefited from the generous assistance of many a kind soul who looked beyond any rates of exchange.

In particular, I would like to thank Jessica Ammon, Richard Bennett, Grant Blank, Richard Breitman, Bob Briggs, David Forde, Brian Forst, Robert Jenkot, Ida Johnson, Robert Johnson, Laura Langbein, Bronwen Lichtenstein, Celia Lo, Eric Lohr, Amanda Matravers, Nicole Muscanell, Sheenal Patel, Michael Sisskin, Michael Wiles, and Jimmy Williams for their encouragement and assistance. Furthermore, this book would not have been possible without the support of The University of Alabama, where I am a proud member of the Department of Criminal Justice.

In addition, I must acknowledge my family and friends, who allow me to take them for granted without resenting it one bit and who were always ready to give me their reactions on some section I'd just written. They are invested in it because I am invested in it, plain and simple.

Finally, I must express my appreciation to a certain four-legged friend who logged the second-most hours on this venture. He was mostly asleep at my feet, dreaming of T-bone steaks and romps in the park while I read, researched, and typed, but he never complained and was simply excellent for morale.

Chapter 1
Human Killing Machines

Despite a certain degree of progress, human history has been regularly marked by violence. People have evolved in many ways over the years, with great advances in politics, art, culture, and science. However, these developments have been offset by our darker side. Simply put—people have gotten smarter, more efficient, and more effective across the board, and tactics for violence have also continued to improve. As one of Mark Twain's more compelling characters explains, "Cain did his murder with a club; the Hebrews did their murders with javelins and swords; the Greeks and Romans added protective armor and the fine arts of military organization and generalship; the Christian has added guns and gunpowder."[1]

Explosives, tanks, submarines, guided missiles, nuclear weapons, and now robotic killing machines—yes, the U.S. military actually expects a substantial fighting force of robot soldiers to be operational in less than a decade. "They don't get hungry," explains Gordon Johnson of the Pentagon's Joint Forces Command. "They're not afraid. They don't forget their orders. They don't care if the guy next to them has just been shot. Will they do a better job than humans? Yes." Robot soldiers are not just a future possibility, says Johnson: they are a certainty.[2]

Ultimately, robotic killing machines may actually prove far less dangerous than their fully human counterparts. Humans do get hungry, they do get afraid. They do forget their orders and they do care if the friend next to them has just been shot. But their biggest weakness is the way they can allow themselves to be trained, indoctrinated, and reprogrammed by powerful organizations which claim to serve the greater good. Ultimately, it is *human killing machines* and the systems which produce them that remain the greatest man-made threat to the world today.

After all, violence is at its most dangerous when it is woven into a larger system. Random violence, spurts of anger, or crimes of passion may cause harm here and there, but when violence becomes the tool of a system that sanctions it as a necessary evil, the real carnage begins.

In such cases, the well-trained agents who carry out violence are usually removed from the decision-making process—they follow orders to storm hills, sack villages, interrogate prisoners, or execute the condemned without fully weighing the implications of their behavior. Sometimes this can be good: armies need disciplined soldiers who do not question every command from above. A purely democratic setup would cripple military effectiveness. On the other hand, such unquestioning obedience can be abused with devastating consequences, as it was during the Holocaust.

The Nazis' institutionalized form of genocide was perhaps the most horrifying element of their campaign. As Tzvetan Todorov attests, "The specificity of these crimes resides . . . principally in the Nazi project of *systematic murder* . . . no real parallel can be found for the systematic destruction of the Jews and of the other groups the Nazis deemed unworthy of existence."[3] In his landmark assessment of the Nazis' deadly system, Raul Hilberg similarly points out that "Never before in history had people been killed on an assembly-line basis."[4] Instead of building cars or sewing machines, the obedient German workers produced death and destruction. Even a commander of Auschwitz confessed, "Our system is so terrible that no one in the world will believe it to be possible."[5] It is no coincidence that he did not say the German people, the Nazis, the Nazi doctors, the SS, the death camp guards, or even Hitler and his associates were particularly evil or terrible. He pointed to the *system*.

It takes a multifaceted system to indoctrinate people and produce a dutifully violent workforce, then fuse it with the best (or worst) that modern technology and modern management strategies have to offer. This is a deadly combination. Alone, even the most bloodthirsty individual could do relatively little damage with Cain's club. Give him modern weapons, and that man's destructive yield increases exponentially, but it is still relatively limited. Perhaps he can blow himself up in a crowded café, attempt to hijack an airliner and use it as a guided missile, or go berserk with a machine gun at a local school. But an ambitious, resourceful, and effective organization could use that man, along with hundreds of other people, to procure a weapon of mass destruction, gather critical intelligence on the patterns, tendencies, and weaknesses of enemies, and obtain the requisite documents and covert transportation for a savage bloodbath of unprecedented magnitude.

And of course, WMDs are not required for genocide or mass killing. A well-run organization can nearly perfect the task of killing by training its agents to carry out pre-programmed missions of violence. While purges, slaughters, and massacres were not new to the twentieth century, the Nazis used the leading weapons, transportation, and administrative techniques of that time to increase the efficiency of their bureaucratic killing process.[6] As Richard Breitman details, the Nazis combined "sophisticated technology and barbaric mass murder . . . in a highly industrialized society," with truly horrible success.[7]

In recent years, terrorist organizations have similarly combined modern technology and advanced management techniques to produce death and destruction. Despite their successes, they have yet to reach their frightening potential. In *Future Jihad: Terrorist Strategies Against America*, Walid Phares envisions the dangerous possibilities if Al Qaeda had waited seven more years before striking the U.S. on 9/11. What if they had prepared more diligently, allowed more operatives to infiltrate America, continued to exploit slumbering U.S. security officials (who only awoke after 9/11), and struck on September 11, 2008? Imagine a 9/11 with twenty-four planes being hijacked, truck and car bombs exploding at the FBI building and other significant targets, hundreds of snipers around the nation, including some armed with shoulder-fired missiles, dirty bombs in shopping malls and other public places, a widespread computer attack, and hostage-taking at local schools. In Phares' nightmare scenario, the U.S. is virtually brought to its knees, and Al Qaeda terrorists strike a much more devastating blow than they did in 2001—one which cripples the U.S. domestically and destroys much of its national infrastructure.[8] A multi-pronged attack that could wreak such devastation could only be produced through a terrorist organization's use of modern management techniques, coordinated resources, and a sufficiently indoctrinated workforce with little concern for traditional moral values.

This book exposes the coercive methods which violent systems employ to condition and control their agents. By applying a model of systematic indoctrination to two famous psychological experiments and detailed case studies of Nazi Germany, Al Qaeda, modern day Iran, and Abu Ghraib, it will reveal how relatively ordinary people in different cultures and contexts can be transformed into obedient, violence-prone agents. The analytical framework is an extension of Stanley Milgram's experiments on *Obedience to Authority*, Philip Zimbardo's Stanford Prison Experiment, Lieutenant Colonel Dave Grossman's research *On Killing*, Ervin Staub's theories on *The Roots of Evil*, Roy F. Baumeister's investigation of *Evil*, James Waller's research on *Becoming Evil*, and other leading scholarship.

The model also builds on Robert Johnson's 1986 article "Institutions and the Promotion of Violence," which outlines common links between institutional violence in a variety of contexts, including death camps, military battlefields, state prisons, police divisions, and industrial work environments.[9] Johnson explains how organizations use specific strategies of authorization, bureaucracy, isolation, insulation, and dehumanization to shape their members:

> The primary condition of institutional violence is some form of authorization to harm others by acts of commission or omission. These authorizations take hold in institutions that are organized in the form of bureaucracies which are isolated

from mainstream moral values or at least shielded from regular review and judgment in light of those values. These organizations, moreover, socialize their personnel so as to insulate them from awareness or appreciation of the moral dimensions of their behavior. Together, authorization, bureaucracy, isolation, and insulation foster dehumanization [which], in turn, is the key condition required to engage in or permit violence "without moral restraint."[10]

When implemented properly, this recipe for violence conditions employees to carry out violence on command. However, not all people are equally well suited for the job, so careful recruitment and training of new workers is critical to ensure reliable productivity. Overall, this model is particularly useful for explaining—without excusing—violence produced in institutional contexts.

While the terms Johnson uses may seem somewhat abstract, they are concepts everyone can connect to. We have all been authorized by parents or bosses to complete tasks without fully understanding why. We have all worked or played in bureaucratic team settings, where we lack control and vision over the complete process. We have all appreciated that distance and isolation allow us to keep our secrets safe. Many of us have been dehumanized by others calling us names or making fun of us, and we may have dehumanized others, calling a dishonest man a "dog" or a "snake," a tattletale a "rat," or a sloppy eater or overweight person a "pig." And many of us have experienced the pressures of overarching systems or organizations that try to influence our behavior in specific ways.

However, this book will reveal a much darker, more insidious threat than subtle social pressures. When many people undergo systematic indoctrination at the hands of an organization with violent intentions, the ethical and social restraints that typically keep them in line seem to disappear. Suddenly, it is a whole new world with "no holds barred." The organizations' new "machines" commit acts of violence without typical moral reflection or hesitation—they obediently perform brutal violence on command, even when it means abusing or killing people.

Systems, Organizations, and Institutions

This book will consider systems, organizations, and institutions in somewhat overlapping terms. For some uses, these words differ—for instance, marriage can be considered a cultural institution, but it is not really an organization. To avoid confusion, this book will primarily refer to systems and organizations, instead of institutions. However, the scholarly experts cited here and the eyewitnesses to torture, terrorism, and genocide often use all three of these terms interchangeably. Thus, the author makes a plea for semantic patience on this issue.

Beyond definitional calisthenics, it is important to recognize that the focus on systems, organizations, and institutions is one some people initially find unsatisfying—perhaps because it seems rather abstract. Waller suggests "to understand the fundamental reality of mass murder we need to shift our focus from impersonal institutions and abstract structures to the actors, the men and women who actually carried out the atrocities."[11] As he further explains, "I am not interested in the higher echelons of leadership. . . . Nor am I interested in the middle echelon perpetrators, the faceless bureaucrats. . . . I am interested in the rank-and-file killers."[12] This is not an uncommon sentiment—if, in the end, guns or systems don't kill people, people kill people, perhaps studies of those people alone are sufficient to shed light on the violent phenomenon.

Of course, life is complicated, and in our efforts to make sense of it we can be tempted by oversimplified explanations. When someone is tortured or killed, we naturally look for the immediate assailant—the guy or girl who administered the electric shocks or pulled the trigger. Not only is that person a potential threat to attack again, but he or she is also the simplest to blame and the most satisfying to punish.

However, when we dig deeper it becomes clear that focusing exclusively on the people—the rank and file killers—does not tell us nearly enough about the overall process. After all, these peoples' behavior was relatively normal until their sudden violent transformation.[13] Not too long ago, they had been rank and file secretaries, waiters, bankers, teachers, and laborers. This point raises a fundamental question: since under regular conditions, ordinary people do not go around massacring innocent populations simply because they were told to do so—by what process, event, or system are ordinary people transformed into obedient mass murderers?

Waller's answer is that it is much more than a system—his comprehensive analysis points the blame at a great range of factors including evolutionary forces and "our ancestral shadow," ethnocentrism, xenophobia, desires for social dominance, cultural belief systems, moral disengagement, rational self-interest, the context of the action, us-them thinking, dehumanization of the victims, and more.[14] There is a lot of truth in this explanation, and yet it is too awkward and unwieldy—it really focuses on much more than just "the people," and as Waller admits, he does not "clarify the relative importance of each of the components in the model."[15] Also, some of the variables Waller mentions may be of minimal value.

Ultimately, *context* appears to be the most crucial factor in explaining why ordinary people can be compelled and pressured into brutally violent acts. Both Milgram and Zimbardo have highlighted the importance of this variable. Milgram's experiments on obedience to authority indicate that in the right (or wrong) context, "ordinary people, simply by doing their jobs, and without any particular hostility on their part, can become agents in a terrible destructive process."[16] In turn, Zimbardo's prison experiments "suggest that ordinary people are capable of cruel behavior if given license by legitimate institutions."[17]

To understand how relatively normal people become rank and file killers, we must understand their context. And the primary force in their socio-psychological context is often a powerful organization with some of the specific features identified by Johnson. We cannot focus solely on the people—we must also focus on the system: the thing that steers, conditions, and motivates people with frightening efficiency and effectiveness.

Applying the Case Study Method

When it comes to social psychological studies of organizational violence, the case study method is usually preferred over quantitative analysis. Beyond Johnson's aforementioned examination of institutional violence and Waller's case studies of killers around the globe, Staub bases his analysis on case studies of the Holocaust, Armenia, Cambodia, and Argentina. Regarding his methodology, Staub recognizes that there "can be no exhaustive test of [his] conception of genocide," but suggests that the qualitative approach will allow him to "provide significant confirmation by demonstrating substantial similarities in the psychological and cultural origins of these four disparate cases."[18]

Studies of terrorist psychology often employ a similar methodology.[19] As Rex Hudson explains, this is mainly because a quantitative approach would be limited and incomplete: detailed "biographical databases on large numbers of terrorists are not readily available . . . [and] such data would be quite difficult to obtain unless one had special access to police files on terrorists around the world."[20] Hudson further notes that existing databases "contain some useful biographical information on terrorists involved in major incidents, but are largely incident-oriented."[21] For instance, in impressive fashion, Gary LaFree and the Study of Terrorism and Responses to Terrorism (START) program have developed a comprehensive database with information on the dates, locations, weapons, targets, casualties, and suspected groups in nearly 80,000 terrorist incidents.[22] And in his book, Richard J. Chasdi provides impressive statistics on Middle Eastern terrorist attacks from 1994-1999.[23] But although these types of quantitative studies can teach us a lot about terrorism from afar, they lack the depth necessary for this subject matter. As Jessica Stern explains, when exploring the violent motives and tendencies of such dangerous people en masse, there are many potential hurdles. "A rigorous, statistically unbiased study of the root causes of terrorism at the level of individuals would require . . . [a] team of researchers, including psychiatrists, medical doctors, and a variety of social scientists" to develop a bevy of surveys and trials for both test and control groups.[24]

Basing this book on quantitative analysis would lead to further problems. The main hypothesis—that specific strategies of recruitment, training, authorization, bureaucracy, isolation, and dehumanization combine to produce successful systematic indoctrination—would be extremely hard to quantify. Why? Because confirming or denying the hypothesis statistically would require a precise measure of organizational members' *willingness* to act violently. Simply the amount of violence carried out would not be enough. After all, the desire to use violence and the demonstrated use of violence are fundamentally different measures. A military division, a national government, or a terrorist group with a fully indoctrinated workforce of agents who are willing to kill on command *might never put those potential killers into action.* Most leaders analyze a range of other factors before commencing a violent campaign, including their financial resources, their weaponry, the strength or vulnerability of their adversaries, and their overall chances for success. Furthermore, some systems with fully indoctrinated agents limit the amount of violence their members are allowed to use. Abuse, but do not torture. Torture, but do not kill. Just because violent agents are willing to kill for the cause, that doesn't mean they will be allowed to do so.

Of course, if a researcher had the opportunity, he or she might try to measure agents' willingness to act violently through surveys. But even this approach would be flawed, for the agents themselves are often not fully aware of how prepared they are for violence until they actually act. In fact, some even remain in denial about their profound psychological transformations *after* they've carried out the violence tasks.

Two primary concerns about the case study method involve objectivity and generalizability.[25] Would an objective researcher trying to replicate the study come up with similar results? And do the case studies provide useful information that extends beyond the given case? When it comes to objectivity, this book's findings are well documented, and the conclusions are clearly referenced and delineated. If a future researcher, when reviewing the case studies, refines the analytical model or develops an improved way to explain systematic indoctrination and organizational violence—that is certainly acceptable. The findings—though structured around the model—can also stand on their own. Furthermore, the conclusions can be generalized—the model, once substantiated, could potentially be used to assess virtually *any* organization which displays the crucial risk factors and would have a strong motive for violence.

Four Powerful Cases

Beyond its review of the existing literature and its reexamination of the two famous psychological experiments, this book applies the analytical framework to four powerful case studies: Nazi Germany, Al Qaeda's global terrorist network, post-revolutionary Iran, and the U.S. military scandal at the Abu Ghraib prison in Iraq. Each case plays a vital role.

Hitler's Nazi Germany is featured in this book because it stands alone as the most horrific example of systematic violence in the modern era. As Michael Mann documents in *The Dark Side of Democracy: Explaining Ethnic Cleansing,*

"In the last 4 years of its 12-year life, the Nazi regime caused the murders of approximately 20 million unarmed persons."[26] Admittedly, in Cambodia, Pol Pot's Khmer Rouge party killed a higher percentage of its population. And in Russia, Joseph Stalin's Soviet government executed millions and is culpable for the starvation of millions more. But in the modern era, no organization has *directly* killed as many unarmed people as the Nazis. Furthermore, the wealth of documents and scholarship on the Holocaust dwarfs the literature on other incidents of genocide, which allows for a more informed and in-depth analysis of the Nazi system.[27]

In turn, the Al Qaeda case represents one of the greatest threats to global security facing the world today. The attacks of 9/11 provided a frightening glimpse of how dangerous terrorists can be, even without nuclear, chemical, or biological weapons. The strikes also provoked the global "war on terror" in response to Al Qaeda's crusade. Furthermore, unlike the other cases, the Al Qaeda case provides an example of systematic indoctrination and organizational violence that has fully transcended direct state sponsorship in a way the Nazis, Iranian extremists, and U.S. military personnel at Abu Ghraib never did. Finally, it emphasizes how clearly the analytical model, which has not been applied to terrorism until now, can explain terrorist organizations.

When it comes to Iran, some fear that if the Islamic state procures nuclear weapons, World War III or a "clash of civilizations" could soon follow. For this book, the Iranian case is important on its own. But it is also significant as a potential modern version of Nazi Germany. Many comparisons are made between the two in geopolitical conversations these days. The recent words of former Israeli Prime Minister Benjamin Netanyahu speak for many, who fear as he does that "It's 1938, and Iran is Germany, racing to arm itself with atomic bombs."[28] Netanyahu has referenced Iranian President Mahmoud Ahmadinejad's numerous claims that the Holocaust never happened and that Iran will soon wipe Israel off the map, and warns that the rest of the world should not discount Ahmadinejad's words as mere bravado. "Believe him and stop him. . . . This is what we must do. Everything pales before it."[29] This book will provide some real evidence and structural clarification for this conjecture—showing how the dominant systems in the Nazi and Iranian cases are, and are not, similar.

The Iranian case is also a chance to look forward and make some sound scholarly predictions. The analytical framework featured here is based on models and theories used almost exclusively to explain what went wrong *after* people are killed or tortured—which is much less risky for scholars, and much less helpful for victims. However, this book will draw on Iran's recent, postrevolutionary history to hopefully save *future* people from horrible suffering. Though making recommendations for the future is an imperfect and potentially embarrassing task (if the future proves the predictions wrong), the projections made here are based on significant findings and cautious comparative analysis, and are no more provocative or alarmist than the data dictate.

The examination of the Abu Ghraib scandal is a natural extension of Zimbardo's famous Stanford Prison Experiment. Today's research standards prohibit social scientists from exposing human subjects to brutal experiments or any forms of abuse. With good reason. However, the Abu Ghraib prison in Iraq is a modern, real-world situation with many of the same systematic features emphasized by Zimbardo. This case also provides a contrast to the other cases because significantly less violence was employed. Despite using tactics of physical and psychological abuse, military interrogators did not resort to lethal force—unlike the murderers and terrorists featured in the other cases. Another important contrast is the nature of the victims: Abu Ghraib's inmates were assumed to be criminals, combatants, and/or "noncombatant" fighters—not fully innocent men, women, and children, like those targeted in the Nazi and Al Qaeda cases. In addition, this case shows how organizations like the U.S. military, which presumably have good intentions, may nonetheless promote extralegal violence to serve their larger goals.

Can We Relate?

This book probes powerful social and structural pressures and will journey to many unfamiliar places. Readers will encounter frightening rituals, shocking training procedures, and some of the most horrific crimes against humanity in the modern era. However, they should try not to dismiss what they see as a distant reality that exists apart from their own. Remember that many of the killers and torturers described in this book were relatively ordinary people before they became brutally violent machines serving a larger system. Could the guy mowing his lawn across the street be a potential torturer, executioner, or terrorist if he were suddenly transplanted to the wrong place at the wrong time? It is hard to be certain.

Even in relatively peaceful organizational contexts, we continue to see people who perform violence on command—not to serve their own needs, but to serve the system. Sometimes the violence might be appropriate, sometimes it is unclear, other times it is more obviously immoral. But the key is that this decision is often made by the organization, whose agent then carries out the act.

For instance, there are countless examples of sports organizations that have pressured their members to carry out violence on command. In February 2005, Temple University basketball coach John Chaney ordered his 6-foot-8, 250 pound player Nehemiah Ingram to "send a message" to the opposing players by intentionally crashing into them and knocking them down. One opponent suffered a broken arm. Later, Chaney apologized, claiming that the aggressive player on his team was not at fault and that as the coach, he was solely responsible for the violence—his player had just been following orders.[30]

On the other hand, in June 2006, Chicago White Sox manager Ozzie Guillen ordered pitcher Sean Tracey to intentionally hit an opposing batter with a fast-ball. Tracey refused to hit the batter, so Guillen removed Tracey from the game, screamed at him in the dugout, and had him demoted from the major league club the very next day. The message from Guillen was clear: serve the organization—or else. Though there was some public outcry about Guillen's behavior, ESPN sports analyst and former professional football player Mike Golic was one of many who quickly applauded it. He insisted that in sports, you follow your coach's orders no matter what they are.[31]

This distorted obedience ethic is just one of the many features of systematic indoctrination. Obviously, these examples are not nearly as serious as the bloodshed and suffering caused by the Nazis, Iranian extremists, Al Qaeda terrorists, or Abu Ghraib guards. However, the parallels are strong and particularly relevant, given that most of these killers and torturers were relatively ordinary people before they were reprogrammed by the system.

As this book examines extreme cases of organizational violence, it is important to remember its relevance to more common social pressures in everyday life. In the sports world, Ingram chose to follow orders to harm others and was protected, while Tracey refused and was punished by his organization. Life is not always fair, but people always have a choice.

Though the torturers and murderers featured in this book may have been recruited, trained, and indoctrinated by corrupt organizations, this does not excuse their behavior. They are still liable for their complicity and for their criminal actions. Many people may be afraid of speaking up, objecting to organizational mandates, or breaking apart from the group, but in every case there have been individuals who did just that. Some people choose to do the *right* thing. They refuse to follow orders, refuse to carry out such evil. Ultimately, the success of violent organizations is rooted in the failure of people to think for themselves and take responsibility for their own actions. Unfortunately, this is a problem that exists everywhere.

Overview

As this study of systematic indoctrination begins, it is helpful to have a general road map. The chapters that follow this one describe the analytical model, apply the model to the famous psychological experiments and each individual case study, examine the patterns of violent transformation found through comparative analysis, and provide specific countermeasures and policy recommendations.

Chapter 2 presents an in-depth explanation of the model and how it extends previous scholarship on violence, torture, mass killing, and genocide. A range of insider facts, evidence, and data, which include accounts of police units' use of force, correctional systems' administration of the death penalty, military sniper desensitization methods, and the strategies which prompted the My Lai massacre in Vietnam, combine to highlight the power of systematic indoctrination.

Chapter 3 examines the famous Milgram and Zimbardo experiments. In Milgram's study, subjects administered what they thought were near-fatal electric shocks to a person seated in the next room, as part of a learning test. In Zimbardo's experiment, young men who were assigned the role of prison guard verbally and physically abused their "prisoner" counterparts to maintain control of a mock prison. These experiments both show that in a controlled environment, relatively normal people can be compelled to use violence to serve the system. But they also show much more than that—they show us *how* this transformation can be achieved. This chapter uses the model of systematic indoctrination to reexamine these experiments, revealing previously overlooked variables and their implications for violence in the real world. In addition, the relatively low-level of violence produced in these contexts—which did not reach the horrors of torture, terrorism, or genocide—provides an important, less extreme contrast to the four major case studies.

Chapter 4 applies the model for systematic indoctrination to the Holocaust and Nazi Germany. This is a particularly powerful case, not only because of the magnitude of human suffering that defined the Holocaust, but also because so much insider information was gathered following the Nuremberg trials, including confessions from Nazi doctors, accounts from death camp commanders, and SS documents offering scientific "evidence" about the "subhuman Jew." Accounts of the Nazis' desensitization training practices are particularly haunting—for instance, some new SS recruits were forced to raise puppies and then strangle them upon maturity, while other recruits were pressured to kill Jewish babies in front of the babies' mothers to prove their mettle.

Chapter 5 tackles the terrorist threat posed by Al Qaeda. More than any other group featured here, terrorists tend to be portrayed as crazy, delusional, and unhinged. In truth, they are calculating and rational thinkers whose extreme values and radical priorities do not limit their effectiveness. Terrorists are built, not born, and personal similarities between members reflect strategic recruitment and training more than anything else. Evidence from captured Al Qaeda operatives, internet recruiting videos, and the official *Al Qaeda Training Manual* show that the terrorist organization essentially operates like a sophisticated multinational corporation, complete with closely managed employees conditioned to produce terror.

Chapter 6 dissects how Iran's radical theocracy promotes unthinking obedience to holy leaders and savage revenge against infidels who supposedly "cause corruption on the earth." The fundamentalist system also capitalizes on traditional rituals of self-flagellation and mutilation that fuse violence, pain, bloodshed, national pride, and religious ecstasy to desensitize young men and glorify the virtues of martyrdom. Beyond its formal armed forces are Iran's Revolutionary Guard and its paramilitary Basij youth groups, which use a specific extremist curriculum to train young boys and men to fight strategically-defined "enemies" by any means necessary: intimidation, harassment, abuse, torture, summary execution, terrorism, or all out war.

Chapter 7 focuses on the abuses at Abu Ghraib. The analysis includes descriptions of the training practices and organizational pressures which led some U.S. guards and interrogators to punch, kick, and slap detainees, stomp on their bare feet, threaten them with loaded guns and potential execution, sodomize them with chemical lights and broomsticks, and place them on boxes with wires attached to their fingers, toes, and genitals, on threats of electric shock torture. Evidence comes from a range of sources, including some within the White House and the Pentagon. Details emerge about the "closing methods" used by military recruiters to challenge young men's egos, the boot camp practices designed to ensure obedience, the confidential emails between military commanders in Iraq, and the guilt-ridden conversations between the abusive MP guards.

Chapter 8 provides a side-by-side comparative analysis of Nazi Germany, Iran, Al Qaeda, Abu Ghraib, and the Milgram and Zimbardo experiments across many key dimensions of systematic indoctrination. The strategic similarities and differences show the power of these violent methods, and help to put these cases in their historical context.

Chapter 9 makes specific policy recommendations and offers several immediate countermeasures we should employ to reduce threats to global security. Many of us wonder: is the U.S. military a danger to itself and others, as it struggles to improve national security and maintain control over its own soldiers? How can we counter the brainwashing employed by terrorist organizations like Al Qaeda? What should the international community do about escalating extremism in Iran? Do any peaceful solutions exist?

Anyone can ask the questions. This book provides some answers.

Notes

1. Mark Twain, *The Mysterious Stranger and Other Stories* (New York: Penguin Books USA Inc., 1980), 233.

2. Tim Weiner, "Killing machines prepare to do warfare's dirty work," *Sydney Morning Herald*, 19 February 2005, http://www.smh.com.au/news/Science/Killing-machines-prepare-to-do-warfares-dirty-work/2005/02/18/1108709439213.html (10 April 2008).

3. Tzvetan Todorov, "The Uses and Abuses of Comparison," in *The Lesser Evil: Moral Approaches to Genocide Practices*, eds. Helmut Dubiel and Gabriel Motkin (London: Routledge, 2004), 32. Emphasis added.

4. Raul Hilberg, *The Destruction of The European Jews* (New York: Holmes and Meier Publishers, Inc., 1985), 863.

5. Richard Breitman, *The Architect of Genocide: Himmler and the Final Solution* (New York: Alfred A. Knopf, Inc., 1991), 4.

6. Michael Mann, *The Dark Side of Democracy: Explaining Ethnic Cleansing* (New York: Cambridge University Press, 2005), 21.

7. Breitman, *The Architect of Genocide*, 3.

8. Walid Phares, *Future Jihad: Terrorist Strategies Against America* (New York: Palgrave Macmillan, 2005), 189-90.

9. Robert Johnson, "Institutions and the Promotion of Violence," in *Violent Transactions: The Limits of Personality*, eds. Anne Campbell and John J. Gibbs (Oxford: Basil Blackwell, 1986), 184. Johnson further extends these ideas in his insightful investigations *Death Work: A Study of the Modern Execution Process* (Belmont, Calif.: Wadsworth Publishing Company, 1998) and *Hard Time: Understanding and Reforming the Prison* (Belmont, Calif.: Wadsworth Publishing Company, 2002), which identify many of these same factors in the U.S. correctional system.

10. Johnson, "Institutions and the Promotion of Violence," 184.

11. James Waller, *Becoming Evil: How Ordinary People Commit Genocide and Mass Killing* (New York: Oxford University Press, 2002), 14.

12. Waller, *Becoming Evil*, 14.

13. Waller himself documents that in most episodes of mass killing, the murderers have been relatively ordinary people. This assertion is almost unequivocally supported by the research of many academic authorities, including Christopher R. Browning in *Ordinary Men: Reserve Police Battalion 101 and the Final Solution in Poland* (New York: Harper-Collins Publishers, Inc., 1998), 188-89 and Fred E. Katz in *Confronting Evil: Two Journeys* (New York: State University of New York Press, 2004), 177.

14. Waller, *Becoming Evil*, 134.

15. Waller, *Becoming Evil*, 277. Emphasis removed.

16. Stanley Milgram, *Obedience to Authority: An Experimental View* (New York: Perennial Classics, 1974), 6.

17. Mann, *The Dark Side of Democracy*, 27.

18. Ervin Staub, *The Roots of Evil: The Origins of Genocide and other Group Violence* (Cambridge: Cambridge University Press, 1989), 7.

19. The staff of the Library of Congress's Federal Research Division also contributed to this publication.

20. Rex. A Hudson, *Who Becomes a Terrorist and Why: The 1999 Government Report on Profiling Terrorists* (Guilford, Conn.: The Lyons Press, 2002), 2.

21. Hudson, *Who Becomes a Terrorist and Why*, 2.

22. "Data," *Start.Umd.edu*, http://www.start.umd.edu/data/ (31 March 2008).

23. Richard J. Chasdi, *Tapestry of Terror: A Portrait of Middle East Terrorism, 1994-1999* (Lanham, Md.: Lexington Books, 2002).

24. Jessica Stern, *Terror in the Name of God: Why Religious Militants Kill* (New York: Ecco, 2003), xxx.

25. Bruce L. Berg, *Qualitative Research Methods for the Social Sciences* (Boston: Allyn and Bacon, 2001), 231-32.

26. Mann, *The Dark Side of Democracy*, 184.

27. Waller, *Becoming Evil*, 22.

28. Abraham Rabinovich, "Weighing up the risks of a second Holocaust: Iran's bid for nuclear capability may force Israel to launch an attack," *South China Morning Post*, 17 December 2006.

29. Rabinovich, "Weighing up the risks of a second Holocaust."

30. Dan Gelston, "Temple's Chaney suspends self for game over 'goon' flap," *USATODAY*, 23 February 2005, http://www.usatoday.com/sports/college/mensbasket ball/atlantic10/2005-02-23-chaney-ban_x.htm (10 April 2008).

31. "Sean Tracey - Chicago White Sox - Player Card," *ESPN.com*, http://sports. espn.go.com/mlb/players/content?statsId=7793 (10 April 2008).

Chapter 2
Strategies of Systematic Indoctrination

People who kill and abuse others have often been characterized as inherently abnormal.[1] This description can be comforting—it implies that as long as we keep the freaks out of our cities, towns, neighborhoods, and homes, we will always be safe. Plus it implies an almost unbridgeable gulf between good and evil, between us and them. Sometimes it's accurate: lone serial killers, for instance, often have severe mental problems rarely found in the general population. But when it comes to organized atrocities like torture, terrorism, and genocide, the evidence indicates that perpetrators of such evil are often relatively ordinary people. The great majority are not scarred by early life traumas or developmental, psychological, or personality disorders.[2]

For instance, even Heinrich Himmler, one of Hitler's top associates and "The Architect of Genocide" in Breitman's eyes, was a rather ordinary individual. "A historian or biographer is tempted to look for some extraordinary, crippling experience in the youth of the man who became the Reich Führer SS . . . [but] Himmler's childhood circumstances were relatively normal, even privileged. There is no simple environmental or psychological explanation as to why Himmler became a mass murderer on an unprecedented scale."[3]

Similarly, Waller references the overwhelming evidence that the Nazi masses were surprisingly ordinary:

> except for a small number of the architects of the extermination process and a few sadists who enjoyed taking part in it—most of the perpetrators of the Holocaust and other cases of mass killing and genocide were extraordinary only by what they did, not by who they were. They could not be identified, a priori, as having the personalities of killers. Most were not mentally impaired. Nor were they identified as sadists at home or in their social environment. Nor were they victims of an abusive background . . . we find educated and well-to-do people

as well as simple and impoverished people. We find church affiliated people as well as agnostics and atheists. We find people who were loving as parents as well as people who had difficulty initiating and sustaining personal relationships. . . . We find ordinary people who went to school, fought with siblings, celebrated birthdays, listened to music, and played with friends. In short, the majority of perpetrators of extraordinary evil were not distinguished by background, personality, or previous political affiliation or behavior as having been men or women unusually likely or fit to be genocidal executioners.[4]

After the Holocaust, the German nation was deeply scarred—as was much of Europe and the rest of the world. Many of these perpetrators, collaborators, and enablers were so profoundly traumatized by their own crimes that they would never be the same. The guilt and confusion were overwhelming. How were they transformed from ordinary people to obedient killers, seemingly overnight?

Relatively normal people do not suddenly become a unified group of killers through a stroke of bad luck, or because it rained yesterday or because the stars are aligned in an odd formation. They turn to violence because they are compelled to do so—not by a random swarm of forces, but by a powerful system with clear goals that can be achieved through violent means. These systems provide the leadership, infrastructure, and resources necessary for mass transformation. As Staub explains, "A monolithic central party, a powerful military, and other organized groups loyal to the government are often necessary. . . . There is a sharp turn towards group violence when institutions are created or existing institutions [are] assigned the task to harm a subgroup of society."[5] Despite wanting to focus on individuals instead of institutions and organizations, even Waller admits that the "binding factors of the group . . . keep people within an evildoing organization or hierarchy."[6] These factors are "often institutionalized in military or paramilitary organizations . . . to help perpetrators disregard or distort the effects of their acts of extraordinary evil."[7]

This book attempts to explain much of what these systems are doing—how they transform relatively normal people into violent agents who serve the system above all else. The model focuses on strategies for recruitment, training, authorization, bureaucracy, isolation, and dehumanization. As seen in Figure 2.1, each strategy makes a unique contribution to the program of systematic indoctrination. In addition, each strategy increases the overall dehumanization of the system's agents, who are transformed from ordinary human beings into killing machines. The crucial significance and explanatory power of these variables has been emphasized by some of the best scientific authorities on violence, killing, and genocide. Some of these scholars find additional factors relevant, while others prefer to focus on just a few of them. However, the evidence shows that these six strategies appear to be the most important elements of systematic indoctrination and the violence it yields. The key subcomponents and nuances of each strategy are explained in the following review.

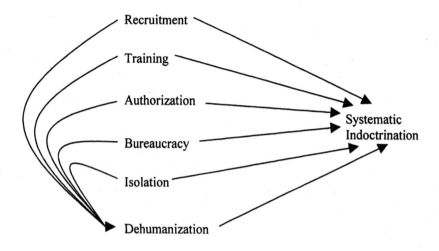

Figure 2.1. Strategies of Systematic Indoctrination

Recruitment

In general, new recruits to almost any group or organization have a strong desire
to fit in. And as Douglas T. Kenrick et al. explain, this craving for "social approval can lead peripheral group members to be especially hostile toward out-
groups" and make them "more willing to adopt [the] group's prejudicial
norms."[8] Unfortunately, this normal psychological tendency is easily exploited.
As previously mentioned, in the right (or wrong) context, many otherwise ordinary people can be compelled to act with brutal aggression, regardless of their
personal history and makeup. Systems arrange for this context to transform their
agents, making it easier for them to accept and perform violence on command.

But as long as the people are rather ordinary, shouldn't they all be suitable
candidates for indoctrination? If the program of indoctrination is effective, why
should it matter who the organization chooses to recruit?

It matters because of who the organization *does not recruit*. The system can
condition relatively ordinary people to perform violence on command, but that
does not mean that all people are equally likely to become killers. Despite Christopher Browning's fear that if men as ordinary as the genocidal policemen he
studied could become killers, "what group of men cannot?"—he admits that
some people simply cannot be compelled to obey.[9] It is the dissenters, these he-
roic individuals, who can become major problems for systems that promote vio-

lence—especially if they are well respected, charismatic, and willing to fight against organizational mandates.

To get around this difficulty, systems try to recruit people who are sufficiently malleable in the first place. As Johnson explains, "Recruitment and selection focus on people who are likely to conform to the institutional regime and accept the 'pejorative stereotyping and indoctrination' . . . essential to carrying out violence, or permitting it to occur, on a more or less regular basis."[10]

These organizations generally look for specific characteristics in recruits that indicate they can be easily sculpted to fit the system's standards. Overall, the favored recruits tend to be young and male, with a shared ideology and respect for authority.[11] It is clear that the recruits who are most susceptible to indoctrination are the youngest ones—though older recruits can be compelled to carry out violent orders as well. As Gwynne Dyer explains, "It's easier if you catch them young. You can train older men. . . . But you can never get them to believe *that they like it*, which is the major reason armies try to get their recruits before they are twenty."[12] Some violent systems try to get them even earlier—as young as ten, eleven, or twelve years old. Although there is plenty of evidence that women can be extremely effective killers, organizations usually prefer men for violent tasks.[13]

When it comes to recruits' values and beliefs, Staub describes how "Strong respect for authority and strong inclination to obedience are other predisposing characteristics for mass killing and genocide. They make it more likely that responsibility will be relinquished and leaders will be followed unquestioningly."[14] Waller agrees: "Indeed, in most cultures, an authority orientation favoring obedience is a major cultural value . . . it is less likely that [obedient] individuals will oppose leaders who scapegoat, or advocate violence against, a particular target group."[15] These recruiting priorities are common to military, police, and prison systems, but guide recruitment for more extreme systems as well.

Training

Once they have joined the system, members are trained in a fashion that specifically increases their willingness to perform violence:

> As training unfolds, the dangers or uncertainties of the job, and the security that can be found in conformity and a show of unity, are emphasized. Hence, soldiers, police, and guards emerge from training with (1) a concern for survival in the face of danger (2) respect for rules and regulations that give shape to the job, and (3) a clearer sense of their roles and mutual obligations to protect and support one another.[16]

Johnson's concise summary of the overall training approach is spot on. However, this strategy is complex and requires exposition.

These organizations begin by indoctrinating new members with a time-tested strategy: they immediately provide them with a big problem. Something outside the group is identified as a serious threat to the recruits' well being—such as rowdy inmates, savage criminals, an enemy nation, or a corrupt religion. This threat can be real and legitimate or false and manufactured. The distinction usually isn't clear cut. Real threats are often exaggerated for effect, while manufactured threats are much more convincing when they are based on some small truth. It really does not matter what the threat is, as long as the recruits are made to feel vulnerable and provided with someone to blame. As Staub asserts, "Sometimes having a scapegoat is the glue in the formation of the group."[17]

This is a critical feature of the system's training strategy. As Baumeister explains, "There is ample evidence that perpetrators of violence learn to detest their victims . . . they are taught that their victims are part of a dangerously powerful movement that aims to destroy."[18] Note that they "learn" and "are taught" that they are in danger. This ensures that recruits share a common enemy, regardless of their varied upbringings, personalities, or past animosities. Once the threat is identified, recruits' self defense instincts are triggered and an overzealous response becomes much more likely. Of course, the system's response is often not self defense at all, but it is framed this way so that agents believe their actions are morally justified.

Having provided recruits with a serious problem that must be overcome, the system offers its other training lessons as part of the solution. To conquer the threat and ensure the system's success, a new recruit must protect and support his colleagues, no matter what they do or ask of him. The system claims that unity is imperative for defeating the enemy, and bonding between recruits becomes a top training priority. Many violent assignments require close coordination in high-pressure environments, so it is especially important that recruits learn to work well together. Furthermore, unity is critical for violent systems because agents are much less likely to abandon their colleagues or resist following orders if they care about their peers on a personal level. Waller cites military science findings which show that "the cohesive bonds soldiers form with one another . . . are often stronger than the bonds they will form with anyone else at any other point in their lifetimes."[19] "[The] individual cares so deeply about his comrades and what they think of him that he would rather die than let them down."[20] Because these bonds are so strong, even when agents are given illegal or unethical orders, they usually follow them anyway. "It is difficult for anyone who is bonded by links of mutual affection and interdependence to break away and openly refuse to participate in what the group is doing, even if it is perpetrating extraordinary evil."[21]

Recruits also learn that they must obey the rules and do their jobs, no matter how distasteful their assignments may be. As long as they follow the rules, the system will prevail. This is a particularly prominent feature of military training—even for the noblest forces, which respect human rights and do not abuse them. However, because obedience is revered within the system, disobeying an order—even a horrible one to torture captured prisoners or kill unarmed children—becomes extremely difficult. As Baumeister explains, "disobeying the command puts the moral burden of proof squarely on you. Obeying might turn out to be wrong, but the burden of proof (and seemingly of responsibility), is not on you, at least not just then."[22] For agents who aren't particularly articulate, the prospect of disobeying becomes even more intimidating because it would require an immediate explanation—the verbal expression of an abstract moral code.

Finally, new recruits are also desensitized to violence so that they will be able to perform it on the spot—without hesitating. The law of diminishing returns takes over—the first time recruits use violence, they are likely to feel the most guilt and psychological angst, and then each subsequent time they attack, torture, or kill, they feel less remorse and find it easier to proceed.

Many organizations try to make training practices as realistic as possible in order to desensitize recruits to the real thing. For example, an Israeli military expert went to great lengths to simulate real killing during training:

> I changed the standard firing targets to full-size, anatomically correct figures because no Syrian runs around with a big white square on his chest with numbers on it. I put clothes on these targets and polyurethane heads. I cut up a cabbage and poured catsup into it and put it back together. I said, "When you look through that scope, I want you to see a head blowing up."[23]

Eventually, shooting at something lifelike no longer feels worthy of a powerful emotional response. A Vietnam veteran explains what it is like to operate as the system's finished product: "Two shots. Bam-bam. Just like we had been trained in 'quick kill.' When I killed, I did it just like that. Just like I'd been trained. Without even thinking."[24] This is precisely the type of human killing machine that the training is designed to produce. It works automatically and kills on command. Of course, sometimes machine-like soldiers are necessary, and sometimes their violence is fully justified by the situation and all commonly shared military ethics and laws. Other times they are used in much more horrible ways.

Authorization

To understand the system's authorizations for violence, it is helpful to divide them into two categories: transcendent and mundane.

Transcendent authorizations emphasize the intended result of the violence, rather than the destructive nature of the acts themselves. As a result, agents do not dwell on the most morally troubling aspects of their behavior. This strategy can help agents gradually come to terms with the system's brutal plans for violence, torture, murder, or genocide.

Johnson finds that transcendent authorizations often come in the form of "vague prescriptions or slogans that can be endorsed without full awareness of the violence they entail."[25] He gives a particularly good example in the military slogan "Victory at any price." In this phrase, the emphasis is on the word "Victory," not "price," because the images of winning, parades, confetti, music, and dancing with pretty women are much better motivators than thoughts of funerals for fallen comrades or being spattered with the blood of your enemies. The key is how the language steers agents' thinking away from the negative and towards the positive. Meanwhile, the very real and very deadly nature of the violence required to *achieve* such ends is at least temporarily obscured, as members of the group are primed for their future accomplishments.

As part of this strategy, violent systems also use euphemisms to mask the pain and suffering their agents inflict. Waller explains that perpetrators benefit from "camouflaging their extraordinary evil in innocuous or sanitizing jargon [so] the evil loses much of it moral repugnancy. In this way, language can obscure, mystify, or otherwise redefine acts of extraordinary evil."[26] These types of transcendent authorizations have been all too common over the years. For example, "Institutional campaigns of oppression and murder have used such . . . terms as *ethnic cleansing* (Bosnia), *final solution* and *special handling* (Nazi Holocaust) . . . and *bush clearing* (Rwanda) to disguise their brutality."[27]

The agents are not completely ignorant or foolish—somewhere beneath the surface, they recognize the true meaning of the language they are encouraged to use. They do not literally think that "cleansing" means they will be helping clean. However, by authorizing violence in pleasant terms, the system ensures its agents do not have to confront the moral implications of their crimes in every discussion of their plans. Members of the system "become bound to a psychologically safe realm of dissociation, disavowal, and emotional distance."[28]

At the same time, mundane authorizations are used to portray violence as an ordinary, acceptable, or even admirable element of agents' overall service to the system. According to Johnson, mundane authorizations can be specific, vague, or come as no direct orders at all, "but only a social climate that condones violence . . . as the Mayor of Detroit recently proclaimed, 'our cops are the toughest gang in town.'"[29]

When specific mundane authorizations are given, violence is spoken about as though it were commonplace and no big deal. For instance, the order to execute a prisoner is given in the same unspectacular fashion as a command to take out the trash. All of the subtle cues support the notion that violence is insignificant: words are spoken in a bored or indifferent tone, and eye contact is quick and passing. Leaders imply that "we've been there, done that" many times before, and that if the violence at hand was ever a big issue or worthy of debate, that time has long since passed.

On the other hand, some leaders prefer to be vague. As Baumeister explains, "ambiguity is often a decisive factor in getting someone started in immoral or cruel acts. This fact is recognized by powerful people who want others to carry out their own malicious wishes."[30] One example he cites is the My Lai massacre in Vietnam, where the military commander on site "apparently implied but did not specifically say that the villages in the area were to be obliterated."[31] "The initial ambiguity was retained and passed along as the orders were transmitted through the chain of command, although at some point a literal and drastic interpretation was made to the effect that the mission involved shooting the villagers en masse."[32]

Systems also create social climates that approve of violence. The glorification of violence has many sources, from individuals to the media to powerful organizations and systems. As Staub explains, "Some cultures (and individuals) idealize aggression. American television programs and films attest to some idealization . . . [as do] organizations such as the National Rifle Association."[33] Of course, none of these organizations are deliberately conditioning agents for campaigns of torture, mass murder, or genocide. It is only in the worst systems that "Brutality comes to be considered an accomplishment, a mark of distinction."[34] Through these mundane authorizations, agents of the system come to feel that violence is not only acceptable—it is an honored sign of strength.

Bureaucracy

When it comes time for members of the organization to carry out authorized violence, the bureaucracy can help them transcend normal moral restraints. Bureaucracies reduce the personal, flexible elements of the workplace and provide formal roles that steer behavior to meet the system's objectives. In addition, violence can become habitual within a bureaucracy, as standard operating procedures, administrative forms, work rituals, and routines make violence seem like normal, unspectacular duties rather than dangerous and powerful acts. Agents can wrongly come to assume that any procedure—even a violent one— that has an existing protocol, appears orderly, and is carefully managed from above must be okay. Because these workers are so accustomed to following procedures which they don't fully understand, they are particularly vulnerable to being misled.

Bureaucratic division of labor also functions to divide up guilt and moral responsibility into easily digestible chunks. This organizational concept is sometimes referred to as the compartmentalization of functions. Each agent performs a portion of the violence and subsequently assumes only a portion of the accountability. As Johnson explains, "no one takes full responsibility for violence":

After all, soldiers don't start wars, and concentration-camp guards didn't design the "final solution." Death-row guards don't sentence the condemned, and many do not participate directly in executions. Police don't write laws or create the social or psychological conditions that drive some men to crime. . . . The statement of a prison warden about his obligation to execute condemned prisoners is quite telling in this regard: "I look at the criminal justice system as a sewer pipe. I'm just at the end of the sewer pipe. The police did their job, the courts did their job, now I have to do my job."[35]

Members of the system are comforted that they are not alone. They have contributed towards the system's violent actions, but so have all of their peers. Literally, morally, and legally, they're all in it together. With sickening circular logic, the system's agents convince themselves that their actions must be morally right and justified because their fellow agents have not objected. Each agent, looking to his left and right and seeing no objections, decides to follow orders. Baumeister suggests that to members of the violent organization, "it surely seems that the entire group could not be making a major moral blunder."[36] "Individual acts may be questioned. . . . But the group itself is above question."[37]

Large bureaucracies also increase the pressure on agents to do their jobs. If the "sewer pipe" is clogged by a disobedient employee who dares to pause for moral reflection, the system backs up and the pressure builds and builds, until, in a violent moment of release, the clog is dislodged, the employee is expelled, and the flow resumes as normal. As Waller explains, these bureaucracies are so effective because members recognize that "refusing to kill would only alienate . . . one's friends and colleagues and, in the end, not deter in the least bit the killing operations. . . . [Thus,] the organization becomes impermeable to the wishes of the individuals within it."[38] For workers, it is much easier just to do their prescribed jobs and avoid clogging up the system than it is to object—especially since they are only responsible for one part of the process. In this way, the bureaucracy keeps rolling along with a life of its own.

Isolation

For any systems that want to quickly transform their members in a significant way, isolation is extremely useful. Whether people are being taught to speak a foreign language, sell the company's product, or adopt a violent ideology, the best method is total immersion. When people are isolated and outside influences are minimized, it becomes much easier to control who they talk to, what they learn, and what they think. Carefully planned activities and exclusive interactions with the ingroup increase the intensity of the experience. It would be easier for a professor to teach calculus if he could round up his students and bring them to an isolated camp, far away from shopping malls, bars, cable television, and iPhones. The same is true for conditioning agents to use violence, only more so. Although math students may be teased or ridiculed by "cool" outsiders for taking their studies too seriously, there are no religious, social, or legal prohibitions against math. On the other hand, torture, terrorism, and genocide are much more controversial, so they must be taught in isolation.

Isolation from outsiders can be literal, where physical distance separates the organization from the rest of the world. Or it can be social, where the system's members choose to ignore the presence, opinions, and values of non-members. Most often, it is both. As Johnson explains, being isolated "protects the institution and its personnel from observation and judgment by the larger society, and conveys the illusion that the institution comprises a separate and unaccountable world with its own moral order."[39]

In this alternate reality, the values of the outside world are rendered meaningless and local values dominate. The psychological buffer between the system and outsiders makes the use of violence much easier, and is one of the most important reasons why military, police, and prison systems strategically remove themselves from the everyday societal context. Their isolation becomes particularly apparent in periods of trouble, when violence is most necessary and potential moral hindrances must be avoided at all costs. Johnson highlights just how dramatic this transition can be:

> For the army, the stress of impending combat converts a "Sad Sack" platoon to a "fighting machine". . . . The prison becomes more monolithic and oppressive, with guards and inmates locked into stereotypical roles, under conditions of crowding (which breeds tension and violence) or where crises such as escapes or riots take place. . . . Police close ranks when confronted with a hostile community. . . . A similar change occurred in some Nazi death camps as well.[40]

This is another reason why violent systems often exaggerate or manufacture external threats: it allows them to justify increased isolation. By closing ranks, organizations further deny the validity of external judgments about their violent tactics.

In addition, by keeping agents isolated from other moral authorities, violent organizations preserve the illusion that the system's values are above reproach. In the contrived reality of the overarching system, new social norms are established and morality is redefined. Increasingly, the agents live in an alternate universe. A new ethos emerges, where the ends justify the means and meeting the system's goals becomes the moral imperative. As Waller states, "the prevailing mind-set becomes how to do it better, not whether to do it at all."[41] Within the isolated system, *what works is right*. And unfortunately, sometimes members of the system discover that crime really does pay. For example, governments that stage oppressive crackdowns on political protestors can effectively keep their corrupt regimes in power, at least for the short term. Brutal violence can be a useful form of coercion and control, and to fully indoctrinated agents, sometimes that's all that matters.

Isolation also helps these agents stay fixated on the system as their moral priority above all others. For instance, Stern describes how people who join terrorist organizations "enter a kind of trance, where the world is divided neatly between good and evil, victim and oppressor. Uncertainty and ambivalence, always painful to experience, are banished. There is no room for the other side's point of view. . . . They know they are right, not just politically, but morally."[42] Through isolation, the system protects agents from "corrupt" counterarguments which might advocate alternatives to violence. It also helps members preserve their righteous rationalizations that violence is morally required. As Kekes explains, most killers have initially been "unintentional evildoers, not moral monsters, because they believed, albeit falsely, that their actions were justified or excused . . . their passions prevented them from questioning the accuracy of their self-understandings."[43] Within violent organizations, self-reflection is reduced so that indoctrinated killing machines can be produced en masse.

Violent systems also isolate their members from one another. Unauthorized interactions between agents are often prohibited, and the details of violent plans are usually kept extremely secret. In particular, these systems often implement the need-to-know principle to control the flow of information. This internal isolation limits discussions of violent orders and options, and low-level agents are kept in the dark about the most sensitive developments. By keeping members isolated and ignorant, systems prevent them from questioning the morality of their orders. It is not allowed, much less expected, for low-level agents to know all of the supposed logic behind their violent duties. In the most extreme systems, organized dissent is rendered nearly impossible. It's no coincidence that suicide bombers don't have worker unions, for example. Like other agents in violent systems, they are left to believe that their leaders can be trusted implicitly and that torturing or killing the enemy is clearly the right thing to do.

Dehumanization

Dehumanization is both a product of the other indoctrination strategies and a strategy unto itself. It has two distinct targets: (1) the members of the system themselves and (2) those who threaten the system.

The agent who takes orders without asking questions, bows to peer pressure, blindly follows the lead of his colleagues, performs his particular role without knowledge or control of the larger process, and is isolated from society and insulated from moral concerns, is thus dehumanized in a fundamental way that numbs his conscience. As Johnson states, "Simply playing one's role in a bureaucracy means relinquishing some autonomy, and hence being less fully human. . . . [A worker] is neither reformer nor villain, but simply an instrument. He means no harm and often sees no harm. If there is responsibility to assign, it lies within the organization."[44] This process is also referred to as deindividuation, and includes "a decreased focus on personal identity, loss of contact with general social norms, and the submergence of the individual in situation-specific group norms."[45] The result is that "people partially lose awareness of themselves as individuals."[46] As Baumeister suggests, the most dangerous effect of internal dehumanization is that "the group may end up doing wilder or more harmful things than the sum of the individual members would lead one to expect."[47] Lacking either the ability or desire to think for themselves, the system's members become more like destructive killing machines and less fully human.

Further dehumanization leads the system's leaders to see their subordinates in impersonal object terms. The workers become pawns, and the "'management team' . . . must somehow 'extract' productivity" from them by steering them towards violence.[48] Waller explains that the "person who becomes invested in the logic and practices of an evildoing organization becomes owned by it."[49] This is by design. The system that owns human tools of violence gains tremendous coercive power. According to Grossman, when these strategies work perfectly, each agent operates virtually "without conscious thought. It is as though a human being is a weapon."[50] Weapons, instruments, and tools have parts—not souls—so this transformation makes low-level agents seem much more expendable.

The targets of violence—people who allegedly threaten the system in some way—are also dehumanized to make harming them easier. Though there are subtle differences between dehumanization, demonization, devaluation, discrimination, us-them differentiation, and ingroup-outgroup bias, all of these concepts refer to the ways people characterize other groups with harmful lies and distortions. In *Demonic Males: Apes and the Origins of Human Violence*, Richard Wrangham and Dale Peterson argue that people are evolutionarily programmed to form groups for survival and that this tendency has developed as "part of the winners' strategy." "The process begins, say social psychologists, with people categorizing, mentally putting people into coarse and general classes that ultimately boil down to Us and Them."[51] This often leads to amazing disregard for traditional moral standards. "Taken to an extreme, ingroup-outgroup bias effectively dehumanizes Them, which means that moral law does not apply to Them and that therefore even ordinary and very moral people can do the most appalling things with a clear conscience."[52] Wrangham and Peterson cite several examples of how dehumanization has led to merciless violence, including the Nazis' orchestration of the Holocaust, Bosnian ethnic cleansing, Spanish conquerors "terrorizing, afflicting, torturing, and destroying" New World natives, the Boers hunting of Bushmen, and the brutal lynchings and mutilations of African Americans in the U.S. before the civil rights movement.[53]

There are many other examples of this strategy in action. Johnson describes how bomber pilots come to see target populations as "distant, anonymous masses . . . statistics or sectors of a map" and that prison guards often see inmates as "in fact sub-human."[54] When those who suffer from violence are viewed as objects, instead of living, breathing human beings, it becomes easier to rationalize that harming them is just part of the job. Torturers and killers sleep easier when they convince themselves that it's business, not personal. This occurs in many contexts. For instance, Grossman cites both sides' use of dehumanization and discrimination during the Vietnam War. U.S. soldiers used a number of slurs for their enemies, such as "gook," while on the other side, as one member of the Viet Cong reported, "My company in the jungle . . . called you Big Hairy Monkeys. We kill monkeys, and . . . we eat them."[55]

Whether or not dehumanization has an evolutionary basis, it is clear that systems use it to condition their agents for violence. Waller describes how in "cases of mass killing and genocide, the dehumanization of victims involves categorizing a group as inhuman either by using categories of sub-human creatures (that is, animals) or by using categories of negatively evaluated unhuman creatures (such as demons and monsters)."[56] Despised groups are often depicted as rats or other vermin, but characterizing enemies as demons can be just as effective. Demonization "solves the problem of how ends justify means. If you are up against Satan, you should not expect the ordinary rules to apply. Murder may be acceptable if you are killing the most wicked and demonic enemies of the good."[57]

Conclusion

History shows us that violent systems can transform relatively ordinary people into torturing, terrorizing, and killing machines. Grossman describes how with "the proper conditioning and the proper circumstances, it appears that almost anyone can and will kill."[58] He further notes that "the history of warfare can be seen as a history of increasingly more effective mechanisms for enabling and conditioning men to overcome their innate resistance to killing their fellow human beings."[59]

The question should no longer be "Can normal people be compelled to use violence on command?" It should be "*How* are they compelled to use violence on command?" This is not merely an academic question—military forces and other violent organizations have been struggling with the question and perfecting their answers for hundreds, if not thousands, of years.

The current model offers the six crucial strategies of recruitment, training, authorization, bureaucracy, isolation, and dehumanization as the recipe for systematic indoctrination. As the preceding review has shown, this model is consistent with evidence from the top experts on violence, torture, terrorism, and genocide. It offers a persuasive explanation for how systems produce obedient, violent machines, and is thus the perfect guide as we analyze two famous psychological experiments, along with the powerful case studies on Nazi Germany, Al Qaeda, Iran, and Abu Ghraib.

Notes

1. This tendency to blame innate, dispositional, or personality characteristics for individual's behavior while underestimating systematic and situational factors is commonly referred to as the fundamental attribution error, as described by Arie W. Kruglanksi in *The Psychology of Closed Mindedness* (New York, Psychology Press, 2004), 73.
2. Waller, *Becoming Evil*, 86-87.
3. Breitman, *The Architect of Genocide*, 9.
4. Waller, *Becoming Evil*, 8.
5. Staub, *The Roots of Evil*, 66. Emphasis removed.
6. Waller, *Becoming Evil*, 212. Emphasis removed.
7. Waller, *Becoming Evil*, 212. Emphasis removed.
8. Douglas T. Kenrick, Steven L. Neuberg, and Robert B. Cialdini, *Social Psychology: Unraveling the Mystery* (Boston: Allyn and Bacon, 1999), 407.
9. Browning, *Ordinary Men*, 188-89.
10. Johnson, "Institutions and the Promotion of Violence," 191.
11. Johnson, "Institutions and the Promotion of Violence," 191.
12. Dave Grossman, *On Killing: The Psychological Cost of Learning to Kill in War and Society* (Boston: Little, Brown and Company, 1995), 264. Emphasis added.
13. Grossman, *On Killing*, xiv.
14. Staub, *The Roots of Evil*, 19.
15. Waller, *Becoming Evil*, 180.
16. Johnson, "Institutions and the Promotion of Violence," 191.
17. Staub, *The Roots of Evil*, 17. Similarly, Peter Glick identifies the strategic use of scapegoating by both genocidal movements and terrorist organizations in "Choice of Scapegoats" in *On the Nature of Prejudice: Fifty Years after Allport*, eds. John F. Dovidio, Peter Glick, and Laurie Budman (Oxford: Blackwell Publishing Ltd, 2005), 259.
18. Roy F. Baumeister, *Evil: Inside Human Cruelty and Violence* (New York: W.H. Freeman and Company, 1997), 183.
19. Waller, *Becoming Evil*, 218.
20. Waller, *Becoming Evil*, 218.
21. Waller, *Becoming Evil*, 220.
22. Baumeister, *Evil*, 268.
23. Grossman, *On Killing*, 255.
24. Grossman, *On Killing*, 233.
25. Johnson, "Institutions and the Promotion of Violence," 185.
26. Waller, *Becoming Evil*, 188.
27. Baumeister, *Evil*, 316-17.
28. Baumeister, *Evil*, 189.
29. Johnson, "Institutions and the Promotion of Violence," 187.

30. Baumeister, *Evil*, 255.
31. Baumeister, *Evil*, 255.
32. Baumeister, *Evil*, 255.
33. Staub, *The Roots of Evil*, 54.
34. Waller, *Becoming Evil*, 210.
35. Johnson, "Institutions and the Promotion of Violence," 193-94.
36. Baumeister, *Evil*, 325.
37. Baumeister, *Evil*, 191.
38. Waller, *Becoming Evil*, 215.
39. Johnson, "Institutions and the Promotion of Violence," 190.
40. Johnson, "Institutions and the Promotion of Violence," 189-90.
41. Waller, *Becoming Evil*, 208-210.
42. Stern, *Terror in the Name of God*, 282.
43. Kekes, *The Roots of Evil*, 236-37.
44. Johnson, "Institutions and the Promotion of Violence," 194-95.
45. Waller, *Becoming Evil*, 216.
46. Waller, *Becoming Evil*, 216.
47. Staub, *The Roots of Evil*, 49-50; Baumeister, *Evil*, 325.
48. Johnson, "Institutions and the Promotion of Violence," 191.
49. Waller, *Becoming Evil*, 227.
50. Grossman, *On Killing*, 233.
51. Richard Wrangham and Dale Peterson, *Demonic Males: Apes and the Origins of Human Violence* (New York, Houghton Mifflin Company, 1996), 195-96.
52. Wrangham and Peterson, *Demonic Males*, 195-96.
53. Wrangham and Peterson, *Demonic Males*, 196-97.
54. Wrangham and Peterson, *Demonic Males*, 195-97.
55. Grossman, *On Killing*, 92.
56. Waller, *Becoming Evil*, 245.
57. Baumeister, *Evil*, 186.
58. Grossman, *On Killing*, 4.
59. Grossman, *On Killing*, 13.

Chapter 3
Violence in the Lab

The model of systematic indoctrination is based on compelling evidence and well-documented research. Supporting data come from a range of eras and cultures, and this further strengthens the model's validity. In addition, the evidence cited in the previous chapter is reinforced by scientific experiments. Two of the most famous psychological studies of the twentieth century are Milgram's experiment on *Obedience to Authority* and Zimbardo's Stanford Prison Experiment. These investigations show that in a controlled environment, relatively normal people can be compelled to use violence to serve the system. But they also show much more than that—they show us *how* this transformation can be achieved. By reexamining these experiments, we can take the model for a useful test drive and show how extensively it explains violence in the lab.

Milgram's Obedience Experiment (1961)

In Milgram's laboratory, subjects were given the role of "teacher" and instructed to administer electric shocks to a "learner" seated in the next room, whenever the learner answered a test question incorrectly. In reality, the learner was an actor and received no shocks whatsoever, but he voiced grunts, protests, screams, and pleas as though he were in pain. The goal of the experiment was to see how far the teacher would go, on a scale of increasingly severe shocks, before he stopped shocking the learner and disobeyed an onlooking scientist's directions. To Milgram's surprise, he found that "Many subjects will obey the experimenter no matter how vehement the pleading of the person being shocked, no matter how painful the shocks seem to be, and no matter how much the victim pleads to be let out."[1] This groundbreaking discovery has critical implications for violence in the real world. However, it is important to recognize that this experiment's brilliance extends far beyond the power of authority. Many of the other elements of systematic indoctrination were built into Milgram's recipe for violence.

Recruitment and Training

To avoid selection bias, Milgram recruited volunteers with a range of backgrounds and occupations. Through newspaper advertisements and direct mail solicitation, he enlisted men in their twenties, thirties, and forties from every walk of life. The recruits ranged from laborers who had not finished high school to engineers and businessmen with advanced degrees.[2] All were from the New Haven, Connecticut area, but it is not clear whether they entered the experiment with the shared ideology and respect for authority that seems to typify particularly malleable recruits.

Training for the experiment took just a few minutes. Subjects were told about the purpose of the experiment and that the shocks they would deliver to the learner "can be extremely painful, [but] cause no permanent tissue damage."[3] Each subject was taught how to administer a basic word-pairing test and assess answers relayed via electronic box. Then he was instructed on how to use an instrument panel with thirty levers for increasingly severe shocks and given a sample 45-volt shock, so that he would have some basis for comparison. It is important to note that the training did not feature an exaggerated threat to the system's security, lessons emphasizing obedience and unity, or desensitization exercises. If it had, the subjects might have been even more willing to administer the electric shocks than they were in these trials.

Authorization

The subjects were provided with both transcendent and mundane authorizations for administering the electric shocks.

The basic transcendent authorization emphasized the importance of the experiment while dismissing the pain experienced by the victim as temporary. Milgram explains that "the idea of science and its acceptance as a legitimate social enterprise provide the overarching ideological justification for the experiment . . . it permits the person to see his behavior as serving a desirable end."[4] Subjects were specifically told that the scientific focus of the experiment had largely gone unstudied and that progress was needed. In addition, once the study began, the scientist's orders were clear, but not explicit. The scientist never said, "Punish him" or "administer the shock." His language was strategically selected to avoid mentioning the violence required, which is typical of transcendent authorizations.

When the subjects would hesitate to deliver a shock, the scientist responded with a series of mundane authorizations or "prods." These directives simultaneously made the experiment seem important and the violence seem like no big deal:

Prod 1: Please continue, *or*, Please go on.
Prod 2: The experiment requires that you continue.
Prod 3: It is absolutely essential that you continue.
Prod 4: You have no other choice, you must go on.[5]

Additionally, if the subject asked about the risks to the learner, the scientist responded, "Although the shock may be painful, there is no permanent tissue damage, so please go on."[6] If the subject pointed out the learner's dismay, the scientist responded, "Whether the learner likes it or not, you must go on until he has learned all the word pairs correctly. So please go on."[7] These authorizations were all said in a calm, polite tone—the scientist's voice did not hint that he was remotely concerned about the violence or the suffering of the learner, which made it easier for the subject to deny the moral implications of his cruel behavior. Furthermore, Milgram emphasizes that "Whatever force authority exercises in this study is based on powers that the subject in some manner ascribes to it and not on any objective threat or availability of physical means of controlling the subject."[8] In other words, the subjects carried out the violence without being physically intimidated or threatened in any way—they could have walked out at any time without consequences. In fact, they were specifically told that the payment they had already received was not at issue and that they could keep it no matter what. We can imagine that—out in the real world—when disobedient agents are threatened with punishment (as they often are), they will be much more inclined to use violence to serve the system and much less likely to object.

Bureaucracy

The bureaucratic organization and structure of this experiment increased the subjects' willingness to use violence. In this case, the bureaucracy was as much a matter of the subject's perception as an actual force. In fact, the experiment only involved three people, but the laboratory setup, the predefined procedures, and the automated behavior of the scientist suggested that a large bureaucracy controlled every detail from behind the scenes.

For instance, the fact that the teaching process was defined by a strict set of rules and procedures made it seem more normal and legitimate. Subjects went through a rather complex routine for each question: they had to read the words and multiple choice possibilities, check the answer box for the learner's electronic answer, check the answer sheet for the correct answer, announce the result, and if wrong, re-read the correct word pair—then read the voltage of punishment shock required and finally administer the shock. This overly complicated process—which is a common feature of bureaucracies—facilitated obedience. By requiring such attention to detail, the system implied that a great deal of care had gone into establishing the process, and that it had been well thought out by those in charge. Rather than examine the larger, moral implications of their actions, subjects focused on the details of doing their job. As Milgram explains, "subjects become immersed in the procedures, reading the words pairs with exquisite articulation and pressing the switches with great care. They want to put on a competent performance, but they show an accompanying narrowing of moral concern."[9]

A specific variation of the experiment shows the importance of this bureaucratic feature. Under normal experimental conditions, over sixty percent of subjects were fully obedient and ended up giving the most severe shocks.[10] But when there were less formal procedures and the subject was free to choose the level of shock he administered, less than three percent decided to shock at the most severe level and most gave very low voltage shocks.[11]

Furthermore, division of labor within the bureaucracy helped to facilitate violence. As Milgram recognizes, "it is psychologically easy to ignore responsibility when one is only an intermediate link in a chain of evil action."[12] He further explains that "there is a fragmentation of the total human act; no one man decides to carry out the evil act and is confronted with its consequences. The person who assumes full responsibility for the act has evaporated."[13] After the experiment, subjects were asked, "How much is each of us responsible for the fact that this person was given electric shocks against his will?" The average respondent attributed approximately forty-three percent of the responsibility to himself, thirty-nine percent of the blame to the scientist, and the eighteen percent to the victim.[14] Subjects who were fully obedient and delivered the most severe shocks attributed *more* blame to the scientist than themselves.[15] These results indicate that the basic division of labor between the supervisor (and his unseen associates), the teacher (subject), and the learner (victim) enabled this division of moral responsibility and thus made the violence easier.

The power of this strategy is even clearer in another variation of the Milgram experiment. When the subject was given a co-teacher role in which he administered the test while a confederate peer delivered the electric shocks, the obedience rate skyrocketed to over ninety percent. As long as he was not directly responsible for delivering the shocks, the subject would almost always continue to the bitter end. As Milgram explains, "They are accessories to the act of shocking the victim, but they are not psychologically implicated in it to the point where strain arises and disobedience occurs."[16] As part of the bureaucratic system, these people enabled the violence, but they did not actually carry it out.

Because the labor of the act was further divided and they played an even more limited role, the subjects felt less morally responsible. The tortured cries of the victim remained exactly the same, but they no longer garnered as much sympathy. In much larger bureaucracies, where division of labor reigns supreme and agents' roles are much narrower, it must be even easier for them to deny their moral culpability and allow brutality to continue.

Isolation

The subjects' willingness to use violence was also increased by the isolation of the research environment. The experiment was held in an impressive, state-of-the-art Yale University laboratory.[17] As Milgram explains, being inside the building's walls and not outside them was important. "The fact that this experiment is carried out in a laboratory has a good deal to do with the degree of obedience exacted. . . . If the experiment were to be carried on outside the laboratory, obedience would drop sharply."[18] The laboratory provided shelter and distance—subjects were comforted that those outside the experiment would not know about their behavior. This isolation gave the illusion that they had entered the well-established world of science where different norms, rules, priorities, and ethics applied.

Beyond attributing importance to the laboratory's general isolation, Milgram ran a few experiment variations that tested related concepts. In the basic experiment, the subject was in a separate room from the victim, which helped to insulate the subject from the pain and suffering he caused. When this buffer was removed and the victim was placed in the same room as the subject, the percentage of subjects who were fully obedient dropped more than twenty percent.[19] Milgram also tested the significance of distance between the scientist giving the orders and the subject carrying them out. When the scientist left the subject's room and instead gave orders over the telephone, obedience dropped more than forty percent.[20] If the scientist reentered the room after obedience began slipping, obedience went right back up, which shows how important the close presence of authority was in this context.

Perhaps because this experiment did not focus on group dynamics, the strategic use of isolation to limit communication between agents was not tested. There was no intra-organizational secrecy, and the scientist never gave the subjects the sense that they had to do what they were told without knowing why. In larger systems, where agents are isolated from one another and information is managed on a need-to-know basis, low-level agents can get so accustomed to following orders without knowledge of the bigger picture that their obedience becomes much more deadly.

Dehumanization

The subjects of this experiment were dehumanized by their role in the system. They did not deliver the shocks because of impatience, personal anger, or sadism—their personal feelings towards the victim had been rendered completely irrelevant.[21] Furthermore, their normal, human emotions of guilt, empathy, and concern were simply dismissed by the experimenter. In this context, it became easier for them to act in as inhuman a way as possible. The stress they experienced during the test dissipated the more they could repress their emotions and numbly complete the task in a robotic, machine-like fashion. In fact, the vast majority of subjects who delivered shocks past the 150-volt mark appeared to just give in and go on autopilot for the remainder of the test, having been fully transformed into a tool of the system.[22] Once the subjects decided to obey, they weren't required to think critically or make any real decisions—they just had to perform a series of predetermined functions, like any machine or basic computer program. As Milgram summarizes, "The essence of obedience consists in the fact that a person comes to view himself as the instrument for carrying out another person's wishes."[23] This psychological transformation for the subjects—from human beings to instruments, tools, and machines—is what made it possible for them to proceed.

On the other hand, there was very little dehumanization of the victims. It is true that both the subject and the victim were referred to by role, instead of by name, which may have facilitated the violence somewhat. If the scientist giving the orders had said "Whether Fred likes it or not, you must go on" instead of "Whether the learner likes it or not, you must go on," it may have triggered some reminder of the victim's humanity and had some small effect on reducing the violence. But in any case, blatant dehumanization was wholly absent. As Milgram asserts, "At least one feature of the situation in Germany was not studied here—namely, the intense devaluation of the victim prior to action against him."[24] He adds that in other, more violent contexts, "Systematic devaluation of the victim provides a measure of psychological justification for the brutal treatment of the victim and has been the constant accompaniment of massacres, pogroms, and wars."[25] Fortunately, in this case, the subjects had no ill will towards the victims whatsoever, and most showed great relief upon hearing (after the study) that the victim was fine and had not suffered at all. Even so, if the experiment had strategically dehumanized or devalued the victim prior to the punishments, the violence probably would have been much more severe. Milgram is quick to cede this point: "In all likelihood, our subjects would have experienced greater ease in shocking the victim had he been convincingly portrayed as a brutal criminal or a pervert."[26]

Zimbardo's Stanford Prison Experiment (1971)

Zimbardo's experiment also teaches us a great deal about how normal human beings can be conditioned to use violence. Zimbardo divided male volunteers into "prisoners" and "prison guards" and placed them in a mock prison environment to see what would happen. The results were startling, as he explains:

> By the end of the first day, nothing much was happening. But on the second day, there was a prisoner rebellion. . . . The guards then quickly moved to psychological punishment, though there was physical abuse, too. In the ensuing days, the guards became ever more sadistic, denying the prisoners food, water, and sleep, shooting them with fire-extinguisher spray, throwing their blankets into dirt, stripping them naked and dragging rebels across the yard. How bad did it get? The guards ordered the prisoners to simulate sodomy. . . . I have no idea how much worse things might have gotten.[27]

Though the experiment was scheduled for two weeks, it was stopped after six days because the guards' behavior had become so abusive. Multiple prisoners suffering psychological trauma had already been released early, and the remaining prisoners and guards were showing pathologically destructive symptoms.

This shocking result has often been interpreted in somewhat oversimplified terms. The experiment is sometimes summarized as only showing the importance of situational context—in Zimbardo's words, "the power of the situation to make good people do evil deeds."[28] Many people have assumed that Zimbardo's leadership, while flawed in not preventing the abuses, was essentially a nonfactor in terms of the experiment's results. He himself states, "The guards were merely told to maintain law and order, to use their billy clubs as only symbolic weapons and not actual ones, and to realize that if the prisoners escaped the study would be terminated."[29] But although the guards did not receive explicit orders to abuse the prisoners, they were not simply acting on their own accord. These volunteers did not magically become evil when they assumed their roles. Though his intentions were not malicious, Zimbardo was the architect of these normal young men's violent transformation.

It was not merely the power of a bad situation that prompted the brutality—it was the precise power of a bad situation created *by design*. Steven J. Breckler notes that "In another similar prison experiment, conducted by social psychologists Alex Haslam and Stephen Reicher, less maltreatment was observed when a less abusive climate was established by the leadership at the outset."[30] Though the Haslam/Reicher experiment has limited value for other reasons, psychologists are correct when they claim that "the guards who behaved as tyrants in the original experiment did so only because they were encouraged to."[31] We cannot conclusively know what the guards in the Stanford experiment would have done under other circumstances, but it is clear that their behavior was authorized from above. Again, both in the real world and in controlled experiments, such perfect storms of corruption and psychological transformation are usually man-made. Even though Zimbardo did not expect to produce such cruel levels of violence and brutality, his orientation for the guards and his design of the mock prison incorporated many of the key strategies of systematic indoctrination.

Recruitment and Training

Unlike the leaders of more violent systems, Zimbardo did not target particularly malleable recruits who would be likely to conform. Approximately 100 people responded to advertisements for the study, and Zimbardo and his staff gave the volunteers a bevy of tests to ensure a relatively normal sample. As he recalls, "We screened out the obvious weirdos, the ones with prior arrests of any kind, and any with medical or mental problems."[32] After Zimbardo's assistants Craig Haney and Curt Banks completed the volunteers' interviews and psychological assessments, they selected twenty-four research subjects. These subjects were then randomly assigned to the roles of prison guard and prisoner. By only recruiting young men, Zimbardo may have increased the likelihood of conflict and abuse, since violent organizations usually prioritize this type. However, these subjects were not particularly respectful of authority or ideologically homogenous in a way that would promote violence.

These mock guards did not get all of the systematic training that typifies real world efforts to produce violent agents. Their training did include authorizations for tough treatment and other lessons they picked up on the job, but they were not formally trained to fear the prisoners or work dangers. They were not trained to be obedient, because they were supposed to be making their own decisions on how to serve the system instead of just following orders. Nor were they desensitized to the hostility or tension they would experience in the prison. They also were not specifically trained to bond with each other or to learn how being unified would increase their security.

However, the guards were quickly shaped by their early experiences in the prison and their interactions with each other. On just the first day, Guard Arnett "doubts that the prisoner induction is having its desired effect. He thinks security on his shift is bad and the other guards are being too polite."[33] He conveys this fear to the night shift when they take over, who promise to handle it. On the second day, when some prisoners begin ignoring the prison's rules, "the prisoners are ordered to remain silent, but 819 and 8612 disobey, talk loudly and laugh, and get away with it—for now."[34] In response, some guards become verbally abusive towards the prisoners and force them to do repeated jumping jacks and push-ups for contrived reasons. They find this method of punishment successful, so others learn and join.

This informal training is quite successful, and even influences the less aggressive guards. Zimbardo notes that "Guard Ceros . . . feels he is too soft to be a good guard, so he tries to turn his urge to laugh into a 'sadistic smile' . . . [and another volunteer] reported that he knew it would be tough for him to be a strong guard, and therefore he looked to the others for clues about how to behave."[35] When shifts change, "The new guard, Burdan, gets into the act even more quickly than did the other guards, but he has had on-the-job training watching his two role models."[36] In turn, Burdan gives a less aggressive guard a "pep talk" on the importance of guard unity and "the necessity for all of them to work as a team in order to keep the prisoners in line and not to tolerate any rebelliousness."[37]

A subsequent attempted rebellion by the prisoners drives home the importance of these very lessons and the danger that the prisoners pose. In the midst of the chaos, one prisoner shouts, "Fight them! Resist violently! The time has come for violent revolution!"[38] In response, extra guards stay on duty to unite and put down the rebellion, shooting some prisoners with spray from a fire extinguisher, taking their clothes and beds as punishment, and dragging a troublemaker across the hall by his ankles, where he is thrown into "the Hole"—a tiny dark closet which serves as solitary confinement.

Through these experiences, the guards became increasingly desensitized to the hostile environment. They began to believe that cruelty was necessary for their own security and the good of the system. Again, these young men lacked much formal training, yet they quickly formed a tight unit of abusive guards in response to a threat. If they had undergone real training to desensitize them to violence, teach them the importance of unity and conformity, and help them recognize the dangers posed by the prisoners, they may have become even more abusive and violent than they actually were.

Authorization

Though they specifically prohibited physical violence, Zimbardo and his staff authorized the abusive treatment of prisoners in several ways. They offered a basic transcendent authorization that emphasized the importance of the experiment and its scientific value, while downplaying what they initially considered minor discomfort and suffering for those involved. Zimbardo told the guards that "the prisoners were likely to think of this as all 'fun and games' but it was up to all of us as prison staff to produce the required psychological state in the prisoners for as long as the study lasted."[39] When he saw that guard John Markus was "not enacting the macho guard image," Zimbardo had his prison warden David Jaffe confront Markus with this message:

[Jaffe:] "The guards have to know that every guard has to be what we call a 'tough guard.' The success of the experiment rides on the behavior of the guards to make it seem as realistic as possible."

Markus challenged him, "Real life experience has taught me that tough, aggressive behavior is counterproductive."

Jaffe gets defensive. He starts saying that the purpose of the experiment is not to reform prisoners but to understand how prisons change people when they are faced with the situation of guards being all-powerful.

[Markus:] "But we are also being affected by this situation. Just putting on this guard uniform is a pretty heavy thing for me."

Jaffe becomes more reassuring; "I understand where you are coming from. We need you to act in a certain way. For the time being, we need you to play the role of 'tough guard.' We need you to react as you imagine the 'pigs' would. We're trying to set up the stereotype guard—your individual style has been a little too soft."

"Okay, I will try to adjust somewhat."

"Good, I knew we could count on you."[40]

Markus did not want to be tough, macho, hostile, or aggressive, but he was told he must do so for the good of the experiment. Most of the other guards did not need as much convincing—the directive from above was quite clear.

Zimbardo and his staff also offered mundane authorizations for the guards' cruelty. As Zimbardo recalls, his guidelines during orientation were pretty plain:

We cannot physically abuse or torture them. . . . We can create boredom. We can create a sense of frustration. We can create fear in them, to some degree. We can create a notion of the arbitrariness that governs their lives, which are totally controlled by us, by the system, by you, me, Jaffe. . . . They will have no freedom of action. They will be able to do nothing and say nothing that we don't permit. . . . In general, what all this should create in them is a sense of powerlessness. We have total power in the situation. They have none. [41]

Through these directions, Zimbardo basically gave the guards the license to be creative and do *anything* that was not physical abuse or torture. The guards were expected to fully dominate the prisoners and make them feel scared and totally helpless. And Zimbardo made it seem mundane, ordinary—like no big deal. He essentially conveyed the message that the guards needed to play the tough guard role, but that because this wasn't who they really were, whatever they did was okay. The tougher, the better.

After this first orientation, Zimbardo had his staff meet with the guards to discuss the goals of the experiment in more depth, dole out specific assignments, and recommend tactics for keeping the prisoners under control.[42] In general, Zimbardo and his staff encouraged a hostile, domineering, aggressive social climate. After Jaffe chewed out a disrespectful prisoner and forced him to do push-ups, Zimbardo and his staff couldn't help but praise Jaffe and "give him a pat on the ego: 'Right on, Dave, way to go!'"[43] Even when specific instructions were lacking, the guards clearly understood this priority of ruthlessness. Zimbardo and his staff were watching the guards around the clock and had the power to intervene at any moment if the guards acted too aggressively. The fact that the staff never did (until finally calling off the experiment) was itself implicit approval of each and every abusive act.

In hindsight, it appears that Zimbardo was so worried that the experiment would fail to seem "real" that he went overboard. The mock prison's social climate intensely authorized abusive behavior. It's easy to understand that as one of the first scholars to test these strategies of systematic indoctrination, Zimbardo had no idea just how powerful these methods would be.

Bureaucracy

The bureaucratic structure of the experiment and the mock prison also helped promote cruelty. Built-in rules and standing operating procedures made confrontations between the guards and prisoners a virtual certainty. Jaffe had agreed upon a list of rules with the guards during orientation, and rule 17 was "Failure to obey any of the above rules may result in punishment."[44] The rules were meant to restrict the prisoners, but they also controlled the guards' behavior. The guards were responsible for enforcing the rules—if they allowed the prisoners to disobey, it meant that they were bad at their job and threatened their power, job security, potential earnings, and the security of the experiment itself. As one guard expressed early on, "The prisoners were getting quite rebellious, and I wanted to punish them for breaking up our system."[45]

These confrontations became routine with prisoner counts at regular intervals. The guards were increasingly prepared to dole out punishment at these counts. As the hostile interactions began to feel more normal, the punishments escalated from verbal abuse to push-ups to other humiliations like simulated sodomy. During counts on the final night, some partially naked prisoners were told to bend over like female camels, while other prisoners were instructed to be male camels and "Stand behind the female camels and [pretend to] hump them."[46] As Zimbardo explains, "the nature of counts is transformed over time from routine memorizing and reciting of IDs to an open forum for guards to display their total authority over the prisoners."[47]

There was also a clear division of labor that made it easier for the guards to abuse the prisoners. After all, they were just doing their jobs as part of an experiment, and were thus only partially responsible for the prisoners' apparent suffering. A Stanford University review board had given the study the green light and Zimbardo and his staff had designed it and authorized the tough treatment. Others who "played along" without demanding that the experiment cease included real police officers who had arrested the prisoners at their homes, a real priest who met with the prisoners, and the prisoners' real parents and friends who had come during visiting hours. From the guards' perspectives, even the prisoners took part of the blame—they didn't have to cooperate with the guards' orders, and could have decided to leave the experiment at any point. In addition, the guards on the other shifts were doing the same types of abusive things. Even if a guard had decided to quit, Zimbardo had two alternate guards waiting as replacements, so it was likely the harsh treatment would have continued. The guards were thus able to rationalize their abusive roles as just a small part of the larger process, and in turn feel a lesser degree of guilt.

Isolation

The isolated nature of the mock prison also made it easier for the guards to abuse the prisoners. Interestingly enough, in early interviews with the volunteers, almost all "had indicated a preference for being prisoners because they could not imagine going to college and ending up as a prison guard. On the other hand, they could imagine being imprisoned for a driving violation or some act of civil disobedience and thus felt they might learn something of value."[48] It took an isolated environment that felt like a totally different world to get the new guards to ignore their "real" values and previous sympathy for prisoners and take on the morality of the system.

In addition, the prison's literal isolation made it easier for the guards to behave badly because they were insulated from outside judgment. Their friends and family members were never around to see their cruel behavior. However, the guards did leave the prison after their eight hour shifts to rejoin their usual lives. This split—that the guards could be sadistic and abusive one moment and relatively normal young men the next has shocked many people. As one prisoner explains, "I was surprised that the guards in general accepted their roles as much as they did after being able to go home each day or night."[49] Of course, there was some carryover, and one guard admitted "that he caught himself bossing his mother around at home" in between shifts.[50] If the guards had been truly isolated—unable to leave the prison during the entire experiment (like the prisoners)—their indoctrination probably would have been much more complete and their actions much more horrible. It is worth noting that there was not significant isolation *within* the system—guards could communicate with each other and the staff, and a need-to-know policy that prioritizes secrecy and reduces information flow was never established.

Dehumanization

The Stanford Prison Experiment certainly dehumanized the guards themselves. The young men were encouraged to repress their personal identities and give in to their tough roles. Zimbardo cites the use of reflective sunglasses as just one example of this transformation—he made sure "all our guards would also be donning the same anonymity-inducing goggles as part of our attempt to create a sense of deindividuation."[51] Guard Mike Varnish explained the dehumanizing process: "I had to intentionally shut off all feelings I had towards any of the prisoners, to lose sympathy and any respect for them. . . . I would not let show any feelings they might like to see, like anger or despair."[52] These strategies worked, and the guards began to feel less morally responsible for their increasingly abusive behavior.

As another explained, they became fully entrenched in their impersonal roles. "I found that I had to defend myself, not as me, but as the guard. [The prisoner] hated me as the guard. He was reacting to the uniform; I felt that was the image he placed on me."[53] In an amazingly insightful moment, one prisoner even dared to ask a guard, "Mr. Correctional Officer, do you think that when this job ends you're going to have enough time to become a human being again?"[54] The guard's automatic response was to shove the prisoner into "the Hole" for solitary confinement. The truth about the guard's dehumanizing transformation must have hit a nerve.

The prisoners were also dehumanized, which made it easier for the guards to abuse them. Upon entry, the prisoners were blindfolded, strip-searched, and made to stand naked. Some were forced to wear bags over their heads. A few guards made fun of the naked prisoners, treating them like helpless bodies with odd appendages, instead of like real human beings.[55] The prisoners soon learned they were not allowed to use their own names or refer to other prisoners by name, but instead they became a number, which decreased their humanity further. As the experiment continued, guards referred to prisoners who cooperated as "sheepish." One recalled that "I thought of them as sheep and I did not give a damn as to their condition," while another admitted that he tried "to dehumanize them in order to make it easy for me."[56] One day after counts, a guard told the prisoners "I've had enough of this, go back to your *cage*."[57]

Ultimately, some of the prisoners began to embody this dehumanized role. After some had been severely punished and others began to believe they could not get out of the experiment, they "decided to become 'good prisoners,' obeying every rule and following all prison procedures faithfully in zombie-like fashion."[58] Though the prisoners' adaptation is understandable, it may have contributed to their abuse by making it even easier for the guards to treat them as targets for contempt and violence, rather than as real human beings.

Conclusion

Despite the fame of these experiments, they have not sparked the full-fledged scholarly awakening or action they merit. Years after Milgram's death, Zimbardo commented on the matter:

> One of my greatest surprises from Stanley came at the height of his career when he confided in me that he felt his research was under-appreciated and not sufficiently respected by his social psychology colleagues. I was at first stunned because his obedience studies are the most cited in every introductory and social psychology text I know. But perhaps what he meant was . . . his work did not generate countless dissertations nor instigate more than a few dozen studies claiming to prove or disprove his theory. [59]

Similar things could be said about Zimbardo's work. Haney, who served as a "psychological counselor" in the experiment, expresses this regret:

> Given the significant head start we had on these issues in the late 1960s and early 1970s . . . we should have made great progress by now—not only in understanding but in actually limiting the potential for institutional excess and abuse that had been highlighted both in Milgram's research and the SPE. Of course, we have not. [60]

This is a peculiar phenomenon—these studies are both extremely well known and surprisingly underutilized, considering their scholarly value and powerful implications.

There are multiple explanations for this result. For one thing, these studies cannot be fully replicated today. [61] Many people rightly consider them unethical, considering the risk of psychological damage for the subjects involved. [62] In turn, institutional review boards have established safeguards that steadfastly protect human subjects from similar risks. These measures are certainly appropriate, but they do put limitations on future research. Thus, some scholars may narrowly see Milgram and Zimbardo's experiments as a dead end, as opposed to a potential launching pad for future discoveries.

Another factor may be denial: some people simply do not want to believe Milgram and Zimbardo's findings. It can be comforting to assume that people who use violence on command are an entirely different breed. If we actively considered the possibility that almost *anyone* we come into contact with might be willing to jolt us with electric shocks or abuse us, we would have an awfully hard time forging trusting relationships.

Still another factor may be our attempts to avoid fatalism. After all, the knowledge that normal people can be transformed into extremely violent and abusive beings is very disheartening if the flaw is rooted in human nature itself.

However, a close re-examination of the Milgram and Zimbardo experiments has shown us that it takes human design, not just bad luck, to compel normal people into an organized outpouring of brutality. These experiments are quite complex and contain subtle, almost hidden information about the recipe for violent transformation. Milgram has not simply shown us that normal people will deliver severe electric shocks to innocents when commanded by an authority. He has shown us many of the specific organizational strategies and mechanisms that influence this obedience and can be used to increase or decrease systematic violence. In turn, Zimbardo did not simply demonstrate that normal people become abusive when they are put in a bad situation. As Breckler explains, "Perhaps most important of all, the Stanford experiment taught us that leadership and oversight plays a significant role in these settings. In some ways, the abusive behavior of the guards in the Stanford experiment was precipitated or allowed to develop because of the ground rules and culture established at the outset."[63]

This point is absolutely critical, but it is often overlooked. Though he did not realize it at the time, Zimbardo was testing a framework for systematic indoctrination. He used his psychological expertise to trigger a violent transformation in the volunteers—only he did it more effectively than any of us could have imagined, with profoundly dangerous results. More than thirty-five years after his experiment, Zimbardo is still coming to terms with his own role in the abuses. He admits that his interests have "widened considerably through a fuller appreciation of the ways in which situational conditions are created and shaped by higher-order factors—*systems* of power."[64] "Systems," he adds, "not just dispositions and situations, must be taken into account in order to understand complex behavior patterns."[65]

Milgram and Zimbardo's tasks were much simpler than the one facing violent systems in the real world, which strive to create longer lasting transformations based on better recruitment and training techniques and deeper, more powerful indoctrination. They need agents who will obey when their leaders are not present. They need agents who will carry out violence when the victims are not separated by a wall, but are bleeding at their feet. They need agents who will use violence even when they could potentially get away with doing much less. And they need agents who will continue to believe in the system's morality when violence reaches its most deadly forms.

The upcoming case studies will show how the same type of system which transformed ordinary people into violent machines in Milgram's laboratory and Zimbardo's mock prison is often the source of organized violence in the real world. It produced torturers for the U.S. military at Abu Ghraib. It produced terrorists for Al Qaeda. It produced killers for radical Iran. And it produced mass murderers for the Nazis.

Notes

1. Milgram, *Obedience to Authority*, 5.
2. Milgram, *Obedience to Authority*, 15-16; In a later variation, Milgram ran the experiments with forty women, who behaved in similar ways.
3. Milgram, *Obedience to Authority*, 19.

4. Milgram, *Obedience to Authority*, 142

5. Milgram, *Obedience to Authority*, 21.

6. Milgram, *Obedience to Authority*, 21.

7. Milgram, *Obedience to Authority*, 22.

8. Milgram, *Obedience to Authority*, xix.

9. Milgram, *Obedience to Authority*, 7.

10. Milgram, *Obedience to Authority*, 35.

11. Milgram, *Obedience to Authority*, 71.

12. Milgram, *Obedience to Authority*, 11.

13. Milgram, *Obedience to Authority*, 11.

14. Milgram, *Obedience to Authority*, 203. The victims may have been deemed partially responsible for their fate because (presumably) they didn't learn well enough, they didn't try hard enough, or because they refused to continue answering questions after shocks reached a certain severe level.

15. Milgram, *Obedience to Authority*, 203.

16. Milgram, *Obedience to Authority*, 118.

17. It was later moved to a less famous laboratory in the New Haven area to control for the influence of academic prestige. Subjects were slightly less obedient at the second institution, but the difference was not large.

18. Milgram, *Obedience to Authority*, 140.

19. Milgram, *Obedience to Authority*, 35.

20. Milgram, *Obedience to Authority*, 60.

21. This distinction was shown in the variation where the subjects were free to choose the shock voltage—their willingness to deliver severe shocks fell dramatically.

22. Jerry Burger, "Replicating Milgram," *APS Observer*, December 2007, http://www.psychologicalscience.org/observer/getArticle.cfm?id=2264 (10 September 2008).

23. Milgram, *Obedience to Authority*, xviii.

24. Milgram, *Obedience to Authority*, 9.

25. Milgram, *Obedience to Authority*, 9.

26. Milgram, *Obedience to Authority*, 9.

27. Claudia Dreifus, "Finding Hope in Knowing the Universal Capacity for Evil," *New York Times*, 3 April 2007, http://www.nytimes.com/2007/04/03/science/03conv.html (10 April 2008).

28. Philip Zimbardo, Christina Maslach, and Craig Haney, "Reflections on the Stanford Prison Experiment: Genesis, Transformations, Consequences," in *Obedience to Authority: Current Perspectives on the Milgram Paradigm*, ed. Thomas Blass (Mahwah, N.J.: Lawrence Erlbaum Associates, Inc., 2000), 196.

29. Zimbardo, Maslach, and Haney, "Reflections on the Stanford Prison Experiment," 200.

30. Steven J. Breckler, "How Can the Science of Human Behavior Help Us Understand Abu Ghraib," *APA Online*, 10 June 2004, http://www.apa.org/ppo/issues/breckler604.html (6 February 2006).

31. David Adams, "Reality TV show recreates famed social study," *Nature* 417 (May 2002): 213.

32. Philip Zimbardo, *The Lucifer Effect: Understanding How Good People Turn Evil* (New York: Random House, 2007), 30.

33. Zimbardo, *The Lucifer Effect*, 47.

34. Zimbardo, *The Lucifer Effect*, 48.

35. Zimbardo, *The Lucifer Effect*, 53.

36. Zimbardo, *The Lucifer Effect*, 49.

37. Zimbardo, *The Lucifer Effect*, 52.

38. Zimbardo, *The Lucifer Effect*, 61.

39. Zimbardo, *The Lucifer Effect*, 55.

40. Zimbardo, *The Lucifer Effect*, 65.

41. Zimbardo, *The Lucifer Effect*, 55.

42. Zimbardo, *The Lucifer Effect*, 54.

43. Zimbardo, *The Lucifer Effect*, 45.

44. Zimbardo, *The Lucifer Effect*, 45.

45. Zimbardo, *The Lucifer Effect*, 60.

46. Zimbardo, *The Lucifer Effect*, 172.

47. Zimbardo, *The Lucifer Effect*, 45.

48. Zimbardo, Maslach, and Haney, "Reflections on the Stanford Prison Experiment," 199.

49. Zimbardo, *The Lucifer Effect*, 188.

50. Zimbardo, *The Lucifer Effect*, 187.

51. Zimbardo, *The Lucifer Effect*, 34.

52. Zimbardo, *The Lucifer Effect*, 86.

53. Zimbardo, *The Lucifer Effect*, 156. Emphasis removed.

54. Zimbardo, *The Lucifer Effect*, 109.

55. Zimbardo, *The Lucifer Effect*, 40.

56. Zimbardo, *The Lucifer Effect*, 157.

57. Zimbardo, *The Lucifer Effect*, 114.

58. Zimbardo, Maslach, and Haney, "Reflections on the Stanford Prison Experiment," 201.

59. Zimbardo, Maslach, and Haney, "Reflections on the Stanford Prison Experiment," 230.

60. Zimbardo, Maslach, and Haney, "Reflections on the Stanford Prison Experiment," 230.

61. There have been some recent partial replications of Milgram's experiment. Perhaps most impressively, in 2007, Burger, "Replicating Milgram," recreated the experiment with several variations. Notably, the subjects were stopped after reaching the 150-volt mark instead of continuing up to 450 volts and beyond. Burger found that today's subjects were just as obedient in delivering shocks as those in Milgram's experiment nearly fifty years earlier. And as mentioned earlier, Haslam and Reicher modeled their prison experiment after Zimbardo's, despite major differences between the two.

62. Indeed, in hindsight, Zimbardo has expressed regret about the experiment, although follow up research apparently revealed no permanent damage to any of the young men involved.

63. Breckler, "How Can the Science of Human Behavior Help Us Understand Abu Ghraib."

64. Zimbardo, *The Lucifer Effect*, 10.
65. Zimbardo, *The Lucifer Effect*, 10.

Chapter 4
Nazi Germany: Blueprints for Genocide

For many, Nazi Germany stands alone as the prime example of evil in the modern era. And for many, Adolf Hitler's surname has become synonymous with the Devil himself. With good reason—the Nazis mobilized millions of Germans for a horrifying campaign of genocide which ultimately left over 50 million people dead. Never before had the masses been successfully programmed on such a large scale, with such scientific precision and such deadly consequences. As the following examination will show, the Nazis used systematic indoctrination to compel relatively ordinary Germans to carry out their brutal plan.

First, however, it is important to say a word on a historical dispute about the Holocaust. In general, those who focus on the system are often categorized as taking a structural functionalist approach to history, because they point to the functions of social structures as responsible for events. This perspective is countered by the intentionalist approach, which attributes the responsibility for historical events to the direct and deliberate plans of people. Interpretations of the Holocaust have similarly been split—with heated political implications.

Structural functionalists generally tend to downplay the importance of Hitler, blaming the German state apparatus and mid-level officials for the mass extermination of Jews. From their perspective, the impetus for the Holocaust grew from society and the state as a whole, and was not planned from above, but simply developed over time in response to strains from World War I and the struggles of World War II. On the other hand, intentionalists generally see the Final Solution as Hitler's premeditated plan, which he successfully got Nazi supporters to buy into and carry out. As Daniel J. Goldhagen explains, "the 'intentionalist-functionalist' debate . . . has become the central fault line dividing academic interpreters of Nazism and the Holocaust. And much of the debate has focused on close, detailed readings of the historical record regarding one particular issue: when the decision to annihilate European Jewry was taken."[1]

Despite this book's focus on the system, it should not be casually aligned with structural functionalist or intentionalist approaches to the Holocaust. Rather, it attempts to provide a synthesis of these perspectives. The assertion here is that Hitler and his associates used the system as a tool. The goal: to produce a Nazi workforce that was conditioned to perform violence on command. Hitler would not have been able to orchestrate the Final Solution without mobilizing the national system. However, the bureaucracies and the mid-level officials running them—as functions of state society—did not organically produce the Final Solution.

This book subscribes to the general interpretation offered by Breitman that "the idea of executing Jews was an essential element from the beginning, although a comprehensive program—the Final Solution—came later."[2] However, even if the possibility of Jewish extermination was not really developed until the later 1930s or early 1940s, the critical point for this book is that Hitler and his fellow Nazi leaders were intentionally designing a violence-prone workforce. To that degree, it fits intentionalist interpretations. As Mann suggests, "Hitler . . . was always prepared to use whatever violence was necessary" "to eliminate Jews and Bolsheviks from a Greater German Reich."[3] Whether his elimination technique du jour was initially forced deportation, forced sterilization, or genocide, from a very early stage he was bent on producing an army of like-thinking Nazis who would do whatever he ordered—no matter how cruel it might be.

To build his workforce, he needed a powerful, complex system that could implement the specific strategies of indoctrination. It was a challenge of unparalleled enormity. As Hilberg explains, "A Western bureaucracy had never before faced such a chasm between moral precepts and administrative action; an administrative machine had never been burdened with such a drastic task."[4]

Recruitment

The Nazis required so much manpower for their campaign that their overall recruitment included many different types of people—they practically mobilized the entire German nation. However, for critical positions, their recruitment reflected many of the priorities outlined in the analytical framework.

The Hitler Youth groups were clearly an attempt to mold pliable kids into loyal warriors for the future, and as Mann explains, the movement deliberately targeted the "cult of youth." He points out that "The main attraction of fascism was the intensity of its message. This always brought committed support from mainly young people."[5] Proven killers were the first option for Dachau concentration camp commander Theodor Eicke, but when "the supply of experienced Nazis dried up, he intentionally recruited young party members, whom he said were more malleable."[6] Although Browning downplays the importance of youth in his study of a murderous reserve police battalion because many men were in their thirties and forties, even in that battalion, the two police captains were young men in their twenties.[7] One of them "had joined the National Socialist Student Union (NS-Schulerbund) in 1930 as a sixteen-year old, the Hitler Youth in 1932 at eighteen, and the SS one year later."[8] The other "joined the Nazi Party and SA" at age twenty and the SS four years later.[9] From an early age, these Nazi captains were classic products of systematic indoctrination.

Beyond their priority on youth, the Nazis only recruited males for roles in which violence was most instrumental. The SS was an all male organization, and all soldiers involved in combat and the extermination of Jews on the Eastern front were men. Mann explains that "The first cohort of recruits . . . were disproportionately students, cadets, athletes, and young working-class rednecks," while fascist "militancy centered on the ability to trap young single men within comradely, hierarchical, and violent 'cages.'"[10]

When it came to ideology, recruits were generally traditionalists—as Klaus Theweleit explains, Nazi "fascists preferred to perceive themselves as the inheritors of millennial traditions."[11] Similarly, Ernst Jünger writes of the Nazis' attempt to connect themselves with the past through violence: "Clutching a weapon from the depths of sleep came easily; it was in our blood, an expression of the primitive within—the same gesture with which Ice Age man grasped his ax of stone."[12] The young men sharing Hitler's vision of a nation of Spartan-like warriors made the best fits for the system's murderous agenda.

Of course, many recruits also shared anti-Semitic beliefs and the sense of belonging to an elite Aryan group. As Waller describes, these beliefs were a critical precursor for violence:

> The role of ideological commitment in shaping perpetrator behavior is perhaps most clearly delineated in the Holocaust. Nazi ideology, first laid out in Hitler's *Mein Kampf* in the fall of 1925, centered on the notion that race is the foundation of all culture . . . it carried dual obligations to promote racial purity whenever possible and destroy whatever—and whomever—threatened racial purity. . . . The committed ideologist, unless he was willing to abandon the comfort of his ideology and admit he was wrong, had to destroy all threats to that ideology.[13]

Anti-Semitism was common throughout Europe during this era, so the Nazis found plenty of new recruits who already held these beliefs.

A final characteristic shared by many Nazi recruits was a deep-seated respect for authority. Adolf Eichmann suggested that this feature was an implicit part of German culture, in general. As he explained, "All my life I have been accustomed to obedience, from early childhood . . . used to being led, in business and everything else. . . . Little by little, we were taught all these things. We grew into them, all we knew was obedience to orders."[14] Indeed, after bad experiences with weak national leadership at the end of World War I and an inefficient Weimar Republic, many Germans craved powerful leadership with clear, decisive policies and demarcated hierarchies with a top-down power structure. In other words, they wanted authoritative leaders who would tell them what to do.

Overall, these qualities—being young, male, committed to tradition, anti-Semitic, and respectful of authority—described those recruits who were targeted by the Nazi system and who proved most susceptible to its indoctrination techniques.

Training

Training was a crucial part of the Nazi system. As Bartov explains, "At home some of [the recruits] might have remained immune to the regime's propaganda, but once in uniform they were sucked into the army's 'melting pot' and forged into Hitler's instruments, becoming the executors of his policies, the conquerors of his empire."[15] Though Bartov's focus is primarily on soldiers, his point applies to all within the Nazi system. The powerful training experiences many recruits went through helped to cement their loyalty and obedience. It is important to note that not all of their training was formal—sometimes new members of the system learned how to behave and what was expected of them simply through interaction with their peers.

New recruits were confronted with immediate threats to their security—most prominently the Russian Bolsheviks and the Jews. Bartov details how the Nazis created and exploited an "irrational, but powerful terror from the Russians. . . . Fear of 'Asiatic Bolshevism,' anchored in long established prejudices and fanned by Nazi propaganda, created the basis for a grotesquely distorted view of reality."[16] The claims about the Jewish threat were steeped in anti-Semitism, and included a frightening medieval myth called the "blood libel."[17] According to the nasty accusation, Jews would regularly steal children in the middle of the night, murder them, and use their blood for secret ceremonies.[18] The Nazis exploited this baseless myth to stir up fears of the Jewish threat. Shlomo Aronson further explains how, overall, "Hitler portrayed himself and his nation—the political-historical framework of his race—as having been victimized, raped, almost murdered by domestic and foreign powers who were dominated by a common sinister racial influence: 'The Jew.'"[19]

As part of this strategy, the Nazis also taught recruits about evidence of *The Protocols of the Meetings of the Learned Elders of Zion*, which supposedly revealed a Jewish conspiracy to take over the world.[20] This text, which was actually a fake, was the Nazis' explicit attempt to cultivate fear and sanction violence. As Robert L. Snow concludes, "It does not take much of a psychologist to see that the *Protocols* was written with the intent of making the reader view Jews as both evil and a dire threat to all non-Jews."[21]

After emphasizing the dangers facing the national system, the Nazis found it easier to sell its followers on the importance of unity. According to many Germans, including Hitler, Germany had lost World War I in large part due to its lack of cohesion. To prevent further failures, the Nazi movement insisted that unity was critical for survival. Leaders regularly preached that "The primary loyalty of the individual was to the German state, which was identified with the Nazi Party."[22] As Mann describes, the Nazi system was successful in "persuading its own members that they were a solidary, comradely elite, willing to take risks for radical goals, and . . . that ritualized 'orderly' violence was needed to solve the country's 'anarchy.'"[23]

The Nazis also prioritized German unity within the army. As Bartov explains, "troops trained and grouped in units together . . . [and] the wounded could expect to rejoin their old comrades once they recovered."[24] Furthermore, "German soldiers could see their unit as a kind of home to which they could always return, a social group made of men they knew and trusted."[25] This emphasis on camaraderie was a strategic part of the Nazis' training program—it made it harder for individuals to quit when faced with orders to commit cruel and terrible violence.

Nazi leaders also stressed that the system's triumph over Jews and Russian Bolsheviks depended on conformity and obedience. As Mann explains, "'certainty,' 'safety,' and 'order' were linked values."[26] In turn, Waller documents how "the first of twelve commandments listed in a primer used to indoctrinate Nazi youth was 'The leader is always right.'"[27] Similarly, Bartov points to the Nazi lesson that "No matter what objections there might be, orders were given to be obeyed."[28]

Though dissenters were sometimes given the option to avoid participating in genocide, they had reason to fear the consequences. George Victor notes that "Hitler demanded blind obedience and created a coercive atmosphere. . . . [He] did threaten people with death for disobedience," even though he may not have followed through on such threats.[29] When faced with soldiers hesitant to conform on the Eastern front, Hitler declared "every courageous man . . . will enforce the execution of orders, if necessary by the force of arms, and will immediately open fire in case of insubordination. This is not only his right, but also his duty."[30] In other words, soldiers were expected to shoot any fellow soldiers who did not follow orders.

Beyond such threats, Browning describes how many policemen refused to "adopt overtly nonconformist behavior" because they didn't want to shirk their duty and leave more work for their peers.[31] As horrible as it sounds, "It was easier for them to shoot."[32] Refusing to give in and obey orders would not only have endangered the mission and the system itself, but it would have been "an asocial act vis-à-vis one's comrades."[33]

The Nazis' most extreme training techniques were designed to desensitize recruits to violence. Victor illustrates how the Nazis trained SS recruits to become hard men by witnessing and growing accustomed to brutality:

> The most extensive training was for the SS. Recruits were required to observe
> and participate as assistants while others beat, tortured, and killed prisoners.
> Those who did not faint were rewarded. And they were subjected to insults,
> humiliations, and violence. Some SS men were given dogs to rear as their own
> and then ordered to strangle them. . . . Still others were forced to kill Jewish
> babies in front of the babies' mothers. Voicing scruples and flinching when
> witnessing or performing such acts were called softness, unmanliness, weak-
> ness, and cowardice before the enemy.[34]

These hurdles were not just some sort of terrible initiation rites—although they
probably did promote bonding among recruits through mutual suffering. These
were strategic attempts at conditioning the workforce to accept and perform violence on command. Thus, to the SS men enlisted with carrying out the execution
of thousands of Jews, "Himmler stressed the idea that doing the most repugnant
tasks made them the best of men."[35] At its core, training prepared men to accept
the opinion that "killing, or being willing to kill, members of another group of
people is necessary for the safety and security of one's own group."[36]

Authorization

The Nazis employed a range of transcendent authorizations to emphasize the
appeal of desired ends and downplay the violence required to meet them.

The supreme German authority was Hitler himself, whose quest to purge the
nation of Jews was portrayed as the path to truth and purity. As Victor details,
"For some, the authority was their own special understanding of what was
'really' happening around them; for others, it was the belief that they were
God's agents. Hitler saw himself as combining both sources of authority."[37] Beyond the goal of a purified country, people were thus encouraged to see pleasing
a god-like Hitler as an end unto itself, a noble pursuit in its own right. Along
these lines, the justice system, which normally serves as a societal moral compass, was specifically recalibrated to serve Hitler's wishes. "To lend an air of
legitimacy to his programs, Hitler used Germany's legal system, bending it to
his will. His authority was imposed on prosecutors by Göring, who told them,
'the law and the will of the Führer are one.'"[38] Thus, what Hitler wanted and
what was morally and legally "right" became synonymous, regardless of the
violence required. The constant greeting "Heil Hitler" only reinforced this message.

Beyond emphasizing the appeal of pleasing Hitler, transcendent authorizations reduced Nazi followers' consciousness of the violence required to meet the
Führer's goals. Victor provides some clear examples of how they made violence

seem like a positive:

> Invading and occupying a country was called "protecting" it (Denmark and
> Norway) and "insuring its neutrality" (Belgium and Holland). . . . Razing a city
> or town to the ground was called "pacifying" it. . . . A proposed measure in
> 1939 to kill mental hospital patients was to be called "The Law for Granting of
> Last Aid" or "The Law for Granting of Special Help". . . . The extermination
> program was called . . . "disinfection," "deportation," "evacuation," "reloca-
> tion," "resettlement" . . . "housecleaning," "special treatment," and "the final
> solution."[39]

Similarly, Waller agrees that "The camouflage vocabulary used by the Nazis to
cover their extraordinary evil was especially striking—'final solution' . . . 'spontaneous actions' . . . [and] 'special installations' among many others."[40]

It is important to recognize how these transcendent authorizations intentionally avoided negative mentions of murder or bloodshed and instead provided
positive images of protection, pacification, aid, help, and treatment. The words
were strategically selected. That people want final solutions to problems is almost a given, and as unarguable as the appeal of victory or pleasing a god-like
figure. Meanwhile, the gruesome nature of the violence required to achieve such
ends was at least temporarily obscured, as the agents were primed to focus on
the positive. Nazi leadership could never appeal to ordinary Germans with
thoughts of millions of ravaged corpses, or the screams of women and children
as they were horded into makeshift gas chambers. They had to lure people in
with positive images and only passing references to the negatives. Once future
perpetrators were so committed to the system that they would not criticize it,
they were finally confronted with their violent assignments.

In order to further prepare people for violence, the Nazis used mundane authorizations. The general call for extreme measures came not only from Hitler
and the Nazi party, but also from educated Germans without direct Nazi affiliation. As Michael P. Ghiglieri explains, "To Hitler, Jews, Slavs, Gypsies, and
even Russians were Untermenschen, 'Subhumans' to be annihilated from the
face of the Earth. . . . [But] documents show that a sobering number of German
scientists agreed with his racist rhetoric."[41]

More specific authorizations were given from various bureaucrats and officers within the Nazi system, who helped cultivate a social climate in which "Order, safety, security, hierarchy . . . [and] national rather than class interest become the primary slogans, while the enemy was demeaned, even demonized, as
the antithesis of all these values, unworthy of democratic or (in extreme cases)
of humane treatment."[42] This emphasis on order and security was extended to
praise and authorize violence. As Mann explains, SS leaders emphasized violence as a form of discipline:

> the SS . . . did blend the notions of violence and order. The SS was committed

to the notion that a paramilitary discipline could generate a new social, political, and racial elite. Thus . . . it attracted many of Germany's young educational and professional elite . . . [and] confused ordinary Germans' responses to Nazism, since it fused together what we normally think of as the legitimate and the illegitimate.[43]

In civil society, order is usually seen as a legitimate goal, while violence is considered illegitimate. But by blurring the two, the Nazis promoted the concept of legitimate violence. In no uncertain terms, Hitler authorized violence as a necessary coercive force that allowed strong people to accomplish great things. Victor recounts that Hitler "espoused violence and ruthlessness over and over . . . shrinking from violence showed moral weakness, while willingness to destroy showed moral strength. And repeated acts of destruction increased one's moral fiber."[44]

Ultimately, these types of mundane authorizations produced a social climate where violence was not only acceptable, it was respected. A perfect example of this mentality came at the opening orientation for the concentration camp Dachau. In typical Nazi fashion, a commander told the guards "Any man in our ranks who can't stand the sight of blood doesn't belong here, he should get out."[45] These brutal values saturated the Nazi system. Violence became an honored sign of strength for those agents with the self-discipline to use it mercilessly.

Bureaucracy

It is clear that German bureaucracies were a critical component of the Nazis' campaign of genocide. Hilberg asserts that as the Final Solution unfolded, "its requirements became more complex and its fulfillments involved an ever larger number of agencies, party offices, business enterprises, and military commands."[46] Beyond logistical concerns, it was the moral hurdles of "destroying the Jews [that] put the German bureaucracy to a supreme test."[47] However, because the Nazis used the bureaucracies to facilitate systematic indoctrination, "No obstruction stopped the German machine of destruction. No moral problem proved insurmountable."[48] Sigrid Meuschel notes how under Nazi control, "Flexible, extra-legal, and extra-bureaucratic agencies institutionalized the terror against fictitious enemies; the fiction of a future civilization and a new moral sense legitimized it."[49]

German bureaucracies were also effective because they made agents feel like small, anonymous parts of the larger system:

[For any given man,] No matter where he looked, he was one among thousands. His own importance was diminished, and he felt that he was replaceable, perhaps even dispensable. In such reflective moments the perpetrator quieted his conscience with the thought that he was part of a tide and that there was very little a drop of water could do against such a wave.[50]

Even if someone felt moral pangs and would have preferred to stop the execution of Jews, the system's momentum opposing him was so daunting that he often felt powerless. Since the Final Solution was such an immense bureaucratic project, most put aside their reservations and simply followed orders.

More specifically, Nazi bureaucracies used routines and rituals to help normalize violence. As Waller asserts, when violence becomes ordered, expected, and regular, a person's "psychological system grows used to events that initially produced a strong reaction, [and] extraordinary evil becomes habitual and routinized."[51] Mann similarly points out that "Rituals were key to Nazi mobilization of militants."[52] Bergerson explains this process as a built-in function of Nazi bureaucracy:

> The bureaucratic quality of the so-called Final Solution to the Jewish Question . . . made "sense" to ordinary people. From their semiotic system of colored triangles, middle names, and tattooed numbers to their schemes for physical relocation, incarceration, and murder, the Nazi regime increasingly administered informal social relations . . . the alleged "willingness" (Goldhagen 1996) of ordinary Germans to participate in Nazi terror and genocide was based not fundamentally on their commitment to Nazi ideology per se but on the degree to which they had grown accustomed, and perhaps even addicted, to Nazi habit while living at home.[53]

People tend to be suspicious of things that are hidden and unpredictable, and trusting of things that are regimented, out in the open, and predictable. Those who may have rebelled against a spontaneous or passionate rush to genocide were conditioned to trust the Nazi system and its well-ordered ways of handling things, so they accepted the more gradual march to mass murder.

Bureaucratic routines and rituals also made horrible acts of violence seem less psychologically significant. As a guilty Nazi doctor explained later, "In the beginning it was almost impossible. Afterward it became almost routine. That's the only way to put it."[54] As part of this strategy, Nazi commander Eicke "instructed guards not to arbitrarily beat or maltreat prisoners according to their mood, but to do so routinely as systematic intimidation."[55] This was the standing operating procedure throughout the death camps: "ritual conduct included the roll calls, camp parades, meaningless physical exercises, and the stripping and beating of victims already marked for death."[56] The regularity of these routines and rituals helped indoctrinate the system's agents—it made their use of violence seem more normal, predictable, and under bureaucratic control.

Finally, the Nazis' bureaucratic division of labor also helped to assuage the moral concerns of their members and encourage the use of violence. This is a point that many scholars have correctly emphasized in their efforts to understand such cruelty. John M. Darley explains how for the Holocaust, "When death, like cars or chairs, is produced on assembly lines, each individual concentrates on the micro requirements of his or her part in the process; the eventual outcome is rarely thought of . . . it is only the final assembly of those subtasks that is horrible, and no individual 'sees' that final solution."[57] Baumeister similarly posits that within the Nazi bureaucracy, "The death of one person was the result of dozens of individual actions by different people, no one of whom felt anything more than a slight responsibility for the lethal outcome. Each person could say something like 'I just drove the train.'"[58]

By avoiding the big picture, perpetrators could console themselves with the knowledge that their violence was only a small part of a larger, unstoppable process. As Hilberg details, "[Bureaucrats] could destroy a whole people by sitting at their desks . . . they never had to see '100 bodies lie there, or 500, or 1,000.'"[59] This made moral transgressions much easier for them. But even for the Nazi doctors, policemen, soldiers, and concentration camp guards with more direct contact with violence and death, the reality that their "contributions" were just a small part of the larger campaign helped to alleviate their moral concerns. And again, for an individual within the system, refusing to follow orders would not only be pointless and ineffective, because the system would quickly replace him, but it would also be socially unpopular among peers. This type of powerful bureaucratic momentum was critical to the Nazis' strategy of systematic indoctrination.

Isolation

The Nazis capitalized on several types of isolation to protect their supporters from critical moral judgments and maintain their acceptance of violence.

In the larger sense, Germany was isolated from the rest of Europe—it had been blamed by Allied powers for World War I and forced to submit to humiliating restrictions in the Treaty of Versailles. Many Germans saw the postwar settlement as an "attempted emasculation" of the nation, which increased their resentment and distrust of foreigners.[60] This rift between Germany and its neighbors allowed Hitler and Nazi leadership to ignore dissenting opinions from the rest of the world as their movement became increasingly radical, and to encourage their followers to do the same thing.

The Nazis used this isolation to build a moral barrier between those within the system and those outside it. Hitler encouraged this isolation by rejecting external values: "Only when the time comes when the race is no longer overshadowed by the consciousness of its own guilt, then will it find internal peace. . . . I am freeing men from . . . the dirty and degrading modification of . . . conscience and morality.'"[61] In the place of traditional standards the Nazis offered the morality of the system. Göring described this credo as "Right is that which serves the German people" and the Academy of German Law deemed that "Right is that which serves the State.'"[62] By this set of moral standards, any act—no matter how violent—that served the system was a good and righteous thing as long as it was *done well*. Thus, through this strategy of social and moral isolation, the Nazis replaced traditional ethics with a merciless work ethic.

The Nazis also increased isolation within the system. They were obsessive about secrecy, and they tried to keep all information about their sinister plans quiet to limit debate. As Hilberg explains, the Nazis "shut off the supply of information from all those who did not have to know it. Whoever did not participate was not supposed to know."[63] Furthermore, "Hitler ordered that officials receive only the minimum [information] needed to perform assigned duties. And they grew afraid to ask for more, to consult each other."[64] For the most part, this strategy worked. Hilberg cites "the prohibition of criticism" and notes that within Germany, "Public protests by outsiders were extremely rare."[65] Again, this was by design: "the bureaucracy wanted to hide its deeds. It wanted to conceal the destructive process not only from all outsiders but also from the censuring gaze of its own conscience."[66]

By increasing isolation within the system, limiting information flow, and barring open discussions about their methods, the Nazis kept their followers' new morality intact. As Mann describes, "The elitism of the SS caged its comrades, protecting them from the reach of conventional morality and legality."[67] Members of the system were isolated from each other in order to protect their newly cultivated Nazi perspective. Ultimately, the system's isolation provided the space and protection for the violent work ethic to supplant traditional values and become established as the norm.

Dehumanization

The Nazis dehumanized members of their own system to the point where their followers became mere objects. Human beings who follow orders instead of thinking for themselves, who lack the freedom to make decisions, who push aside their true passions, and who repeatedly perform isolated tasks without grasping the bigger picture are missing out on the full human experience. Though the Nazi masses can in no way be excused for slaughtering millions of innocents in horrid fashion, it is important to recognize the extent of their transformation. The Nazis' emphasis on becoming free from morality and desensitized to violence actually led its agents away from what it means to be human.

Of course, Nazi followers should also be held responsible for dehumanizing themselves, which was a coping mechanism for times when being fully human was inconvenient or uncomfortable. Hilberg notes that often a killer within the Nazi system convinced himself that "he did not act out of personal vindictiveness . . . duty was an assigned part; it was his 'fate.'" [68]

Nazi leadership also viewed many of those within their ranks in object terms—members of the system were weapons, instruments, or pawns that should be treated in a utilitarian manner and sacrificed if any benefit could be gained. Of course, this mentality was not advertised to the populace, but it existed nonetheless. Victor cites perhaps the most obvious example: "Like other charismatic leaders, Hitler impressed his followers as devoted to them but . . . [as] in the Röhm purge, during crises he killed his followers."[69] The murder of hundreds of SA Nazis helped strengthen the SS and gave Hitler more power, so he authorized it. These men were not valued as human beings, but seen as expendable means to an end, nothing more.

However, by far the most blatant dehumanization was that of the Jews—the prime targets of Nazi violence. In general, as Browning explains, perceived differences between two groups of people makes it psychologically easier for one group to brutalize the other one: "a struggle between 'our people' and 'the enemy' . . . creates a polarized world in which 'the enemy' is easily objectified and removed from the community of human obligation."[70] The Nazis encouraged their members to view the Jews in dehumanized terms so that it would become easier to harm them.

Nazi leaders made sure that Jews were not seen as just different, but as *literally* sub-human. Leonard Berkowitz cites how many people "in the Nazi campaign to exterminate Jewry during World War II clearly regarded Jews as less than human, or even as dangerous nonhumans who had to be destroyed. . . . [This] made it easier for German soldiers to slaughter the innocent by the millions."[71] Similarly, Todorov asserts that "In the German camps . . . humiliation and degradation took place as if the very goal of the system were to reduce men and women to less than animals."[72] In fact, the Nazis actually used human beings "as guinea pigs for medical experimentation, because they were 'undermen,' incomplete men."[73] Another example of this dehumanization is SS officer Franz Stangl, who reportedly saw the "men, women and children about to be gassed as cattle" and encouraged others to feel the same way.[74] By the Nazi rationale, killing a Jew was supposed to be no more morally objectionable than killing an animal, and indeed, Jews were often compared to lice, rats, or other vermin. All were seen as dangerous pests that threatened to contaminate the nation.

Of course, any person with common sense might be expected to doubt such conjecture: to the average German, Jews certainly *seemed* human. After all, they looked, behaved, and functioned pretty much just like everyone else. Ever prepared, the system quickly addressed this concern. As an SS pamphlet explained, "The subhuman man—that creation of nature appearing wholly identical in all biological respects, with hands, feet, and a species of brain, with eyes, and a mouth, *is in reality something quite different*, a dreadful creation, a mere draft of a human being . . . mentally and spiritually inferior to any animal."[75] Jews were thus dehumanized and portrayed as a particularly terrible type of creature because of their close resemblance to man. The Nazis contended that like the wolf in sheep's clothing, the Jews appeared to be harmless in their convenient human disguises, all the while lurking as a deadly and treacherous threat.

Conclusion

As this chapter has shown, Hitler's goal of eliminating the Jewish presence in Germany was a big project, and the Nazis needed a powerful system to carry out the mission. Hilberg explains that "The destruction of the Jews was a total process, comparable in its diversity to a modern war, a mobilization, or a national reconstruction."[76]

However, the Nazi system was important beyond its logistical efficiency and its ability to organize mass murder. It controlled more than poisonous gas, lodging for soldiers, transportation for captured Jews, and the details of the killing process. It controlled the very souls of the Nazi killers. It was the Nazi system that transformed relatively ordinary men into weapons of genocide. By combining strategies of recruitment, training, authorization, bureaucracy, isolation, and dehumanization, the Nazis built an army of loyal soldiers from a society that was not particularly aberrant. As Victor reminds us, "Nations as anti-Semitic as Germany and even more anti-Semitic ones did not perpetrate the Holocaust."[77] The difference was that in Germany, a powerful system indoctrinated people with time-tested strategies.

Unfortunately, it worked.

Notes

1. Daniel Jonah Goldhagen, "The Road to Death," *The New Republic* 205, no. 19 (November 1991): 35.
2. Breitman, *The Architect of Genocide*, 32.
3. Mann, *The Dark Side of Democracy*, 211.
4. Hilberg, *The Destruction of The European Jews*, 1011.
5. Michael Mann, *Fascists* (New York: Cambridge University Press, 2004), 359, 364.
6. Mann, *The Dark Side of Democracy*, 201.
7. Browning, *Ordinary Men*, 46.
8. Browning, *Ordinary Men*, 46.
9. Browning, *Ordinary Men*, 46.
10. Mann, *Fascists*, 359, 364.
11. Klaus Theweleit, *Male Fantasies*, Vol. 2, *Male Bodies: Psychoanalyzing the White Terror* (Minneapolis, Minn.: University of Minnesota Press, 1989), 385.

12. Theweleit, *Male Fantasies*, 385.

13. Waller, *Becoming Evil*, 185.

14. Waller, *Becoming Evil*, 181.

15. Omer Bartov, *Hitler's Army: Soldiers, Nazis, and War in the Third Reich* (New York: Oxford University Press, 1991), 183.

16. Bartov, *Hitler's Army*, 181.

17. Jay Y. Gonen, *The Roots of Nazi Psychology* (Lexington, Ky.: The University Press of Kentucky, 2000), 54.

18. Gonen, *The Roots of Nazi Psychology*, 54.

19. Shlomo Aronson, "Nazi Terrorism: The Complete Trap and the Final Solution," in *The Morality of Terrorism*, eds. David C. Rapoport and Yonah Alexander (New York: Columbia University Press, 1989), 170.

20. Robert L. Snow, *The Militia Threat: Terrorists Among Us* (New York: Plenum Trade, 1999), 116.

21. Snow, *The Militia Threat*, 117.

22. Leo Braudy, *From Chivalry to Terrorism* (New York: Alfred A. Knopf, Inc., 2003), 426.

23. Mann, *Fascists*, 175.

24. Bartov, *Hitler's Army*, 30.

25. Bartov, *Hitler's Army*, 30.

26. Mann, *Fascists*, 356.

27. Waller, *Becoming Evil*, 182.

28. Hilberg, *The Destruction of The European Jews*, 1024.

29. George Victor, *Hitler: The Pathology of Evil* (Washington, D.C.: Brassey's, Inc., 1998), 94.

30. Bartov, *Hitler's Army*, 100.

31. Browning, *Ordinary Men*, 184.

32. Browning, *Ordinary Men*, 184.

33. Browning, *Ordinary Men*, 185.

34. Victor, *Hitler*, 111.

35. Victor, *Hitler*, 112.

36. Waller, *Becoming Evil*, 186.

37. Victor, *Hitler*, 85.

38. Victor, *Hitler*, 115.

39. Victor, *Hitler*, 114.

40. Waller, *Becoming Evil*, 189.

41. Michael P. Ghiglieri, *The Dark Side of Man: Tracing the Origins of Male Violence* (Reading, Mass.: Perseus Books, 1999), 218.

42. Mann, *Fascists*, 357.

43. Mann, *Fascists*, 175.

44. Victor, *Hitler*, 91.

45. Mann, *The Dark Side of Democracy*, 200.

46. Hilberg, *The Destruction of The European Jews*, 994.

47. Hilberg, *The Destruction of The European Jews*, 1011.

48. Hilberg, *The Destruction of The European Jews*, 1011.

49. Sigrid Meuschel, "The Institutional Frame: Totalitarianism, Extermination and the State," in *The Lesser Evil: Moral Approaches to Genocide Practices*, eds. Helmut Dubiel and Gabriel Motkin (London: Routledge, 2004), 122.

50. Hilberg, *The Destruction of The European Jews*, 1028.

51. Waller, *Becoming Evil*, 209.

52. Mann, *Fascists*, 173.

53. Andrew S. Bergerson, *Ordinary Germans in Extraordinary Times: The Nazi Revolution in Hildesheim* (Bloomington, Ind.: Indiana University Press, 2004), 255.

54. Waller, *Becoming Evil*, 209. Emphasis removed.

55. Mann, *The Dark Side of Democracy*, 201.

56. Waller, *Becoming Evil*, 207.

57. Waller, *Becoming Evil*, 214.

58. Waller, *Becoming Evil*, 214.

59. Hilberg, *The Destruction of The European Jews*, 1024.

60. Caleb Carr, *The Lessons of Terror* (New York: Random House, 2002), 183.

61. Victor, *Hitler*, 88.

62. Victor, *Hitler*, 116.

63. Hilberg, *The Destruction of The European Jews*, 1013.

64. Victor, *Hitler*, 114.

65. Hilberg, *The Destruction of The European Jews*, 1013.

66. Hilberg, *The Destruction of The European Jews*, 1012.

67. Mann, *The Dark Side of Democracy*, 200.

68. Hilberg, *The Destruction of The European Jews*, 1025.

69. Victor, *Hitler*, 105.

70. Browning, *Ordinary Men*, 162.

71. Leonard Berkowitz, *Aggression: Its Causes, Consequences, and Control* (Philadelphia: Temple University Press, 1993), 118.

72. Todorov, "The Uses and Abuses of Comparison," 33.

73. Todorov, "The Uses and Abuses of Comparison," 33.

74. Kekes, *The Roots of Evil*, 236.

75. Victor, *Hitler*, 111. Emphasis added.

76. Hilberg, *The Destruction of The European Jews*, 994.

77. Victor, *Hitler*, 132.

Chapter 5
Al Qaeda: Terror By Design

Terrorism can be a tactic of personal violence. For instance, "The Unabomber" Ted Kaczynski used homemade bombs to wage a savage, solo campaign against American scientists and businessmen. He saw America's technological society as an ever-increasing threat to individual freedom. To understand Kaczynski, it is natural to focus on his individual psychology—his painful family life, his early success as a brilliant mathematician, his growing frustration and ideological alienation, and his retreat to a hidden mountain shack in Montana.

On the other hand, when terrorism is the tool of a large group, organization or system, as is more commonly the case, the psychological analysis of individuals is of limited use. After all, just like in other large systems, the different members of a terrorist organization each have their own histories, tendencies, and personal peculiarities. This is why Robert A. Pape centers his analysis of suicide terrorism on groups and campaigns rather than on individual perpetrators. As Walter Laqueur notes, "there has always been a great variety in character traits, mental makeup, and [personal] psychology among terrorists," which is why situational and social psychological explanations of terrorist behavior are significantly more useful.[1]

When it comes to organizations like Al Qaeda, *terrorists are built, not born,* and personal similarities between members reflect strategic recruitment and training more than anything else. Al Qaeda essentially operates like a sophisticated multinational corporation, complete with closely managed employees conditioned to produce terror.

It must be emphasized that despite antiquated theories to the contrary, the leading scholars recognize that most terrorists are not raving lunatics or mentally deranged—they are relatively normal individuals capable of rational and coherent thought. As longtime terrorism expert Bruce Hoffman came to realize after years of study, "Many [terrorists] are in fact highly articulate and extremely thoughtful individuals for whom terrorism is (or was) an entirely rational choice."[2] In turn, the design and structure of Al Qaeda reflects rationality, intelligence, and careful planning, with an emphasis on cost-effective efficiency, productivity, and "best practices" like any business.

For example, Osama bin Laden's complex analysis of the social and economic costs of 9/11 highlights the similarities between his network and other profit-oriented organizations:

> According to [U.S.] admissions, the share of the losses on Wall Street market reached 16%. . . . The gross amount that is traded in that market reaches $4 trillion. So if we multiply 16% by $4 trillion, it reaches $640 billion of losses from stocks. . . . They have lost this, due to an attack that happened with the success of Allah lasting one hour only. The daily income of the American nation is $20 billion. The first week they didn't work at all due to the psychological shock of the attack. . . . So if you multiply $20 billion by 1 week, it comes out to $140 billion, and it is even bigger than this. If you add it to the $640 billion, we've reached how much? Approximately $800 billion. The cost of the building losses and construction losses? Let us say more than $30 billion. Then they have fired or liquidated until today . . . from the airline companies more than 170,000 employees. That includes cargo plane companies and commercial airlines, and American studies and analysis have mentioned that 70% of the American people even until today still suffer from depression and psychological trauma after the incident of the two towers, and the attack on the Defense Ministry, the Pentagon—thanks to Allah's grace. One of the well-known American hotel companies, Intercontinental, has fired 20,000 employees . . . so watch as the amount reaches no less than $1 trillion by the lowest estimate— thanks to Allah's grace—due to these successful and blessed attacks.[3]

In this passage, bin Laden sounds like a company's CEO or financial analyst— like a well-educated businessman carefully analyzing the losses of a rival corporation and assessing financial competition on the business battlefield. He does not sound like some stereotypical raving terrorist lunatic—probably because he is not one. What is extreme about bin Laden is his politics, religious ideology, and murderous tactics—on the other hand, many of his management techniques and strategies for running an organization are actually rather conventional.

Because Al Qaeda is in a violent business, it uses the same proven framework for systematic indoctrination as other violent systems.

Recruitment

Al Qaeda's recruitment strategies reflect the violent priorities outlined in the analytical framework. In general, terrorist recruits tend to be young and male, and Al Qaeda and its many terrorist branches seek the same types.[4] Syed Sala-huddin, a commander of the Muttahida Jihad Council in Pakistan, makes this point quite clear:

> We have our own monthly publication. Once a young man subscribes to our journal, we know he is mentally prepared. We prefer to recruit children at the age of eleven or twelve. We start preparing them mentally and physically. They are usually not ready to fight until age eighteen or twenty, although some children develop muscles early. Lots of Saudis have joined the jihad. Osama bin Laden is a great force. He goes from organization to organization, persuading people to donate money or donate their lives to jihad. . . . We select people on the basis of character.[5]

The desire to attract young, committed males is a central feature of the recruiting strategy. Paul L. Williams finds that beyond the adolescent stages of indoctrination, "Typical recruits for Al Qaeda and its sister groups are unmarried males between ages 17 and 25."[6] This makes sense: since unmarried males do not have nuptial ties to the outside world, they are easier to isolate.

An Al Qaeda training film posted on Islamist websites in December 2005 also highlights these priorities. Only males are featured in the film, and at one point a ten-year-old boy is shown happily firing an automatic rifle at some off-screen target, while grown men sing passionately in the background. Like a caring father, a bearded man walks behind the boy, watching and pointing out where he should shoot, even leaning over to cover the boy's left eye so he can improve his aim.[7]

These internet and multimedia recruitment campaigns are particularly effective for connecting with young men, who tend to be more technologically inclined than older generations, particularly in less modern societies. Madeleine Gruen points out the advantages of the internet, which "can be used to disseminate the same elements of a propaganda campaign that are employed in the physical world. Through audio and video streams, downloadable leaflets, discussion boards, and links to hundreds of other extremist sites, the internet can be used to indoctrinate, fundraise, [and] recruit."[8] In addition, Brigitte L. Nacos highlights evidence of "other tools and methods to win new recruits, namely cassettes, CDs, videotapes, and DVDs, that terrorist groups and their supporters produce themselves."[9] As part of this effort to recruit young men, Al Qaeda quadrupled its production of propaganda-filled videos from 2005 to 2006 and used an estimated 4,500 jihadist websites to spread its violent messages.[10] Inspired by the success of such methods, Al Qaeda has continued to expand its internet and multimedia recruitment campaigns.[11]

Beyond its deliberate attempts to attract young males, Al Qaeda targets recruits who share the organization's general beliefs. The ideal recruits agree with Islamic fundamentalists' goals to recreate a past seen as pure and highly ordered, while avoiding trends of modernization, globalization, and democratization that threaten to upset traditional ways. Ideologically committed young men are often selected from religious schools called madrasahs, local seminaries and mosques, mainstream Islamic associations, and charitable agencies.[12]

This is a critically important job, because potential dissenters or spies must be screened out at all costs. As Stern explains, "Identifying reliable recruits is considered the most difficult job. Among Al Qaeda's most well known and successful recruiters of elite operatives [were] Muhammed Atef, who was reportedly killed by U.S. bombs in November 2002, and Abu Zubaydah, a Palestinian born in Saudi Arabia, now in U.S. custody."[13] No doubt other members of the system have risen to take their place.

Training

Al Qaeda's training program is absolutely critical to the system's success. It provides a seemingly endless procession of suicide bombers for acts of terror around the globe, while at the same time producing the terrorist operatives who will train and lead future generations.

Once recruits are identified, "The raw talent is then sent to a camp, where it is assessed on various dimensions: commitment to Islam, psychological reliability, intelligence, and physical prowess."[14] Before 9/11 and the subsequent U.S. military response (Operation Enduring Freedom), Al Qaeda training camps were primarily run in Afghanistan, though there were also camps in Somalia, Yemen, Indonesia, Chechnya, and several other countries.[15] More recently, however, Al Qaeda has reestablished its main bases for terrorist training in Pakistan and Iraq, while continuing to support smaller bases around the world, including some in Western nations.[16]

These new locations have some built-in advantages. As Bruce Riedel explains, "Al Qaeda's relocation to Pakistan has also provided new opportunities for the group to expand its reach in the West" because travel between the UK and Pakistan is so common it does not arouse heightened security suspicions.[17] "Visitors from Pakistan have relatively easy access to the Pakistani community in the United Kingdom, and Pakistani-born Britons can readily travel to Pakistan and back—facilitating recruitment, training, and communications for jihadists.[18] Furthermore, recent political turmoil in Pakistan has made it difficult for the government to control what goes on in remote parts of the country.

Meanwhile, the U.S. presence in Iraq has made it an ideal place for new trainees to go to rise and be tested. Bin Laden has called on Muslims throughout the Middle East to go to Iraq to fight imperialist U.S. forces, and some Iraqis themselves have joined Al Qaeda in order to defend their homeland and support the radical jihad. However, with Iraq becoming increasingly secure, it now appears more Al Qaeda recruits are streaming back into Afghanistan and Pakistan. But this could change at any point—particularly if the fledgling Iraqi government proves unable to control significant portions of its territory. In any case, with Pakistan, Iraq, and Afghanistan established as the major centers of Al Qaeda training, the organization has plenty of places to implement systematic indoctrination on a large scale.

Al Qaeda puts a great deal of emphasis on the importance of psychological training. *The Al Qaeda Training Manual* defines that the "necessary qualifications and characteristics" of an Al Qaeda member include "commitment to Islam and the organization's ideology, maturity, sacrifice, listening and obedience, keeping secrets, health, patience, 'tranquility and unflappability,' intelligence and insights, caution and prudence, truthfulness and counsel, ability to observe and analyze, and the 'ability to act.'"[19]

These traits are rooted in mental toughness, not physical strength. The training program is based on the belief that any man can become an Al Qaeda warrior, as long as he has the proper perspective and willpower. Stern tells of this crucial point of emphasis:

> The most important aspect of training . . . is mental training and religious indoctrination. Religious indoctrination includes Islamic law and history and how to wage a holy war. The story that recruits must learn is about their identity—it is about who *we* are as distinct from *them*, to whom Zawahiri, bin Laden's deputy, refers to as the "new Crusaders." Most importantly, camps are used to inculcate "the story" into young men's heads. The story is about an evil enemy who, in the words of Zawahiri, is waging a "new Crusade" against the lands of Islam. This enemy must be fought militarily, Zawahiri explains, because that is the only language the West understands.[20]

Stern is not the only one who identifies indoctrination and psychological conditioning as the most critical part of training. "Al Qaeda puts great stress on the fact that its members should be psychologically trained for war," explains Rohan Gunaratna, "which is considered far more important than battlefield or terrorist combat training."[21] "The organization believes that this policy produces fighters with the requisite mental resilience to sacrifice themselves . . . [and] that commitment to the ideology of the organization frees its members from 'conceptual problems.'"[22] The conceptual problems which Gunaratna refers to could be a lack of religious faith, a lack of respect for authority, or—worst of all—a fair conscience and moral sense that would stop an operative from committing savage violence on command. Al Qaeda's training system is specifically engineered to rub out these dangerous possibilities.

Al Qaeda confronts new members with a serious problem, which is the emotional center of the story. The danger of America, as depicted by bin Laden, is from a "greedy, materialistic, dominant, and arrogant infidel power," that is "evil in its essence."[23] Phares describes the U.S. as a very real threat in the eyes of Al Qaeda members: "Seen from their angle, the United States bore the sins of Las Vegas, New Orleans, Hollywood, the presidential scandals, the pleasures, materialism, liberalism, sexual freedom, wealth, women's equality, and military arrogance worldwide"—a disease feared to be highly contagious.[24]

New recruits learn that bin Laden's solution—to destroy America—requires psychological strength, a united workforce, blind conformity, a clear sense of one's role and responsibilities, and a strong work ethic.[25] Al Qaeda's psychological training is actually desensitization in action—the organization attempts to dull the moral senses which can cause members to hesitate in the line of duty. It further desensitizes some of its members by training them to perfect their killing skills against substitute targets like dogs.[26] Having become comfortable killing animals during training, the recruits will find it easier to kill their real enemies when the system demands it.

Al Qaeda also makes bonding and unity among members a central feature of training. Williams explains how the terrorist system shares these priorities with other tightly-knit groups, although with much more disturbing implications:

> The young men were conditioned to come together by the same mechanics that pull together a football team, a boy scout troop, or an army platoon. The coming together was sealed through blood initiations—rites of passage in which the young men cried out their loyalty to Allah, to the emir, and to one another. They took solemn oaths with daggers to their breasts. Following this initiation, they emerged as members of an elite and holy fraternity of suicide bombers.[27]

Stern cites similar aspects of the system's training program: beyond tactical and weapons training, the camps help "create social ties, so that operatives feel committed to the cause on both the ideological and solidarity grounds."[28]

According to captured Al Qaeda terrorist Mohamed Rashed Daoud Al-Owhali's recollection of his own training, recruits were also divided into small groups where they "collectively pored over passages from the Koran and chanted religious slogans . . . [and were instructed] to repeat and memorize certain passages from the Koran five times a day at services."[29] As Williams describes, these training features were specifically designed to "create a sense of belonging and mystical cohesion and to grant the recruits a distinct identity as members of a spiritual brotherhood."[30]

In addition, to increase bonding and unity among members, Al Qaeda emphasizes the importance of a cooperative work ethic, and often uses teams to complete tasks, rather than individuals.[31] When they eventually graduate and begin carrying out strikes, the terrorists rely on the trust and relationships they built during training. Even relatively low-level Al Qaeda attacks involve many agents working together. "First, intelligence teams mount surveillance. . . . Next an Al Qaeda support team arrives in the target area and organizes safe houses and vehicles, bringing with it the necessary weapons and explosives. Lastly, Al Qaeda's strike team arrives and withdraws after completing the mission, unless it's a suicide attack."[32] Naturally, these collaborative assignments add to the pressure on each fighter to do his specific job, do it well, and not let his brothers down.

New members are also taught that their security depends on total obedience and unquestioning respect for organizational rules. As Gunaratna describes, "to maintain internal security . . . [a] member should not be curious or inquisitive about matters that do not concern him; he should not discuss with others what he knows or hears."[33] This robot-like conformity is often referred to as "the blind march of jihad."[34] Ultimately, knowing one's roles, duties, and obligations is critical for survival and overcoming the dangerous infidel threat—which is why Al Qaeda encourages a strong work ethic defined by "perseverance, patience, steadfastness, and adherence to a firm set of principles."[35] It's through these training lessons that Al Qaeda operatives are conditioned to perform violence on command.

Authorization

Al Qaeda employs transcendent authorizations to guide the thinking of its members. Instead of emphasizing victory for its own sake or a "final solution," the terrorist organization points to Allah and how he will certainly be pleased by the result of their activities. In the short paragraph where bin Laden calculates the costs of 9/11, he mentions Allah three separate times, both to thank Allah for his support of their mission and to underscore that the attacks were carried out for him.

For someone within the system to disagree with Al Qaeda's actions, he or she would have to discount the existence of Allah, deny that pleasing Allah is a good thing, or argue that Al Qaeda's missions would not please Allah. For the terrorist organization's agents, all three arguments are powerless. The first is blasphemy and would never be proposed by Islam's true believers. The second is unthinkable, for pleasing God could never be a bad thing. And the third is impossible to prove—for if Allah does not support Al Qaeda, the group's successes in previous missions would never have been achieved.

Al Qaeda members see evidence of Allah's approval in events like the collapse of the World Trade Center's twin towers. As bin Laden admitted in a video interview several months after 9/11, he expected the twin towers to be damaged by the hijacked airliners, but he had not anticipated their total collapse.[36] Naturally, this fortunate turn is chalked up to the power and will of Allah.

Through these authorizations, the means—which involve violent killing, mass murder, and suicide—are downplayed, while the ends—which are to please Allah—are emphasized. As Phares explains, from early on, the "neo-Wahabi organization . . . shaped its vision of the future solely on what it perceived as direct signs from Allah . . . only Allah could stop the will to jihad."[37]

Gunaratna emphasizes that for Al Qaeda operatives, "Killing and dying for Allah are viewed as the highest form of sacrifice."[38]

As the infamous leader of Al Qaeda, bin Laden is another critical source of authority. He has long been worshipped and beloved. As a former bodyguard confessed, "I place Sheik Osama on the same level as my father, and I love him perhaps even more than my father."[39] Similarly, Lebanese Sunni cleric Fathi Yakan expresses the type of dedication to the terrorist leader that is common among radical Islamists:

> There is no doubt that Sheik Osama bin Laden has a high level of faithfulness, trustworthiness, and transparency. He is faithful to his religion and to Jihad for the elevation of the word of Allah. . . . This man has a pure, honest, and believing personality. He defends all that belongs to Islam and . . . renounces anything that is not Islamic, and therefore, he is a man after my own heart.[40]

How significant bin Laden remains in terms of directly planning, orchestrating, and authorizing current Al Qaeda operations is unclear. But the prevailing wisdom is expressed by Riedel, who suggests that "Bin Laden continues to influence [Al Qaeda's] direction and provide general guidance and, on occasion, specific instructions."[41] Though some have downplayed bin Laden's importance due to Al Qaeda's decentralized cell structure, he remains an extremely powerful symbol. The fact that bin Laden has been able to avoid capture or assassination at the hands of desperate U.S. headhunters only adds to his appeal and mystique.

A key point is how Al Qaeda and its subsidiary Islamist terrorist groups regularly carry out attacks in bin Laden's name. For instance, when questioned about bin Laden's long absence from media pronouncements and confronted with the possibility that bin Laden may have died, Taliban Military Commander Mullah Dadallah was quick to reject such speculation:

> Allah be praised, [bin Laden] is alive, and we have information about him. Allah be praised, he formulates the plans in Iraq and Afghanistan. You may recall the martyrdom operation in the Baghram base, which targeted a senior American official [Vice President Dick Cheney]. No Afghan can reach the Baghram base. This operation is the result of his blessed planning. He is the one who formulated the details of this plan and who instructed us. The operation was successful, and, Allah willing, you will hear him speaking. As the operations intensify, a video statement by him will be released, Allah willing. We have information that he is alive, and that he is in constant contact with the mujahideen.[42]

At best, Dadallah seems to be basing his conjecture about bin Laden's direct support and involvement in Afghanistan and Iraq on hearsay. Nothing in this quote indicates that the Taliban commander has personally seen or communicated with bin Laden. But Dadallah and other radical Islamists like him make the most of the *symbol* of bin Laden. By portraying him as a powerful, nearly godlike figure with almost supernatural skills for planning terrorist strikes, they can simultaneously inspire their followers and authorize a range of violent attacks. Pleasing bin Laden and fulfilling his calls for jihad become the primary focus, while the brutal means required to meet this goal are initially downplayed.

Like Allah, bin Laden gets credit for things done in his name, whether or not he is directly involved. His purported support of every aspect of the campaign makes it easier for operatives to follow their violent orders. Riedel speculates that "The death of bin Laden and his senior associates in Pakistan and Iraq would not end the movement, but it would deal al Qaeda a serious blow."[43] This is because authorization is such a critical element of Al Qaeda's systematic indoctrination. Caleb Carr notes that the 9/11 hijackers were "programmed by years of rhetorical exhortation," and Gunaratna describes how "no other group has invested so much time and effort as Al Qaeda in programming its fighters for death."[44] Above all others, Allah and bin Laden are the sources of the system's authority.

When it comes to actually carrying out their missions, Al Qaeda members are given direction in the form of mundane authorizations. The general orders come from select Islamic scholars who have sanctioned the struggle against the U.S. and its allies. As Phares recounts, "The doctrine of jihadism had to build a case for why they should turn the guns against their former ally [the U.S.]. The case was duly built, piece by piece, by the scholars of jihad and takfir from within the Saudi kingdom."[45] Along these lines, Al Qaeda employs "mobilization rhetoric" which suggests "a cross-national military alliance of national liberation movements working together against what they see as a common imperial threat."[46]

More directly, Al Qaeda leaders plan and authorize specific attacks against enemy targets, while also supporting a social climate that not only condones violence, but also extols the virtue of self-sacrifice in pursuit of the system's goals. Like the military, like other religious organizations, and like many corporations, terrorist groups such as Al Qaeda encourage members "to sacrifice themselves for a cause greater than themselves."[47] In an interesting combination of transcendent and mundane authorizations, terrorist organizations like Al Qaeda do not explicitly mention the suicidal nature of such attacks, but instead use a label that emphasizes both the morality of self-sacrifice and the certainty that Allah will appreciate such acts. As Gunaratna explains, "Although the media refer to 9/11 and the USS Cole attacks as 'suicide' operations, Islamist military groups consider them to be 'martyrdom' attacks, given that suicide per se is forbidden in Islam."[48]

Bureaucracy

Al Qaeda and its subsidiaries also use bureaucracies to make it easier for their members to carry out violence. Individual terrorists learn that they are just cogs in the machine, part of something much bigger than themselves. Al Qaeda is known to be a powerful international network, akin to a successful multinational corporation, with local branches, local command, and jihadists recruited from all over the world for its "main striking missions on the planet."[49] As Phares explains, it has "international and also regional command centers . . . [and] its own central units, deployed in many places."[50] Jerrold M. Post extends the allusions to Al Qaeda bureaucracy as big business: "Osama bin Laden is seen to be in effect the Chairman of the Board of Radical Islam, Inc., who has grown his corporation through mergers and acquisitions and has a flat organizational structure."[51]

The size and power of Al Qaeda's system thus helps ease normal guilt associated with violence because there is a sense of institutional momentum. Operations seem certain to proceed with or without the participation of any single member. As the familiar saying goes, "If you can't beat them, join them." Even a dissenting member of Al Qaeda would be essentially powerless to stop the grand machine, so he might as well go with the flow and do his part.

The procedural nature of Al Qaeda bureaucracy also makes violence more acceptable for members of the system. As Phares recounts, "the jihadists, including bin Laden's Al Qaeda and the myriad of other radical Islamist warriors, have a system of reference for their actions. Their clerics and 'legislators' have an entire system of laws and regulations, including war codes and traditions."[52] This existence of laws, regulations, and codes gives crucial legitimacy to Al Qaeda and to the violence authorized by its leaders.

Al Qaeda has at least three detailed training manuals which document precisely how members of the organization are expected to carry out their violent campaigns: *The Encyclopedia of Afghan Jihad*, *The Declaration of Jihad against the Country's Tyrants*, and *The Al Qaeda Training Manual*.[53] These documents draw lots of their material from U.S. and British military manuals and combine military science with religious teachings and traditions. In general, many people tend to trust transparency and be suspicious of secrecy, so violence based on well-known traditions, established laws, and published rules becomes easier to perform. The popularity of these manuals among radical Islamists also makes violence seem more like a carefully considered and rationally thought-out political strategy and less like a primal lust for revenge. As Stern observes, "Terrorism becomes a career as much as a passion. What starts out as moral fervor becomes a sophisticated organization."[54]

In addition, other procedures are used to help overcome terrorists' natural hesitancy to commit suicide attacks. As Pape explains, "Suicide terrorist organizations commonly cultivate 'sacrificial myths' that include elaborate sets of symbols and rituals to mark an individual attacker's death as a contribution to the nation."[55] These established practices not only make it easier for members to act violently, but they provide a sense of order and predictability to such violence. Suicide terrorists know what to expect in the hours and minutes leading up to an attack, what to expect during the violence, and what events will transpire after their deaths.

For instance, 9/11 ringleader Mohammed Atta followed the system's protocol and wrote detailed letters to the other 9/11 hijackers. These letters were found in their luggage after the attacks. The letters offer detailed, sixteen-point instructions for how the operatives should behave in the days leading up to the attacks, including specific orders on prayer, bathing, and dress rituals. As Williams explains, "The document does not read like a political manifesto or an expression of rage, but rather like a religious tract that is meant, not to further a cause, but to fortify faith."[56] Pages and pages of more detailed tasks, duties, and rituals follow these instructions, so a terrorist could easily become so focused on following the recipe for martyrdom that he would not stop to think about the moral implications of his violent assignment. These types of symbols and rituals are a key feature of systematic indoctrination. Al Qaeda's bureaucracy thus manufactures cognitive clarity and moral certainty for its operatives, which makes it easier for them to carry out violence.

It is similarly clear that Al Qaeda benefits from bureaucratic division of labor. On the macro-level, Al Qaeda leaders divided the organization "into four distinct but interlinked entities" at some point in 1998.[57] As Gunaratna details, "The first was the pyramidal structure to facilitate strategic and tactical direction; the second was a global terrorist network; the third was a base force for guerilla warfare inside Afghanistan; and the fourth was a loose coalition of transnational terrorist and guerilla groups."[58] Further divisions were also made, including "four operational committees: military; finance and business; fatwa and Islamic study; and media and publicity, which ensure the smooth day-to-day running of Al Qaeda, each being headed by an Emir."[59] This complex web highlights how profoundly bureaucracy defines Al Qaeda's operations, and suggests that even for mid-level terrorist leaders, it's possible to find moral shelter in the great expanses of the system.

In the wake of 9/11, the global war on terror, and the wars in Afghanistan and Iraq, Al Qaeda has been forced to rebuild and restructure its organization. However, Al Qaeda's new system is even more decentralized and truly international than it was before. As Stern explains, "The Al Qaeda network of networks is at the cutting edge of organizations today."[60] She further documents how the division of labor exists within regional divisions and cells, with an obvious chain of command:

Al Qaeda has a clear hierarchy. There are commanders, managers, and cadres; and cadres consist of both skilled and unskilled labor. Foot soldiers are likely to

be found in schools or mosques, and only the best and brightest make it to the
top. Some mid-level operatives are paid enough within the organization that
they may find it difficult to leave, while for others—generally those who come
from wealthier families—the spiritual and psychological attractions of jihad are
sufficient.[61]

It is easy to imagine that, like the executioner who isn't responsible for the police arrest or the judicial sentencing of a death row inmate, and thus performs his
dirty job with relatively little guilt, Al Qaeda's commanders, managers, cadres,
foot soldiers, suicide bombers, and support personnel all appreciate the division
of responsibility that reduces their role and culpability in the overall orchestration of violence. In this fashion, the system's bureaucracy makes it considerably
easier for them to unleash carnage on civilian populations.

Isolation

At first glance, it may seem easy to assert that terrorists are isolated from society
and traditional moral values. However, some experts argue that the picture is
more complex. Pape actually suggests the opposite of isolation. He contends that
suicide terrorism "is typically the result of close integration of suicide terrorist
groups with the surrounding society."[62] He considers suicide terrorism to be a
form of altruistic suicide, where "society venerates the person who commits the
act as a martyr or hero that others should emulate."[63] Pape bases this argument
on evidence that the politics of Al Qaeda are endorsed by the masses: "within
Saudi Arabia there is little debate over Al Qaeda's objection to American forces
in the region, and over 95 percent of Saudi society reportedly agrees with bin
Laden on this matter."[64] These figures seem suspiciously high, but it is clear that
some level of support for bin Laden is common to segments of Muslims all
around the world. According to Pew Research Center surveys, "71 percent of
Palestinian residents of Gaza and the West Bank [and] 58 percent of Indonesians
. . . expressed confidence in the 'world figure' bin Laden 'to do the right thing'"
in 2003, while "Sixty-five percent of Pakistanis, 55 percent of Jordanians, and
45 percent of Moroccans viewed the Al Qaeda leader favorably" in 2004.[65]

But regardless of the precise figures, Pape is dramatically oversimplifying
and overestimating societal acceptance of terrorism, even in the Middle East. As
he admits, "there is a major debate among Islamists over the morality of suicide
attacks," which is one reason terrorist organizations withdraw and isolate themselves.[66] In addition, much of society simultaneously disapproves of U.S. intru-
sion into the region *and* of terrorist groups like Al Qaeda. Iraq is a perfect example of a place where many people resent both the U.S. soldiers on their streets
and the terrorist bombings that inject fear into their daily lives and regularly
threaten them and their families. Increasingly, Iraqi people, including Sunnis,

have taken up arms against Al Qaeda fighters, despite sharing some common goals with the organization on a macro-geopolitical level.[67] The Machiavellian notion that "The enemy of my enemy is my friend" is imperfect and does not accurately apply to these cases.

Al Qaeda actually functions more like the suicidal cults described by Pape—it uses social isolation, strong authorizations from charismatic leaders, undermined individual autonomy within the system, rigid discipline, rituals, and codes to encourage members to ignore normal moral constraints and act violently, even if it means killing themselves.[68] James J. F. Forest agrees: "Similar to cults, terrorist organizations need to establish control over the new recruit's personal social environment, time, and sources of social support . . . social isolation is promoted."[69] Al Qaeda is able to maintain such dominant control over its members by separating the system from the rest of society.

Furthermore, even when Al Qaeda gets some support from local communities, the system still remains isolated in many ways. As Phares summarizes, Al Qaeda jihadists are socially and morally isolated—they "simply do not recognize any system the international community has reached since the Peace of Westphalia; no conception of sovereignty, human rights, humanitarian rights, the Geneva Convention, or even Red Cross agreements. . . . [These things] are to them all 'products of the infidels.'"[70] Al Qaeda has deliberately isolated itself to avoid the moral ramifications of international judgment, which could hinder or undermine its justifications for violence. Phares adds that "When mounting operations in the 1990s, Osama bin Laden and his men had no limits with regard to international relations and did not take world opinion into consideration."[71]

Rather than seek solace, guidance, or support from their fellow man, terrorists have historically made clear distinctions between those inside the system and those outside it. As Eddin Ibrahim Saas explains, hatred of outsiders and outside views is a fundamental part of the strategy because "That gets the process of recruitment under way. . . . Then [the recruits] are insulated from the mainstream, brainwashed, and indoctrinated until they become deployable."[72] In this manner, the system uses isolation to protect terrorists' confidence and moral conviction about their mission. As Laqueur further emphasizes, "The political terrorist of recent vintage may preach the brotherhood of man and sometimes even practice it. [But] More often he has liberated himself from moral scruples and persuaded himself that all is permitted since everyone is guilty but himself."[73] The Al Qaeda system not only isolates and insulates its members, but it also encourages them to take pride in this arrangement. Laqueur explains that "Terrorists, it is true, have usually claimed to act on behalf of the masses, but they also believe that the 'liberation of the masses' is the historical mission of a chosen few."[74]

Beyond social and moral distance, Al Qaeda engineers more tangible forms of isolation to indoctrinate its members. Many terrorist training camps are literally isolated. Forest notes "in many cases new recruits are brought to a geographically remote location to ensure they have contact only with other members of the group during this formative period.[75] Far away from the rest of the world, Al Qaeda leaders can force the system to the center of its agents' minds and souls. The power of literal isolation is perhaps most apparent when it comes to training new Al Qaeda members abroad. As Williams explains, "Muslims in the West . . . are especially vulnerable to militant Islamic movements. . . . They can feel as if they have no home," and are thus more likely to be swayed by local branches.[76]

In addition, Al Qaeda's agents are often commanded to act in absolute secrecy.[77] Perhaps most importantly, they are usually ordered not to inform their parents of their missions.[78] By cutting off young recruits from their parents, Al Qaeda keeps the people who care most about their welfare and future at a safe distance. Family members can no longer influence their confused, coerced, and co-opted loved ones. In a tragic irony, the recruits who are most undecided about carrying out terrorist attacks, who miss their families the most, and who would have been most likely to consult their parents for guidance may also be the quickest to embrace their new "brotherhood" as an emotional replacement, a surrogate family. Eager to please and feel accepted, they quickly become willing to do whatever they're told.

But even within the Al Qaeda brotherhood, members are deliberately isolated from each other. Gunaratna details how "Al Qaeda's training program is designed to create self-contained cells that operate independently of central command."[79] He explains further that "Al Qaeda's global terrorist network strictly adheres to the cellular (also known as cluster) model, 'composed of many cells whose members do not know one another, so that if a cell member is caught the other cells would not be affected and work would proceed normally.'"[80] This isolation is a key feature of the system's strategic design. Beyond the aforementioned security benefit, agents who do not know one another are much less likely to question the morality of violent orders from above. There is very little opportunity for the organization's rare dissenters to meet each other and combine efforts to change the system.

In addition, Al Qaeda restricts the flow of information between members. "To preserve operational effectiveness at all levels of Al Qaeda compartmentalization, the 'need to know' principle and secrecy are paramount."[81] This mandate is common to many violent organizations, including national militaries and covert intelligence agencies such as the CIA. In no uncertain terms, *The Al Qaeda Training Manual* demands that operatives on a mission "exercise extreme caution and apply all security measures to the other members."[82] In other words: you can trust almost no one. Once you have your orders, you are literally—and morally—on your own.

Ironically, *The Al Qaeda Training Manual* warns that isolation gives *enemy organizations* power over individuals. It cautions that upon capture, a member may face psychological torture at the hands of the enemy. The infidels' tactics include "Isolating the brother socially, cutting him off from public life, placing him in solitary confinement, and denying him news and information in order to make him feel lonely."[83] Here, the terrorist organization is warning its members that the enemy may strategically use isolation to control people—to pressure them to do things they otherwise would not do, such as rat on their Islamic brothers or confess the details of a terrorist plot. The sad reality is that Al Qaeda uses isolation to control its members' behavior in much more profound ways: towards savage acts of violence against innocents, carried out on a moment's command.

Dehumanization

In order to facilitate violence, Al Qaeda dehumanizes both the members of its own organization and the targets of its attacks. As Gunaratna details, in addition to all the other dehumanizing features of their system, Al Qaeda has rules that restrict the normal human emotions of its agents in the name of security. For example, "Covert members must avoid attracting unnecessary attention by advocating one thing or denouncing another, or by getting too passionate about their cause, thereby criticizing or praising the organization."[84] As much as Al Qaeda wants support for its international objectives—it strategically *discourages* its members from getting passionate in public or private. After all, being human in all the usual ways could attract attention and jeopardize the system's objectives.

Further dehumanization leads terrorist leaders to look down on their subordinates, seeing them simply as the means to an end, instead of as individuals. This is clear in suicide bombing campaigns like those carried out by Hamas, but also applies to Al Qaeda. As Netanyahu explains, "suicide attacks require a significant infrastructure, and the people who provide it are anything but suicidal. On the contrary, they very much want to live; they want to kill, and not be killed."[85] For the leaders of terrorist organizations like Al Qaeda, the young men blowing themselves up are dehumanized instruments—a type of advanced weaponry more destructive and customizable than a grenade or homemade bomb. These instruments must be carefully prepared and fine-tuned, and it requires the system's bureaucracy, codified rules and rituals, and extensive training to make these weapons usable. As Netanyahu put it, indoctrinated terrorist recruits literally "become walking human time bombs. And one day, they explode."[86]

Eventually, Al Qaeda terrorists are ordered to attack targets that have also been dehumanized. Pape explains how terrorist campaigns use religious differences for the "extreme demonization" of alleged enemies. Targets are seen as "misguided, amoral, immoral, or even actively evil. . . . [The] religious inferiority of the enemy can promote a feeling that he is less than fully human."[87] As he further documents, "Demonization encourages the two main features of suicide terrorism—the willingness to die and the willingness to kill innocents."[88] "The more the foreign culture is viewed with scorn and revulsion, the more malignant sentiments can justify cruel treatment of even innocent members of the foreign society."[89] Of course, from Al Qaeda's perspective, even unarmed men, women, and children are anything but innocent—they're part of the larger problem because they support America. Again, dehumanization functions to make the terrorist themselves feel less human, while also making it easier for them to harm others without normal empathy or guilt.

Along these lines, Akbar Ahmed describes how Egyptian activist Sayyid Qutb, an Islamic fundamentalist whose teachings inspired bin Laden and the Al Qaeda campaign, has denounced the West by exaggerating cultural differences. In Outb's words, "Humanity today is living in a large brothel! One has only to glance at its press, films, fashion shows, beauty contests, ballrooms, wine bars, and broadcasting stations! Or observe its mad lust for naked flesh, provocative postures, and sick, suggestive statements in literature, the arts and mass media!"[90] Strictly speaking, this is not dehumanization, but it is a similar strategic attempt to define Westerners as wholly different in nature from Qutb's followers and as a terribly corruptive force.

Al Qaeda also uses more precise dehumanization. Ruth Stein documents how Al Qaeda has characterized the West as a "world of contaminants" which needs to be purified.[91] The terrorist organization also tells its members "that they are fighting on behalf of Islam against the enemies of God, epitomized by Western civilization, and especially the United States—[who is] the 'Hubal of this age' and literally 'Satanic,' being in league with the Devil."[92] Al Qaeda has also dehumanized Westerners and Jews by referring to them as lowly animals. "A knight from the state of Islam . . . reached the heart of the Green Zone . . . the temporary headquarters of the mice of the infidel parliament and blew himself up among a gathering of the infidel masters," one Al Qaeda website bragged.[93] In another case, Al Qaeda suicide bomber Abu Muhammad Al-San'ani relayed in his martyrdom video that "I pray to Allah that this operation will be vengeance upon the American pigs and their apostate collaborator dogs, for their assault on the home of Mulawi Nur Muhammad."[94] These labels were certainly not of his own invention: they reflect they way he was programmed to think about the enemy. The images of Americans and their allies as a disease, as satanic, and as mice, pigs, and dogs is classic dehumanization—for if your enemies are not regarded in human terms, it is much easier to exterminate them. Like the other systems that promote violence, Al Qaeda encourages its members to see their targets in object terms, instead of as living, breathing people who have fears, hopes, and dreams.

Conclusion

Increasingly, scientists are coming to terms with the fact that "fanatical ideo-logical commitment to destructive ideologies" can be produced through "'normal' social psychological processes."[95] Nowhere is this more apparent than in the case of Al Qaeda. Before coming into contact with terrorist propaganda and beginning their systematic indoctrination, most of Al Qaeda's terrorists were relatively ordinary people. Some, like 9/11 ringleader Mohammed Atta, may have even grown up disliking violence and opposed to terrorism.[96] Though it may be very hard for us to accept, a great deal of evidence supports these conclusions.

First, there is no terrorist-specific profile and no evidence of any personal peculiarities, such as childhood trauma, sadism, mental illness, or a death wish, which make people more likely to become terrorists. And for many recruits, becoming a terrorist is not even a particularly risky way to fight for the cause. Indeed—as Larry Iannaccone points out, even factoring in the suicidal element of terrorist systems, "the number called upon to die is very small relative to the total number working for the firm. Ex ante, the typical worker may face risks no greater than those endured by most criminals or war-time soldiers."[97] In addi-tion, the characteristics of Al Qaeda's ideal recruits—being young, male, and intrigued by Islamic fundamentalism—are common to millions and millions of people. Most of them live rather ordinary lives. In fact, perhaps due to the wholesale success of its systematic indoctrination, Al Qaeda now seems willing to accept a more diverse range of recruits, including more women.[98] It is confi-dent it can compel them to serve the system as well.

By contrast, if terrorist recruits entered the system fully committed—if they would not hesitate to kill innocent people or blow themselves up—indoctrination would not be necessary. In that case, Al Qaeda's operations would be much more streamlined, practical, and focused on logistics. Instead of the constant psychological conditioning, the system would only emphasize weapons training and mission training. The reason Al Qaeda spends so much time, money, and effort on systematic indoctrination is because it is necessary: they must transform relatively normal recruits into loyal, obedient killers who will do whatever they're told.

Notes

1. Walter Laqueur, *A History of Terrorism* (New Brunswick, N.J.: Transaction Publishers, 1977), 130.

2. Bruce Hoffman, *Inside Terrorism* (New York: Columbia University Press, 1998), 7.

3. Rohan Gunaratna, *Inside Al Qaeda: Global Network of Terror* (New York: Columbia University Press, 2002), 225.

4. Gunaratna, *Inside Al Qaeda*, 74; Laqueur, *A History of Terrorism*, 120-21; Robert A. Pape, *Dying to Win: The Strategic Logic of Suicide Terrorism* (New York: Random House, 2005), 207; Phares, *Future Jihad*, 201.

5. Stern, *Terror in the Name of God*, 210.

6. Paul L. Williams, *Al Qaeda: Brotherhood of Terror* (Upper Saddle River, N.J.: Alpha Books and Pearson Education, Inc., 2002), 10.

7. "Children Train with Weapons in Al Qaeda Film," *MEMRITV*, December 2005, http://www.memritv.org/clip/en/971.htm (10 April 2008).

8. Madeleine Gruen, "Innovative Recruitment and Indoctrination Tactics by Extremists: Video Games, Hip-Hop , and the World Wide Web," in *The Making of a Terrorist: Recruitment, Training and Root Causes*, Vol. 1, *Recruitment*, ed. James J. F. Forest (Westport, Conn.: Praeger Security International, 2006), 14.

9. Brigitte L. Nacos, "Communication and Recruitment of Terrorists," in *The Making of a Terrorist: Recruitment, Training and Root Causes*, Vol. 1, *Recruitment*, ed. James J. F. Forest (Westport, Conn.: Praeger Security International, 2006), 48.

10. Bruce Riedel, "Al Qaeda Strikes Back," *Foreign Affairs* 86 (2007): 26-28.

11. Craig Whitlock, "Al-Qaeda's Growing Online Offensive," *WashingtonPost.com*, 24 June 2008, http://www.washingtonpost.com/wp-dyn/content/article/2008/06/23/AR2008062302135.html (7 August 2008).

12. Stern, *Terror in the Name of God*, 259; Williams, *Al Qaeda*, 9.

13. Stern, *Terror in the Name of God*, 259.

14. Stern, *Terror in the Name of God*, 259.

15. Stern, *Terror in the Name of God*, 260.

16. Riedel, "Al Qaeda Strikes Back," 26-31.

17. Riedel, "Al Qaeda Strikes Back," 30.

18. Riedel, "Al Qaeda Strikes Back," 30.

19. Stern, *Terror in the Name of God*, 249.

20. Stern, *Terror in the Name of God*, 261.

21. Gunaratna, *Inside Al Qaeda*, 73.

22. Gunaratna, *Inside Al Qaeda*, 73.

23. Phares, *Future Jihad*, 121, 165.

24. Phares, *Future Jihad*, 165.

25. Phares, *Future Jihad*, 154.

26. Pape, *Dying to Win*, 224.

27. Williams, *Al Qaeda*, 10.

28. Stern, *Terror in the Name of God*, 260.

29. Williams, *Al Qaeda*, 14.

30. Williams, *Al Qaeda*, 14.

31. Gunaratna, *Inside Al Qaeda*, 74; Pape, *Dying to Win*, 185.

32. Gunaratna, *Inside Al Qaeda*, 77.

33. Gunaratna, *Inside Al Qaeda*, 78.

34. Phares, *Future Jihad*, 120.

35. Gunaratna, *Inside Al Qaeda*, 224.

36. George P. Fletcher, *Romantics at War: Glory and Guilt in the Age of Terrorism* (Princeton, N.J.: Princeton University Press, 2002), 149.

37. Phares, *Future Jihad*, 120-21.

38. Gunaratna, *Inside Al Qaeda*, 91.

39. "Former Bodyguard of Osama Bin Laden: I Love Him More Than I Love My Own Father," *MEMRITV*, 4 May 2007, http://www.memritv.org/clip/en/1462.htm (10 April 2008).

40. "Top Lebanese Sunni Cleric Fathi Yakan: Bin Laden a Man After My Own Heart; I Am Not Sad Because of 9/11 and I Have Never Condemned this Attack," *MEMRITV*, 16 March 2007, http://www.memritv.org/clip/en/1408.htm (10 April 2008).

41. Riedel, "Al Qaeda Strikes Back," 35.

42. "Taliban Military Commander Mullah Dadallah: Bin Laden Planned the Baghram Base Attack on American VP Cheney," *MEMRITV*, 30 April 2007, http://www.memritv.org/clip/en/1437.htm (10 April 2008).

43. Riedel, "Al Qaeda Strikes Back," 35.

44. Carr, *The Lessons of Terror*, 11; Gunaratna, *Inside Al Qaeda*, 91.

45. Phares, *Future Jihad*, 121.

46. Pape, *Dying to Win*, 104.

47. Laqueur, *A History of Terrorism*, 196.

48. Gunaratna, *Inside Al Qaeda*, 73.

49. Phares, *Future Jihad*, 128-31.

50. Phares, *Future Jihad*, 128-31.

51. Jerrold M. Post, "When Hatred is Bred in the Bone: The Sociocultural Underpinnings of Terrorist Psychology," in *The Making of a Terrorist: Recruitment, Training and Root Causes*, Vol. 2, *Training*, ed. James J. F. Forest (Westport, Conn.: Praeger Security International, 2006), 27.

52. Phares, *Future Jihad*, 162.

53. Rohan Gunaratna and Arabinda Acharya, "The Terrorist Training Camps of Al Qaeda," in *The Making of a Terrorist: Recruitment, Training and Root Causes*, Vol. 2, *Training*, ed. James J. F. Forest (Westport, Conn.: Praeger Security International, 2006), 179-80.

54. Stern, *Terror in the Name of God*, 282.

55. Pape, *Dying to Win*, 29.

56. Williams, *Al Qaeda*, 134.

57. Gunaratna, *Inside Al Qaeda*, 57.

58. Gunaratna, *Inside Al Qaeda*, 57.

59. Gunaratna, *Inside Al Qaeda*, 57.

60. Stern, *Terror in the Name of God*, 279.

61. Stern, *Terror in the Name of God*, 250.

62. Pape, *Dying to Win*, 181.

63. Pape, *Dying to Win*, 181.

64. Pape, *Dying to Win*, 42.

65. Nacos, "Communication and Recruitment of Terrorists," 43.

66. Pape, *Dying to Win*, 42.

67. Ammar Karim, "Sunni fighters take on Qaeda in Baghdad," *Yahoo! News*, 1 June 2007, http://news.yahoo.com/s/afp/20070601/wl_mideast_afp/iraq (14 June 2007).

68. Pape, *Dying to Win*, 178-79.

69. James J. F. Forest, *The Making of a Terrorist: Recruitment, Training and Root Causes*, Vol. 1, *Recruitment* (Westport, Conn.: Praeger Security International, 2006), 8-9.

70. Phares, *Future Jihad*, 162.

71. Phares, *Future Jihad*, 163.

72. Kenneth R. Timmerman, *Preachers of Hate: Islam and the War on America* (New York: Crown Forum, 2003), 303.

73. Laqueur, *A History of Terrorism*, 222.

74. Laqueur, *A History of Terrorism*, 219.

75. Forest, *The Making of a Terrorist*, 8-9.

76. Williams, *Al Qaeda*, 112.

77. Williams, *Al Qaeda*, 11.

78. Williams, *Al Qaeda*, 11.

79. Gunaratna, *Inside Al Qaeda*, 78-82.

80. Gunaratna, *Inside Al Qaeda*, 76.

81. Gunaratna, *Inside Al Qaeda*, 78-82.

82. Williams, *Al Qaeda*, 14.

83. Williams, *Al Qaeda*, 10.

84. Gunaratna, *Inside Al Qaeda*, 78.

85. Benjamin Netanyahu, *Fighting Terrorism: How Democracies Can Defeat Domestic and International Terrorists* (New York: Farrar Strauss Giroux, 1995), 108.

86. Timmerman, *Preachers of Hate*, 303.

87. Pape, *Dying to Win*, 90.

88. Pape, *Dying to Win*, 90.

89. Pape, *Dying to Win*, 90.

90. Akbar Ahmed, *Islam Under Siege* (Cambridge: Polity Press, 2003), 110.

91. Ruth Stein, "Evil as Love and as Liberation: The Mind of a Suicidal Religious Terrorist," in *Hating in the First Person Plural*, ed. Donald Moss (New York: Other Press LLC, 2003), 291. This rhetoric is remarkably similar to the language of Nazi propaganda.

92. Gunaratna and Acharya, "The Terrorist Training Camps of Al Qaeda," 176.

93. Bushra Juhi, "Iraqi Insurgents Claim Parliament Blast," *ABCNEWS.go.com*, 13 April 2007, http://abcnews.go.com/International/wireStory?id=3039023 (10 April 2008).

94. "An Al Qaeda Released Video of Attacks in Afghanistan," *MEMRITV*, 4 May 2006, http://www.memritv.org/clip/en/1131.htm (10 April 2008).

95. Glick, "Choice of Scapegoats," 259.

96. John Cloud, "Atta's Odyssey," *Time.com*, 30 September 2001, http://www.time.com/time/magazine/article/0,9171,1101011008-176917,00.html (10 April 2008).

97. Bryan Caplan, "Terrorism: The relevance of the rational choice model," *Public Choice* 128 (2006): 5.

98. Diaa Hadid, "Al-Qaida uses women as suicide attackers," *FoxNews.com*, 4 January 2008, http://www.foxnews.com/wires/2008Jan04/0,4670,IraqFemaleBombers, 00.html (10 April 2008).

Chapter 6
Iran: Manufacturing Martyrs

When you mention the violence of Nazi Germany, most people think of the Holocaust and understand the magnitude of that tragedy. When you mention Al Qaeda, most people think of 9/11 and the terrorist attacks on the World Trade Center and the Pentagon, and recognize the nature of the threat. When you mention Abu Ghraib, most people think of U.S. forces torturing prisoners in Iraq, and the resulting political scandal. But when you mention violence in Iran, there is no clear consensus on what you're referring to. The hostage crisis of the early 1980s? The war with Iraq? The nation's threats against Israel and its nuclear ambitions?

To many, it may seem that Iran has actually been rather peaceful in recent years. Sure, its leaders have made inflammatory public statements. Sure, it wants nuclear power and perhaps even nuclear weapons, but many Western countries and respected allies around the world have acquired these capabilities, and no disasters have resulted. What violence has Iran actually performed in recent times? What killing has it done? If despite Iran's speeches and controversial politics, it practices peace, not war, perhaps it doesn't matter that it indoctrinates and dehumanizes its people.

Unfortunately, this perspective overlooks important elements of Iran's track record. Before examining Iran's methods of indoctrination, we should review some of the many ways the radical regime has used violence to achieve its goals.

Since its sudden rise in 1979 and steadily since then, the Islamic revolution of Iran has brought more violence than harmony. Primarily through its Iranian Revolutionary Guard Corps and its Basij militia forces, Iran's theocratic system has regularly used intimidation, torture, murder, and terrorism to maintain its power and pursue its stated goal of world domination.[1] To be fair, over the last twenty years, most of Iran's violence has been domestic and its foreign activities have been somewhat limited. Attacks beyond Iranian soil have mainly been secretive and carried out by proxies or covert agents, and violence has not escalated into open battle or full-scale war. However, the nation's nuclear ambitions and recent inflammatory statements by its leaders suggest that it will be a much more dangerous threat to global security in the years to come. As current Supreme Leader Ayatollah Ali Hossayni Khameini has preached to his followers, "it is incumbent on us to fight until the entire humanity either converts or submits to Islamic authority."[2] This battle cry is based on a distorted, extremist interpretation of the true goal of Islam. It may just be rhetoric, or it may express Iran's real aspirations.

It's clear that Iran has made violence the primary tool for its national system. In the early 1980s, it executed hundreds of religious and political opponents, and in 1988, Iran murdered more than 4400 people in prison massacres.[3] A report by Human Rights Watch provides additional evidence that "the Iranian government summarily and extrajudicially executed thousands of political prisoners held in Iranian jails."[4] Because the Iranian government has never admitted that these murders took place or released any details on the matter, it is certainly possible that this is a low estimate. It is also important to recognize that these killings were not the result of random violence or internal chaos—they were carefully orchestrated and carried out in what Human Rights Watch labels a "deliberate and systematic manner."[5]

Ten years later, government-authorized murder was still the norm. In 1998, Iranian agents carried out serial murders of many high-profile liberal activists. After initial attempts at a cover-up were exposed, Iran admitted that high-ranking government officials had ordered the assassinations, but it directed the blame towards low level agents and protected many of the critical figures involved.[6] Even today, Iran continues to execute prisoners—including children—at an extremely high rate and for conveniently vague crimes such as "enmity against God" or "being corrupt on earth."[7] Of course, since anyone who opposes the system can be found guilty of these crimes, it has virtually unlimited power over the life and death of its citizens.

Amnesty International has also documented a range of other human rights abuses committed by Iran in 2007 and 2008, including "large-scale arrests, incommunicado detention," the "detention of human rights defenders and other prisoners of conscience, unfair trials, torture and mistreatment in detention, deaths in custody," and a "widespread crackdown on civil society, targeting academics, women's rights activists, students, journalists, and labor organizers," as well as religious minorities and homosexuals.[8]

Iran has also been one of the world's most enthusiastic state sponsors of terrorism. As Daniel Byman recounts, "Tehran has armed, trained, inspired, organized, and otherwise supported dozens of violent groups over the years. Iran has backed not only groups in its Persian Gulf neighborhood, but also terrorists in Lebanon, Israel, Bosnia, the Philippines, and elsewhere."[9] Perhaps most well known is Iran's formation of the terrorist group Hezbollah, which it funds, supports, and helps train to this day. As Amir Taheri explains, beyond its role in fighting internal enemies, the Iranian Revolutionary Guard Corps is in charge of these types of violent operations abroad:

> The IRGC also controls the lucrative business of "exporting the revolution," estimated to be worth $1.2 billion a year. It finances branches of the Hezbollah movement in at least 20 countries, including some in Europe, and provides money, arms, and training for radical groups with leftist backgrounds. In recent years, it has emerged as a major backer of the armed wing of the Palestinian Hamas and both Shiite and Sunni armed groups in Iraq, Afghanistan, and Pakistan.[10]

Taheri adds that these attempts to spread Iran's radical version of Islam are usually violent, and require "highly trained men and women specializing in 'martyrdom operations,' a code word for guerrilla war, armed insurgency, and terrorism."[11]

In addition, there is significant evidence that despite religious differences, Iran has supported Al Qaeda on the basis of their shared goals and mutual enemies.[12] Unfortunately, many people are extremely close-minded to this possibility. Having been misled by the Bush administration's claims of links between Iraq and Al Qaeda, people are naturally skeptical about similar U.S. charges against Iran. Fool me once, shame on you—fool me twice, shame on me, right? Cognizant that they may come across as the boy who cried wolf, U.S. politicians themselves have downplayed this angle. However, the facts are (1) that the bipartisan *9/11 Commission* found ties between Al Qaeda and Iran (2) eight of the nineteen 9/11 hijackers traveled to Iran in the year before the attacks and (3) after 9/11, Iran and Hezbollah worked extremely hard to conceal all evidence of their past cooperation with Al Qaeda.[13] Where there's smoke, there may be fire. As Bob Woodward reports, CIA director George Tenet's initial response to the attacks was to look for ties to Iran:

> [Tenet] believed that eventually they might find Iranian tracks in September 11. The Revolutionary Guard has a sophisticated network, and they had both motivation and capability. . . . Al Qaeda bought services wherever it could find them. So the classic model of direct support and control of terrorism no longer applied. Tenet had everything but proof that there was state sponsorship.[14]

This connection would not imply that Al Qaeda is controlled or managed by Iran, but simply that they have cooperated in some form to orchestrate past attacks.

If the U.S. eventually discovers more concrete evidence of Iran's involvement in 9/11, it wouldn't be the first case where it took a long time to prove responsibility for terrorism. For instance, the U.S. suspected Syrian involvement in the Pan Am Flight 103 bombing for nearly ten years before it established that the true sponsor was Libya. Similarly, the U.S. initially believed that Al Qaeda was solely responsible for the 1996 Khobar Towers bombing in Saudi Arabia. This was one of the most destructive terrorist attacks of the twentieth century, with nineteen U.S. servicemen killed and nearly four hundred people wounded. As it turns out, Iran so successfully disguised their involvement that it wasn't until 2006—after the separate confessions of six captured terrorists—that the truth finally came out. In December of that year, a U.S. federal judge cited "overwhelming" evidence to rule that "the Khobar Towers bombing was planned, funded, and sponsored by senior leadership in the government of the Islamic Republic of Iran."[15]

Despite remaining questions about Iran's involvement in terrorism, the radical nation's regular use of violence over the years is not up for debate. Naturally, its assassinations, large-scale executions, political crackdowns, and campaigns of terror require a great deal of manpower. As the following examination reveals, Iran has continuously used systematic indoctrination to transform normal Iranian citizens into loyal agents who will use violence on command. This is a central feature of the system's governing policy.

Nikola B. Schahgaldian's report on *The Clerical Establishment in Iran*, written for the RAND Corporation and the Office of the Under Secretary of Defense for Policy, makes this point quite clear:

> an integral part of the clerics' general management pattern is illustrated by their preoccupation with ideological/religious indoctrination, conformity, and political repression. . . . For this purpose, the clerics have required the government to place all its available resources at their disposal. In addition, they have made indoctrination a primary function of all Islamic revolutionary organizations, regardless of their nature and other functions. At present, these include the revolutionary committees, Islamic associations and societies, charitable and welfare organizations, the IRGC, the *Basij* (the Mobilization Army), and the country's entire private educational network.[16]

This strategy's success speaks for itself. Iran's hardliners have remained in control of the Islamic nation, and its agents have repeatedly proven themselves willing to strike anyone or anything that threatens the system's plans. And as Robert Spencer explains, "Anything that may advance that goal—nuclear weapons, burning embassies—is permitted."[17] If Iran continues to use these strategies to build its membership and the rest of the world continues to struggle in vain to do anything about it, Iran's future may be even more violent and deadly than its past.

Recruitment

Although Iranian leaders attempt to market their nation as having one clear mind and one strong voice, they work carefully to get malleable recruits for their violent system.

As the first part of their strategy, the violent system targets young members. As Schahgaldian explains, "the regime hopes that the younger generation will be socialized rapidly enough to ensure the continued existence of the Islamic government in Iran."[18] The youngest paramilitary group is the infamous Basij corps. Reza Aslan describes it as a combination of "pimply thugs" and "a street gang" that fits somewhere between "Hitler's Nazi Youth and the children of the Khmer Rouge."[19] Since the government requires all males to serve in some military group, many high school boys join the Basij as the most prestigious and exciting option for their age.[20]

In turn, the IRGC has its own high schools and universities to enlist and train young recruits.[21] As Kenneth Katzman explains, the Guard initially recruited many experienced, hard-line fighters to aid in the revolutionary movement and the war against Iraq, but it "also provided an opportunity for advancement for ambitious youths"—many of whom "viewed the Guard as a vehicle for upward mobility."[22] For young Iranians, it is a tempting career path offering increased power, prestige, and a range of tangible benefits, including "access to rare goods and services, from color TVs to more decent housing . . . [and] a fast track to social, political, and economic success."[23]

Beyond prioritizing youth, Iranian leaders prefer to recruit males for violent roles. Their reasons are rather straightforward, given the regime's ideology. As Jean B. Elshtain observes, "Within radical Islamism, women are unclean persons who must be kept hidden, covered entirely, and made subordinate."[24] Similarly, the Quran warns that "women [are] erotic creatures, continually giving trouble to man."[25] Thus, military and paramilitary forces are almost entirely reserved for men, because men are assumed to be stronger and smarter warriors, more worthy of the honored right to defend one's homeland, and because letting women into the system would presumably distract and corrupt the membership. In reality, allowing a significant number of female members inside Iran's violent organizations might well lead to increased moral reflection and less unthinking obedience regarding violent orders—which is exactly what the Islamic leaders want to avoid.

Recruits also tend to share a conservative, religious mindset.[26] President Mahmoud Ahmadinejad, a former Guard member and Basij instructor himself, is the kind of working class man that typifies the membership.[27] Like their current president, many members of the Basij and IRGC were recruited "from dispossessed classes loyal to the principles of the Islamic Republic."[28] For these recruits, Islamic codes and Islamic law are an extremely important part of daily life. Aslan explains that, even for those who aren't "exceptionally religious,"

"Islam is ingrained in [their] social consciousness. . . . It is a part of their national identity. It defines their morals and shapes their view of the world."[29] As we will see, it can also be distorted to facilitate their indoctrination.

Finally, many recruits for Iran's violent system come with a shared respect for authority. In part, this is based on the Iranian tradition of divine leadership, which provides comforting cognitive clarity for true believers. As Nader Ahmadi and Fereshteh Ahmadi explain, "when those who are in power are supposed to be the deputies of God on earth, adorned by divine grace, divine knowledge, and infallibility, there would be no sense in the fallible, ignorant masses, who are in desperate need of guardianship . . . questioning—still less . . . opposing—the deeds and wills of these authorities."[30] However, respecting Iranian authorities is not just about seeking guidance—it is also important to avoid being punished. Those who oppose the system meet a quick and brutal end, as the "series of political assassinations in Iran that began in 1998 . . . [where] individuals who advocated reforms and liberalism were murdered," reminded everyone.[31] Recruits are very aware of the coercive power in Iran. By joining the violent system and respecting their superiors, they hope to gain some control over their lives and some newfound power over the lives of others.

Training

Iran's violent system goes to great lengths to ensure the comprehensive training of new recruits. The Revolutionary Guard's first high school, the Imam Sadegh School, began teaching young Iranians in 1982 with a curriculum that combines "general education, military training, and the teaching of Islamic ideology."[32] Extending this successful model, the IRGC has built similar high schools throughout the country. At the college level, the Guard opened Imam Hussein University in 1986, which churned out its first graduating class two years later and is designed "to enhance the strategic, scientific, and religious knowledge of the members of the IRGC."[33] As Katzman documents, "Its training includes courses on Islamic ideology, military strategies, defense policies, defense strategic management, military interventions, and Iranian military history."[34] Naturally, these lessons portray the violent system in a very favorable light.

Beyond high school and college education, the IRGC also has military training programs that require a minimum of three months of tactical and weapons instruction. However, by far their top priority is the indoctrination of new recruits. As Katzman explains, the training program is "heavily imbued with Islamic ideology and the Guard's militant revolutionary rhetoric."[35] It is "less a vehicle for developing military proficiency than for perpetuating the Guard's revolutionary militance."[36] The Basij puts a similar premium on devout ideological training.[37]

Both the Basij and the IRGC are quick to crack down on substandard recruits. Any of them who show resistance to indoctrination are seen as a major risk for future missions. They might object to performing violence on command, or even more dangerously, provoke others to object. In the past, the Basij has dealt with this by expelling the troublemakers so that only the fully committed ones remain in the unit, but more deadly remedies cannot be ruled out.[38] Even high-level IRGC agents who become unwilling to serve the system face immediate danger. Taheri cites evidence that "An unknown number were purged because they refused to kill anti-regime demonstrators in Iranian cities."[39] When the system sends this type of message, recruits pay close attention. Do what you're told—or else.

As a prime feature of their indoctrination, recruits are taught to fear external enemies. The system portrays the U.S. and Israel as the primary threats to the Islamic way of life. This message has a long history. As Shay explains, Ayatollah Ruhollah Khomeini "presented the United States as 'the main enemy,' and the battle against it as 'a confrontation between Islam and the infidels.'"[40] Under Khomeini, "the United States was considered the 'Great Satan,' due to its presence and involvement in Iran and in the Middle East, and its attempts to instill the influences of its corruptive culture in Muslim states."[41] In turn, Israel is viewed as the "Little Satan"—a less mighty but more proximate threat to the Islamic Republic's daily existence. Recruits are taught that Iran's leaders are totally innocent and blameless, and that the West plots against Iran out of spite, envy, and pure evil. A perfect example of this self-serving distortion comes from Prosecutor General Qorban-Ali Dorri-Najafabadi. In January 2007, he explained to Iranian agents that "the enmity and hostile approach of the U.S., Israel, and Britain to Iran is rooted in the Iranian nation's independence-seeking and love for freedom."[42]

Echoing similar sentiments, a senior member of the Revolutionary Guard warned young fighters that "The axis of blasphemy is an axis against Allah and the Muslims" and that "the Jews and Christians further their goals by means of oppression and violence."[43] The only protection, he instructed, comes from groups like the Revolutionary Guard, which have violent means at their disposal:

> We have written strategy aimed at destroying Anglo-Saxon culture and uprooting the Americans and the English. Our missiles are ready to strike at their culture, and when the orders come from our leader (Ali Khameini) we will launch our missiles at their cities and facilities . . . There are 29 sensitive sites in the United States and the West. We have examined these sites and we know how we'll attack them.[44]

Iran's violent system has continued to support and exploit these notions over the years. As part of this strategy, leaders have regularly marketed the Zionists and their supporters as a grave threat, and the willingness to fight back as the sole solution.

Having increased fears of the threat, the Iranian system emphasizes the importance of unity for its members. One arrangement that encourages bonding and camaraderie among new IRGC and Basij agents is that both organizations deliberately train and station recruits near their hometowns—unlike most national armies, where recruits are shipped out to different units all over the country.[45] Thus, the members of a given unit can be more quickly molded into a collective entity—one with a common background and shared local reference points. Leaders also exploit Islam's limited regard for individuality to train new recruits to unite. As Ahmadi and Ahmadi explain, "The Iranian Shi'i Muslim who historically has been used to seeing some divine authorities ruling over him . . . never gains the opportunity of thinking of himself as an individual. He is an integrated part of a predetermined system, both metaphysically and socially."[46]

New recruits are also trained to conform and be obedient. Ahmad Beheshti, one of the most influential Shi'a ulama, is a perfect example of an Iranian leader who has emphasized this point. He claims that it is appropriate that "the government demands absolute obedience from the people, and . . . the integrity of society depends on this obedience."[47] He further insists that "in Islam the government actually belongs to God. Obedience to the Prophet and the imams is the same as obedience to God."[48] This notion has historical roots—according to some Islamic scholars, one's actions are *always* ethical as long as he or she defers to legitimate religious authorities. Ahmadi and Ahmadi explain that "obeying the ulama [Islamic clergy] would bring salvation upon the believer and grant him heavenly reward *regardless of the Mujtahid's being right or wrong.*"[49] This point is critical—it provides the ultimate moral blank check for blind obedience because *any act* may be permitted.

This lesson is also tied to the central Iranian notion of religious leaders as guardians of the common man. The system emphasizes that these guardians are necessary because the masses are "incapable of acting for their own good and thus are in need of someone who can tell what is right and what is wrong."[50] As Khomeini wrote, "*Velayat-e faqih*—the guardianship of the Islamic jurist—is the same as the appointment of a tutor for minors. The tutelage of the nation regarding responsibility and authority does not differ at all from the tutelage of the under-aged."[51] Like children who have been conditioned to shut their mouths and do exactly what they're told, recruits are expected to serve the system with complete obedience—no questions asked. They are taught that Allah will reward their obedience, even if their actions appear to be wrong.

New members of Iran's violent system are also trained to be willing to sacrifice themselves for its goals. Youssef Ibrahim describes the "common sight" of Basij "teenagers clustered in prayer groups led by a mullah or sitting quietly listening to religious indoctrination."[52] While "proclaiming their willingness to become martyrs for Islam, they listen to the same message that is taught at Qom's seminaries: they are the soldiers of Islam, battling blasphemous armies of infidels. This is their destiny. Paradise is their reward."[53]

Finally, recruits are desensitized to violence by actually practicing it on civilians. As Aslan explains, they are "totally unimpeded by the law—indeed, encouraged by the law—to force Iranians to observe the Supreme Leader's moral guidance."[54] Their regular oppression and intimidation of the populace prepares them for more extreme violence at some later date. The IRGC and Basijis serve as "protectors" of Islamic law, which means they police the streets and search homes, "looking for transgressors, such as women who refused to strictly conform to Islamic dress, youths playing Western music, and those eating during the daylight hours of the holy month of Ramadan."[55] By flexing their muscles and bullying people who cannot defend themselves, young recruits become accustomed to the use of violence.

A seventeen-year-old member of the Basij corps gives a typical example: he and his fellow thugs "arrived at a party full of drunk college students and forced them to take off their clothes and roll around in the snow as punishment" for drinking, which is against Islamic law.[56] Another time, "when they cornered a girl who had violated the Islamic Republic's modest dress code, they had her take off her shoes and put her bare feet in a dirty bucket filled with worms."[57] The system encourages this type of desensitization training so that some day in the future, when this boy is called upon to execute a prisoner or carry out a terrorist attack against a foreign nation, he will find it easier to complete his task. He has already learned to numb his conscience and act brutally to serve the system.

Beyond their on-the-job training as protectors of Islamic culture, the system's recruits are desensitized to violence through the Muharram rituals. In these religious rites, they engage in self-flagellation and self-mutilation to show their loyalty and dedication. During these events, they experience simultaneous feelings of national pride, religious ecstasy, physical suffering, and pain, all with an eye on martyrdom. As a member of the Iranian parliament explains, "There's a saying in Iran, 'You die once, you cry once.' . . . Iran has over 500,000 martyrs who defended our land."[58] Bloodshed and death are not new to these young men, and by desensitizing them, the system makes it even easier for them to attack the enemy.

Authorization

The Iranian system uses many sources of authority to legitimize violence.

While Allah is the ultimate authority for Iranian society, the system's leaders claim his spiritual and moral licenses. After the successful Islamic revolution in 1979, Khomeini officially became the Supreme Leader of Iran, seen as an extension of God himself and as much more than a mere politician. Khomeini tapped into sacred rumors of the twelfth, "Hidden Imam," who would someday return to Iran and restore its glory. By encouraging people to call him "Imam" and view him in this honored way, Khomeini's status rose to that of the "semi-divine 'saints' of Shiism who can intercede on behalf of God, heal the sick, and grant forgiveness of sins."[59] Some Iranians still believe the doctrine quite literally, and cite "evidence" of Khomeini's miracles. For instance, during the war between Iran and Iraq, some Iranian soldiers claimed to have seen the twelfth imam in person—he was gallantly riding a horse at battle alongside them, providing guidance and aid.[60] When Iran repelled the Iraqi onslaught, this legend became proof that Allah supports Iran and its holy leaders.

The superhuman authority of Iran's leaders did not die with Khomeini—Supreme Leader Ayatollah Khameini and the Council of Guardians continue to justify their decisions based on privileged connections with Allah. The types of divine wisdom bestowed on the imams and denied to ordinary people include "transmission from the previous Imam, knowledge acquired in a hereditary fashion, knowledge acquired from books whose contents are known only to the Imams, and knowledge acquired through direct contact with an angel."[61] Apparently, Allah's messenger does not actually appear before the Imam, but instead speaks to him in his dreams.[62] Opinions vary about how much privileged information Iranian leaders actually get, but many members of the system believe that they have sacred authority and must be obeyed.

Ahmadinejad also frames his presidency and control over the system as a divine product. A perfect example is his assertion that, through Allah's direct guidance, approval, and support, Iran has now grown strong enough to handle a confrontation with the West.[63] Ahmadinejad's combination of radical Islamicism, Iranian nationalism, and anti-Americanism has significantly raised the president's status as a traditional crusader. As Gary Sick suggests, "by quoting Ayatollah Ruhollah Khomeini and continuing to parrot anti-Israel slogans that have become ritual since 1979, Ahmadinejad . . . has attained rock-star status."[64] Despite concerns that Ahmadinejad's "religious zealotry and bellicose rhetoric" might provoke a premature clash with the West, "many Iranians, nonetheless, find an undeniable allure in seeing their country expand its influence on the world stage and square off with the foremost military and economic powers."[65] Ahmadinejad's uncompromising political stance fits with his image. He portrays himself as a religious warrior on a divine mission who gets cues from Allah himself.

Iran's management strategy is thus based on the relentless promotion of Allah and these leaders of his choosing as supreme authorities. This is the basis for a fundamental transcendent authorization. The Iranian system teaches members of the IRGC and Basij to think of Allah and how he will be pleased by their acts, rather than dwell on the brutality, violence, and sacrifices demanded of them.

A key example is how the radical regime accentuates the appeal of martyrdom attacks and refuses to name the suicidal nature of such violence. For years, the Iranian system has successfully marketed martyrdom as a most honorable undertaking:

> Following [Shi'ite] tradition, children as young as 12 were sent to the front lines during the war with Iraq in the 1980s to clear minefields with their bodies. Thousands of these young soldiers, recruited by religious leaders as part of the Basiji movement, marched to their deaths, eager to die as directed for the glory of God and in expectation of a heavenly reward. The cult of religious martyrdom remains strong in Iran, and one of its most ardent promoters is President Mahmoud Ahmadinejad. [66]

As recently as May 2006, Iran celebrated the graduation of 150 potential suicide bombers at a public media event. These graduates were apparently just a small sample of those recruited, indoctrinated, and trained by the IRGC and Basij corps over several months.[67] This is all made possible by a transcendent authorization that obscures the horrible nature of suicide attacks or the fact that suicide is forbidden by Islamic doctrine. Instead, the virtues of martyrdom are emphasized, along with the claim that these sacrifices please and honor Allah.

As part of this strategy, Iranian leaders capitalize on the story of Muhammad's grandson, Imam Hussein, to further glorify the virtues of martyrdom. Legend has it that Hussein was killed in a battle in 680 after he defiantly refused to swear allegiance to a corrupt government, despite being outnumbered by enemy forces. For many Iranians, Hussein's death "forged a set of principles which Iran defines today as its divine mandate to fight oppression and to glorify those who die doing so."[68] As one Iranian citizen summarizes, "The message we take from Ashura is that we should always stand up against oppression, even if you are a small group. . . . Hussein would not accept being oppressed."[69]

Members of the IRGC and Basij get plenty of opportunities to show their resolve. Iranian leaders exploit this religious authorization to challenge oppressors by making constant parallels between current geopolitical conflicts and Hussein's plight. As Michael Slackman documents, "By referring to the United States as the 'World Oppressor,' [Iranian leaders have] consistently invoked the intense feelings associated with their people's deepest religious convictions, and tapped into a moral framework that pervades even the secular parts of society."[70] As part of this transcendent authorization, Iran's hardliners emphasize the honor in standing up for what you believe in and refusing to abandon your religious principles. Meanwhile, they downplay the terrible pain and suffering that this violent form of confrontation is sure to cause.

Other transcendent authorizations frame violence against so-called enemies of Islam as a matter of cleanliness, instead of what it actually is: oppression or brutal aggression. Iran has often labeled such missions as "moral cleansing" to promote the "propagation of virtue."[71] The stated goal is thus to "purify the society from all sinful habits of urban life."[72] Similarly, Khomeini strategically depicted Islamic jihad as a struggle that is "primarily focused upon the purification of Islamic society from within . . . [that] does not end in the Islamic arena but it is also designated to obliterate the 'source of evil'—the superpowers that cause the corruption of the world."[73] These authorizations exploit the fact that spreading virtue, cleansing and purifying society, and stopping corruption are noble goals in the abstract. At least on the surface, they are pursuits that no one could argue against. Led to think in this manner, Iranian agents focus on the system's goals, rather than on the violence required to meet them.

The Iranian system also employs mundane authorizations to ready its followers for violence. Beyond the authorizations from God, the Supreme Leader, the Council of Guardians, and the president—various clerics, commanders, and administrators throughout the system give both specific and vague orders.

These authorizations combine to produce a social climate in which violence is no longer extraordinary. Instead, it becomes the standard, justified response to insults or oppression. Members of the system are taught to endorse Hammurabi's code, which is a fundamental part of the Islamic legal system. As a result, values like "an eye for an eye and a tooth for a tooth" are widely accepted.[74] (In fact, in September 2006, an Iranian man found guilty of blinding another man in a street fight was actually sentenced to have his left eye gouged out, painfully personifying the oft-quoted saying.[75]) When the system calls on the IRGC or Basij to attack enemies accused of some crime, their agents find it easier to respond with violence because it is well established as the social norm. Through the legal system's mundane authorizations, violent retributive justice seems commonplace and like no big deal.

The system further authorizes violence with references to the *Hirabah* verse from the Quran. This infamous selection suggests that the "punishment of those who wage war (*yuharibun*) against God and His Prophet, and strive to cause corruption on the earth (*yasawna fi al-ardi fasadan*) is that they be killed or [tied to a tree] or have a hand and foot cut off from opposite ends or be exiled in the land."[76]

Scholars continuously debate how to interpret this verse. Are its calls for punishment metaphorical or literal, who exactly does it apply to, and what constitutes such sins? As Khaled Abou El Fadl points out, the passage is easily exploited: "Theoretically, the language 'cause corruption on earth' could be applied to a wide range of activities including anything from writing heretical poetry to raping and pillaging."[77] Iranian leaders point to this verse as a religious authorization for virtually *any* violence that serves the system.

Bureaucracy

The overarching Iranian bureaucracy helps national leaders condition the system's agents for violence. One key factor is the tremendous size of the system, which can make individual members feel small, anonymous, and powerless to disobey. Beyond the offices of the Supreme Leader, the president, and the Council of Guardians, Iran possesses more than ten agencies just to handle the issue of national security.[78] One of these agencies, the Ministry of Intelligence and Security, contains twelve sub-departments manned by over 20,000 agents operating inside and outside of Iran, while the Revolutionary Guards have at least 120,000 members, and their own land, air, and sea forces that are run separately from the national military.[79] The Basij boast of having up to 20 million members, with units in every Iranian city and town, though the exact number is hard to document and is probably much smaller. But in any case, since orders for violence may come from the very top, channeling down the chain of command, agents often feel overwhelming pressure to fulfill their roles in the system.

This type of bureaucratic pressure may well have been critical in the 1992 assassination of four Kurdish politicians in a German restaurant. As Shay asserts, the case "constitutes a prominent example of the Iranian decision-making chain, and the German court unequivocally indicated the responsibility of the Iranian government's top leaders for the terror activity."[80] The court also cited "the personal and direct involvement of the Iranian Intelligence Minister Falahian in the planning and implementation."[81] By the time the assassins, who were trained at a commando camp in Iran, got their orders from above, the system's pressure on them to obey must have been immense. The system is so large, with so many thousands of members, that a dissenting opinion would have seemed pointless and insignificant. Even if the agents had objected, others would have been called on to carry out the assassinations, and the disobedient Iranians would have been, at the very least, extremely unpopular with their peers and Iranian leadership. More likely, they would have been immediately executed for disobeying orders. Faced with these pressures, it's easy to see why they did what they were told.

Under Ahmadinejad, Iranian bureaucracy has grown even larger and more violent. As Abbas Milani details, upon election, the president undertook a "kind of purge and revamping of the whole upper echelon of the bureaucracy" and installed a "vast network of Revolutionary Guards, Basiji commanders, and some dangerously strident right-wing clergy."[82] Mark Kukis further describes the refashioned Iranian bureaucracy:

> Since taking office, Ahmadinejad has restructured the government more extensively than almost anyone suspected he could have. . . . Ahmadinejad wasn't content simply to install new heads in the national ministries . . . [his] government has seated new leadership in almost every university. Virtually all of the ambassadors who served in the last government are gone. Ahmadinejad has even gone so far as to replace sitting undersecretaries, governors, and city managers with his loyalists.[83]

By replacing top bureaucrats throughout the country with administrators who think like he does, Ahmadinejad has only stoked more of the systematic group-think that propels violence into action. Potential dissenters can no longer trust the man to the left or right of them for support—that person may be a strict de-votee to Iranian leaders and the system.

Within the Iranian bureaucracy, symbols and rituals help to normalize vio-lence for agents. For example, in the late 1970s, Islamic leaders used religious rites to mobilize the violent uprising against the Shah. As Nir Rosen explains, "an exiled Ayatollah Khomeini appropriated the Muharram rituals to inspire the fall of the shah's regime. Khomeini accused Mohammad Reza Shah of acting as a modern Yazid, an enemy of the Shi'as, thus sanctioning the uprising against him."[84] After the revolution, the bureaucracy established these customs as the "primary means for promoting the legitimacy and revolutionary program of the new state."[85]

In order to further indoctrinate its agents, the Iranian Ministry of Culture and Religious Guidance organizes "hundreds of religious events and rituals every year."[86] Veteran agents, who are already fully trained and indoctrinated, are mobilized for these mass demonstrations to support the regime and help shape the system's new members. Thematically, the system exploits Ashura and the death of the Imam Hussein to portray Iran "as being the defender of the op-pressed masses of the world from imperialist domination and oppression."[87] As part of the bureaucratic framework, these militant demonstrations are portrayed as a normal, state-administered part of life.

One of the most violent examples is the annual Muharram ritual, which is characterized by self-flagellation and mutilation. Rosen describes the scene in 2004:

> After dawn prayers on the morning of March 2, the 10th of Muharram, the same day the Battle of Karbala was believed to have started in 680 CE, trum-pets blared and drums beat in a military cadence. "Haidar, Haidar, Haidar," cried thousands of men dressed in white gowns, calling out to the 7th-century caliph Ali, the father of the martyred Shi'ite leader Hussein, by his nickname. They waved their swords in the air, dancing and beating their newly shaved heads with the blades, slowly drawing blood that soaked their white garb and splattered everyone around them. Men brought their young sons, some not yet 10, whose heads had also been shaved to make the scalp easier to get to. The boys cringed in terror as their fathers held their hands on the sword, and drew first blood, proudly congratulating the relieved and bloody children after-wards.[88]

Although this ritual may sound like something from hundreds of years ago, it is an annual event that still takes place today. The mutilation and flagellation may seem frightening to outsiders, but it is part of a government-run event and serves the system's violent purpose. Through these events and demonstrations, IRGC agents, Basij members, and regular citizens are familiarized with violence as a central feature of the system. Thus, for the agent who may one day be called upon to execute a so-called agitator, assassinate an enemy politician, or blow himself up in a foreign cafe, there is an existing subconscious psychological association between violence, pain, bloodshed, the clerical system, and religious ecstasy.

In addition, Iran's regular Friday sermons have become "a major vehicle for reinforcing the revolutionary ideology and legitimacy of the state."[89] The system's explicit approval of violence is a point of emphasis at these religious ceremonies. As Kamran S. Aghaie details, clerics often "hold machine guns at their sides while giving the Friday sermon, a symbol of the connection between the war of words and armed struggle in the path of God."[90] It is on occasions such as these that Islamic leaders as high as Khameini himself have led Iranian crowds—laden with IRGC and Basij members—in chants of "Death to America." The government makes sure to broadcast the sermons on television and the radio and to publish them in newspapers for any Iranians who may have missed the not so subtle message. Again, the system specifically uses these bureaucratic rituals and symbols to promote its violent mandate and conditions agents accordingly.

The division of labor within the Iranian bureaucracy also makes it easier for agents to serve the system. Violence is often the combined product of formal security departments, mid-level bureaucrats, legitimate members of the IRGC and hired thugs or mercenaries. The system often uses "unofficial groups and paramilitary organizations (hezbollahis and basijis) to carry on vigilante actions," so that it can innocently claim that such violence was outside of government control.[91] In turn, many members of the violent system can conveniently deny their own roles in atrocities. Reza Afshari explains that there are "two familiar faces" of the Iranian system, "the visible and the invisible."[92] This arrangement allows systematic violence to carry on without typical moral hindrances. For years, "Technobureaucrats who were publicly visible rendered themselves unaccountable for the human rights abuses that were taking place. Those who were hidden beyond the walls of the security apparatus remained out of reach."[93]

In reality, these distinctions are not clear-cut. Within the Ministry of Intelligence and Security for example, there are three major departments—one that handles internal security, one that handles popular intelligence and supervision of public places, and one that handles external security and foreign operations. All three of these departments have overt and covert missions, and all three use violence to serve the system.[94] For the system's agents, playing a demarcated role in larger campaigns of violence, terrorism, or jihad is made easier by the bureaucracy, which shields them from the distasteful comprehension of the total, brutal picture.

For instance, Iranian diplomats do not personally stage terrorist attacks, but they do provide "diplomatic camouflage for the activity of intelligence members and terror activists, [and aid] in the provision of documentation (passports, visas, etc.) and in the transfer of combat means and equipment via diplomatic pouch," which cannot be inspected.[95] Diplomats also "deal in the gathering of intelligence and surveillance of potential targets against which Iran intends to perpetrate attacks."[96]

A typical example is the 1994 bombing of a Jewish community center in Buenos Aires, which left 85 people dead and hundreds injured. Fourteen years later, in 2008, the investigation is still going on. Argentinean officials claim that the terrorist attack was planned by high-ranking members of the Iranian government and carried out by Hezbollah operatives, with the help of Hadi Soleimanpour, the Iranian ambassador to Argentina.[97] Interpol has joined the effort to arrest some of the key Iranian officials involved. Meanwhile, Iran dismisses the charges as a "Zionist plot."[98] Psychologically, diplomats such as Soleimanpour can rationalize the violence they facilitate, telling themselves that they are not responsible for terrorist attacks because they did not plant the bombs or pull the guns' triggers.

At the same time, the IRGC and Hezbollah agents who do plant the bombs use the same type of rationalization to minimize their moral culpability, claiming that they didn't pick the targets or supply the weapons. They only played a limited role in the overall scheme, and thus bear limited responsibility for the violent results. As Katzman finds, IRGC leaders have "appeared to compartmentalize their responsibilities to best cope with the demands of war."[99] Afshari similarly emphasizes that the ongoing attempt to export the Islamic revolution has "also created a division of responsibility for the state security apparatus," with "the means of repression and violence" becoming the product of a complex, combined effort.[100]

Isolation

Iranian leaders have used several types of isolation to make it easier for their agents to perform violence on command.

After the Islamic revolution, Khomeini attempted to increase Iran's social isolation so that violence could be used indiscriminately. He publicly insisted that Iran "did not recognize the superpowers' values and norms . . . such as liberalism, democracy, human rights, socialism, and others."[101] He further claimed, "the UN is simply a tool whose reason for existence is to bestow legitimacy upon interests and concepts that serve the superpowers."[102] Through these statements, Khomeini rejected the moral authorities of the outside world. This was by design. If outsiders had been allowed to influence the Iranian masses, they might have jeopardized Iran's production of fully obedient human killing machines.

Over the years, Iran has reestablished some ties to the UN and the Western world, but it is still quite dismissive of international opinion. Ahmadinejad's public attempts to antagonize foreign leaders highlight his desire to maintain Iran's social isolation. By rejecting the views of others, Iran preserves the moral buffer between its agents and the outside world.

This strategy is particularly apparent in Iranian leaders' manipulation of the media. Iran ensures that its members are literally isolated by keeping outside information from penetrating its borders and keeping internal critics silent. Over the years, Iran has shut down newspapers that allegedly "spread lies against the government," closed a political journal for publishing a poem by a female dissident, strictly controlled the phone system, and censored the internet to prevent criticism of the system's violent morality. In addition, according to Human Rights Watch, in 2004, "Tehran's prosecutor general, Saeed Mortazavi, orchestrated the secret detentions and alleged torture of 21 bloggers and staff of internet news sites known to be critical of the government."[103] Once in prison, four of the men were forced to confess to crimes such as "participation in formation of groups to disturb national security," "propaganda against the state," "dissemination of disinformation to disturb public opinion by writing articles for newspapers and illegal internet sites," and "interviews with foreign radio broadcasts."[104] Even more brutally, the system has authorized assassinations and torture to control the media. During the 1990s, "Writers, artists, and intellectuals were murdered in their homes. Newspapers were shut down, and student protesters savagely beaten on the streets by the Basij and the Revolutionary Guards."[105]

In turn, Iran's isolation allows it to direct the information that its people do get. Leaders regularly use the media to redefine the conditions for justified violence on their own terms. Today, the Islamic Republic News Agency, or IRNA, stands alone as the system's propaganda machine. Its government-approved messages further isolate mainstream Iranians from the rest of the world. The IRNA adamantly claims that it is an objective agency and that the government "defends the free circulation of information and opposes censorship, self-censorship and government pressure on the media."[106] Yet at the same time, the IRNA's own website blatantly admits that, along with its news-related objectives, its first goal is "promoting the interests and objectives of the Islamic Republic of Iran."[107] Its second goal is the "Promotion of the Islamic culture as far as possible and encountering the cultural onslaught of enemies of the Islamic Revolution.[108] Providing accurate news or diverse perspectives, much less promoting a culturally and intellectually *connected* (instead of isolated) society, are ideals noticeably absent in their list of institutional guidelines. Through this control of information and the media, Iran further isolates its agents and establishes its violent ethics as pure and undisputed.

To further ensure their agents' isolation, Iranian leaders prioritize secrecy within the system. When members of the system are kept uninformed about many of Iran's deadly activities, it becomes easier for them to do their jobs. Afshari describes how former President Akbar Hashemi Rafsanjani maintained "a delicate balance between the two sides of the state. He did not allow himself or his (nonsecurity) ministers to pry deeply into the affairs of the secret side, often defending both the security apparatus and the judicial system that were together the main violators of human rights."[109] As agents deny their own roles in the system's use of torture, murder, and terror—both to themselves and to others—their ignorance truly becomes bliss. In addition, the system's internal isolation is designed to make it harder for agents to spread dissent, even if they object to the orders they've received. For Iranian leaders, "Keeping internal matters secret . . . is seen as essential to preserving the clerical system, while mutually protective silence among clerics lessens strife within their own ranks."[110] By keeping agents from discussing the moral dimensions of their behavior, Iran ensures that their indoctrination remains uncompromised and that they will continue to perform violence on command.

Ironically, Iran's self-imposed isolation, rejection of the outside world, and violent track record have led many countries to cut off ties with the radical nation, which only further isolates Iran and its indoctrinated membership. In particular, one of the U.S.'s main strategies over the past thirty years has been to isolate Iran with sanctions and political restrictions.

Our understanding of systematic indoctrination is absolutely critical here. By recognizing the dangerous effects of isolation, we can see how the current international effort against Iran may actually be helping the hardliners' agenda and supporting their violent system. As Jacob Weisberg suggests, sanctions can actually be advantageous for radical regimes because their people "already suffer from global isolation."[111] "Fed on a diet of propaganda, they don't know what's happening inside their borders or outside of them. By increasing their seclusion, sanctions make it easier for dictators to blame external enemies for a country's suffering" and thus justify violent measures.[112] Instead of facilitating change and reform in Iran, the "more likely effect of a comprehensive sanctions regime is that it will push dissatisfied and potentially rebellious Iranians back into the arms of the nuke-building mullahs."[113] Fortunately, there are ways we can act to correct this strategic misstep and counter Iran's radical agenda. This point is addressed in more depth in the final chapter.

Dehumanization

Through its overall implementation of systematic indoctrination, Iran dehumanizes its own agents in several ways. Members of the system become objectified tools to be used, exploited, or sacrificed as the leaders deem appropriate. As discussed earlier, Iran's religious and political tradition reduces individuality for almost everyone, leaving "no opportunity for the will of the individual to step forward onto the scene of social and political life."[114] It even restricts the way members of the system think about themselves. Though IRGC and Basij agents are empowered to use violence, most of them are still essentially powerless in the larger sense. Within the system, they continue to lack both the freedom to express themselves openly and the power to control their own lives.

One of the key reasons that Basij training is so "rich with ideology" is that their members have been viewed "as essentially expendable soldiers of Islam and the revolution."[115] They are not valued as real human beings, but instead weighed as the simple means to an end. And the same could be said of the IRGC. Iranian leaders see low-level agents as a resource, plain and simple. Once they have been fully indoctrinated, these young men become dehumanized weapons for the larger jihad.

Never was this clearer than during the Iran-Iraq war, when young Basij members were given toy keys that would supposedly let them enter heaven, and then instructed to rush Iraqi forces in human waves, clearing land mines with their bodies. This fatal task was originally assigned to donkeys and cows, "but when the animals saw other animals getting blown to pieces, they got scared and ran away."[116] The tragic irony is that the *animals* were too smart and put too much value on their own lives to be effective mine clearers, so the dehumanized Basijis were given the job instead. As Yossi Melman and Meir Javedanfar explain, "The Basijis obliged faithfully because they were believers. They ran in waves over the mines and were slaughtered. IRGC soldiers watched from a distance, and as soon as the Basijis were blown up and the mines were cleared, they launched their attacks."[117]

The dehumanized young men were so machine-like in their mass sacrifice that even some enemy soldiers could hardly stand what they were witnessing. As one Iraqi fighter exclaimed, "You can shoot down the first wave and then the second. . . . But at some point the corpses are piling up in front of you, and all you want to do is scream and throw away your weapon. Those are human beings, after all!"[118] Clearly, this foreign observer was not a product of systematic indoctrination—to his credit, he retained his human feelings of empathy, even in battle.

To outsiders like him, the Basijis were recognized as human beings, but to leaders of the system, that classification was no longer relevant. The Basijis became useful tools, more valuable than donkeys and cows only because they were more obedient. As Melman and Javedanfar affirm, systematic indoctrination turned these young boys into "cannon fodder"—they were seen as "sacrificial sheep."[119] Of course, Iranian leaders put much more value on their own lives. As a French intelligence officer once remarked, "Ayatollah Khomeini thinks martyrdom is great—for other people. You don't live to be eighty-eight years old with a death wish."[120] One day, the same thing may be said of Khameini or Ahmadinejad.

The Iranian system also dehumanizes and demonizes its enemies. As A. M.

Rosenthal explains, Khomeini used dehumanization to justify violence against the opposition:

> Khomeini and his preachers light the flame of hatred with a word: Death. Death to America! Death to Zionists! Death, death, death. Not just death to nations but to all who oppose. Death to the hypocrites! Death to the traitors! And, of course, the curse meant to cast the enemy out of humanity and into the pits of hell: Satan. Satan America. The satanic powers. The forces of Satan.[121]

By this rationale, the enemy who serves Satan is no longer human, so he deserves no respect, compassion, tolerance, or mercy. Since the enemy corrupts and defiles in accordance with his evil nature, any weapon or violence against him is justified. Beyond employing demonic imagery, Khomeini also called leaders of enemy Muslim countries "infidels and animals."[122]

The Iranian system's strategic use of dehumanization certainly did not die with Khomeini—it has been continuously used to justify brutality against all enemies. For instance, the previously referenced Islamic authority Qutb turned to dehumanization to frame his contempt for enemies of Islam. As Stern reports, "Qutb's outlook on the West changed dramatically after his first visit to America, where he was repulsed by Americans' materialism, racism, promiscuity, and feminism."[123] "Americans behave like animals, he said . . . [emphasizing] the need to cleanse Islam from impurities resulting from its exposure to Western and capitalist influence."[124]

Similarly, in 1997, "leaders of the Iranian Revolutionary Guard Corps called for 'removing the tumorous cancer Israel off the region's map.'"[125] Through their dehumanizing language, they implied the Jewish state is a disease and that violence is the only cure.

More recently, speaking to supporters at Tehran University in December 2006, Mullah Ahmad Khatami portrayed Israeli Prime Minister Ehud Olmert as a direct danger to Muslims, labeling him a "blood-thirsty butcher" and a "wild and brainless animal," while supporters chanted "Nuclear technology is our obvious right" in the background.[126] He also depicted Americans, the British, and the Israelis as dangerous animals instead of humans, claiming "These wolves are prepared to burn the world for their own interests, like they did in Iraq, Afghanistan and Lebanon."[127]

These are just some scattered public examples—countless others exist. Even today, Iranian leaders still use dehumanization to justify violence against their enemies.

Conclusion

As Ahmed astutely observes, "God took a gamble by creating human beings. . . . Man has the capacity to kill and destroy just as easily as to be just and compassionate."[128]

The wide range of man's moral options is quite apparent in Islamic history. Many great things have been achieved in the name of Muhammad, and the Islamic empire has a glorious tradition of cultural and intellectual enlightenment. Muslims have made many impressive contributions to science, mathematics, and the arts. There is nothing inherently bad or dangerous about the Islamic religion or a national system based on its religious teachings. Unfortunately, the recent behavior of Iran—and Al Qaeda—has assured that "Islam, which sees itself as a religion of peace, is now associated with murder and mayhem."[129]

For nearly thirty years, Iran has used systematic indoctrination to help its agents repress their consciences and commit violence for the good of the system. This strategy has been extremely successful. As the nation's leaders have come to realize, "Ideological indoctrination, combined with conformity and political repression, mobilizes the masses and crushes all resistance, making it likely that the regime will continue in power."[130]

As bad as Iran's post-revolutionary record of murder, terrorism, torture, and other human rights abuses has been, there are worrisome signs that the future could be worse. This is a reality we cannot afford to ignore or deny. Spencer explains that "Westerners may find it hard to believe that this cleric-controlled regime would so cravenly trample upon what are accepted in the non-Muslim world as universal moral principles, but in Tehran 'it all depends on the goal.'"[131]

In the past, the radical regime believed that "Nothing could rival a human mind that has been infused with a powerful religious ideology."[132] Now it is ready to pair its committed fighters with the most destructive weaponry known to man. Iran's current goal appears to be the acquisition of nuclear weapons, so that it will have the military technology to go along with its unrivalled force of indoctrinated warriors. As Taheri documents, "The crown jewel of the IRGC's business empire is the Islamic Republic's nuclear program, which has cost the nation over $10 billion so far. This is part of a broader scheme of arms purchases and manufacture, which in total accounts for almost 11% of the annual national budget."[133] This financial commitment implies that Iran's long-term plans are even more frightening than its violent past, and could include terrorism, genocide, or even World War III.

Notes

1. Iran's reliance on the IRGC and Basij militias, which exist separately from the Iranian military, parallels Nazi Germany's use of the SS and other Nazi paramilitary groups for many of its violent operations.
2. Timmerman, *Preachers of Hate*, 126.

3. "Ministers of Murder: Iran's New Security Cabinet," *HRW.org*, http://hrw.org/backgrounder/mena/iran1205/index.htm (8 January 2008).
4. "Ministers of Murder."
5. "Ministers of Murder."
6. "Ministers of Murder."
7. "Iran: Amnesty International appalled at the spiraling numbers of executions," *AmnestyUSA.org*, 5 September 2007, http://www.amnestyusa.org/document.php?lang=e&id=ENGMDE131102007 (10 April 2008).
8. "Iran: Human Rights Concerns," *AmnestyUSA.org*, http://www.amnestyusa.org/By_Country/Iran/page.do?id=1011172&n1=3&n2=30&n3=922 (18 January 2008).
9. Daniel Byman, *Deadly Connections: States that Sponsor Terrorism* (Cambridge: Cambridge University Press, 2005), 79.
10. Amir Taheri, "Who Are Iran's Revolutionary Guards?" *Wall Street Journal*, 15 November 2007, Eastern Edition.
11. Taheri, "Who Are Iran's Revolutionary Guards?"
12. "Former Bodyguard of Osama Bin Laden."
13. "The Attack Looms," *National Commission on Terrorist Attacks Upon the United States*, 26 August 2004, http://www.9-11commission.gov/report/911Report_Ch 7.htm (1 July 2008).
14. Bob Woodward, *Bush at War* (New York: Simon & Schuster, 2002), 317.
15. Carol D. Leonnig, "Iran Held Liable In Khobar Attack: Judge Orders $254 Million Payment," *WashingtonPost.com*, 23 December 2006, http://www.washingtonpost.com/wp-dyn/content/article/2006/12/22/AR2006122200455.html (7 July 2008).
16. Nikola B. Schahgaldian, *The Clerical Establishment in Iran* (Santa Monica, Calif.: The RAND Corporation, 1989), 33.
17. Robert Spencer, "Iran's Broken Moral Compass," *Human Events* 62 (2006): 15.
18. Schahgaldian, *The Clerical Establishment in Iran*, 34.
19. Reza Aslan, "A weeklong journal of a writer in Iran—Entry 3," *Slate Magazine*, 9 September 2004, http://www.slate.com/id/2106317/entry/2106465/ (10 April 2008).
20. Aslan, "A weeklong journal of a writer in Iran—Entry 3."
21. Kenneth Katzman, *The Warriors of Islam: Iran's Revolutionary Guard* (Boulder, Colo.: Westview Press, 1993), 91-92.
22. Katzman, *The Warriors of Islam*, 9.
23. Taheri, "Who Are Iran's Revolutionary Guards?"
24. Jean B. Elshtain, *Just War Against Terrorism* (New York: Basic Books, 2003), 39.
25. Vern Bullough, et al., *The Subordinated Sex* (Athens, Ga.: The University of Georgia Press, 1988), 116.
26. Rebecca Cann and Constantine Danopoulous, "The military and politics in a theocratic state: Iran as case study," *Armed Forces and Society* 24 (Winter 1997): 276; Gary Sick, "A Selective Partnership: Getting U.S.-Iranian Relations Right," *Foreign Affairs* 85 (November/December 2006): 145.
27. "No clear winner in Iran poll trends," *AlJazeera.net*, 26 June 2005, http://english.aljazeera.net/English/Archive/Archive?ArchiveID=20208 (10 April 2008).
28. Cann and Danopoulous, "The military and politics in a theocratic state," 275.
29. Aslan, "A weeklong journal of a writer in Iran—Entry 3."

30. Nader Ahmadi and Fereshteh Ahmadi, *Iranian Islam: The Concept of the Individual* (London: Macmillan Press Ltd., 2004), 167.

31. Shaul Shay, *The Axis of Evil: Iran, Hizballah, and the Palestinian Terror* (New Brunswick, N.J.: Transaction Publishers, 2005), 234.

32. Katzman, *The Warriors of Islam*, 91-92.

33. Cann and Danopoulous, "The military and politics in a theocratic state," 275-76, Katzman, *The Warriors of Islam*, 92.

34. Katzman, *The Warriors of Islam*, 92.

35. Katzman, *The Warriors of Islam*, 92-93.

36. Katzman, *The Warriors of Islam*, 92-93.

37. Cann and Danopoulous, "The military and politics in a theocratic state," 282.

38. Cann and Danopoulous, "The military and politics in a theocratic state," 282.

39. Taheri, "Who Are Iran's Revolutionary Guards?"

40. Shay, *The Axis of Evil*, 166.

41. Shay, *The Axis of Evil*, 20.

42. "Prosecutor general considers promotion of security as gov't duty," *Islamic Republic News Agency*, 21 January 2007, http://www.irna.com/en/news/view/line-17/07 01210284165127.htm (24 January 2007).

43. Shay, *The Axis of Evil*, 256.

44. Shay, *The Axis of Evil*, 256.

45. Katzman, *The Warriors of Islam*, 88.

46. Ahmadi and Ahmadi, *Iranian Islam*, 131.

47. Ahmadi and Ahmadi, *Iranian Islam*, 166.

48. Ahmadi and Ahmadi, *Iranian Islam*, 166.

49. Ahmadi and Ahmadi, *Iranian Islam*, 163. Emphasis added.

50. Ahmadi and Ahmadi, *Iranian Islam*, 144.

51. Ahmadi and Ahmadi, *Iranian Islam*, 167. Emphasis added.

52. Katzman, *The Warriors of Islam*, 93.

53. Katzman, *The Warriors of Islam*, 93.

54. Aslan, "A weeklong journal of a writer in Iran—Entry 3."

55. Katzman, *The Warriors of Islam*, 84.

56. Aslan, "A weeklong journal of a writer in Iran—Entry 3."

57. Aslan, "A weeklong journal of a writer in Iran—Entry 3."

58. Michael Slackman, "Invoking Islam's Heritage, Iranians Chafe at 'Oppression' by the West," *New York Times*, 6 February 2006, Late Edition East Coast.

59. Reza Aslan, "A weeklong journal of a writer in Iran—Entry 2," *Slate Magazine*, 8 September 2004, http://www.slate.com/id/2106317/entry/2106413/ (10 April 2008).

60. Ahmadi and Ahmadi, *Iranian Islam*, 131.

61. Ahmadi and Ahmadi, *Iranian Islam*, 143.

62. Ahmadi and Ahmadi, *Iranian Islam*, 143.

63. Associated Press, "Ahmadinejad warns Iran is ready for any possibility over nuclear row," *USATODAY*, 18 January 2007, http://www.usatoday.com/news/world/2007-01-18-iran_x.htm?csp=34 (18 January 2007).

64. Sick, "A Selective Partnership," 145.

65. Mark Kukis, "Ahmadinejad the Aggrandizer," *National Journal*, April 22, 2006, 54-55.

66. Editor's Desk, "Talking to Iran," *The Christian Century*, 13 June 2006, http://www.christiancentury.org/article.lasso?id=2112 (12 December 2006).

67. Kasra Naji, *Ahmadinejad: The Secret History of Iran's Radical Leader* (Berkeley, Calif.: University of California Press, 2008), 194.

68. Slackman, "Invoking Islam's Heritage, Iranians Chafe at 'Oppression' by the West."

69. Slackman, "Invoking Islam's Heritage, Iranians Chafe at 'Oppression' by the West."

70. Slackman, "Invoking Islam's Heritage, Iranians Chafe at 'Oppression' by the West."

71. Reza Afshari, *Human Rights in Iran: The Abuse of Cultural Relativism* (Philadelphia: University of Pennsylvania Press, 2001), 21.

72. Afshari, *Human Rights in Iran*, 21.

73. Shay, *The Axis of Evil*, 23.

74. "'An eye for an eye—Iran hands out gruesome punishment,'" *IranFocus.com*, 27 September 2006, http://www.iranfocus.com/modules/news/article.php?storyid=8765 (10 April 2008).

75. "'An eye for an eye—Iran hands out gruesome punishment.'"

76. Khaled Abou El Fadl, *Rebellion and Violence in Islamic Law* (Cambridge: Cambridge University Press, 2001), 48. Emphasis added.

77. Abou El Fadl, *Rebellion and Violence in Islamic Law*, 48.

78. Shay, *The Axis of Evil*, 30.

79. Shay, *The Axis of Evil*, 31-32.

80. Shay, *The Axis of Evil*, 35.

81. Shay, *The Axis of Evil*, 35.

82. Kukis, "Ahmadinejad the Aggrandizer," 54-55.

83. Kukis, "Ahmadinejad the Aggrandizer," 54-55.

84. Nir Rosen, "The Passion of Hussein," *Jerusalem Report*, 5 April 2004, 24.

85. Kamran S. Aghaie, *The Martyrs of Karbala: Shi'i Symbols and Rituals in Modern Iran* (Seattle, Wash.: University of Washington Press, 2004), 156.

86. Aghaie, *The Martyrs of Karbala*, 135.

87. Aghaie, *The Martyrs of Karbala*, 131.

88. Rosen, "The Passion of Hussein," 24.

89. Aghaie, *The Martyrs of Karbala*, 133.

90. Aghaie, *The Martyrs of Karbala*, 133.

91. Afshari, *Human Rights in Iran*, 29. Emphasis removed.

92. Afshari, *Human Rights in Iran*, 26.

93. Afshari, *Human Rights in Iran*, 26.

94. Shay, *The Axis of Evil*, 31-32.

95. Shay, *The Axis of Evil*, 33.

96. Shay, *The Axis of Evil*, 33.

97. "Iranians sought for Buenos Aires bomb," *BBC News*, 15 March 2007, http://news.bbc.co.uk/2/hi/americas/6454917.stm (12 July 2008).

98. "Iranians sought for Buenos Aires bomb."

99. Katzman, *The Warriors of Islam*, 104.

100. Afshari, *Human Rights in Iran*, 28.

101. Shay, *The Axis of Evil*, 20.

102. Shay, *The Axis of Evil*, 20.

103. "Iran: Alarming Increase in Executions," *HRW.org*, 27 February 2006, http:// hrw.org/english/docs/2006/02/27/iran12724.htm (10 April 2008).

104. "Iran: Alarming Increase in Executions."

105. Reza Aslan, "A weeklong journal of a writer in Iran—Entry 4," *Slate Magazine*, 10 September 2004, http://www.slate.com/id/2106317/entry/2106413/ (10 April 2008).

106. Nir T. Boms and Elliot Chodoff, "Orwellian Censorship," *Washington Times*, 10 November 2006.

107. "About IRNA: Guidelines," *Islamic Republic News Agency*, http://www.irna .ir/en/content/view/menu-240/id-24/ (15 January 2007).

108. "About IRNA: Guidelines."

109. Afshari, *Human Rights in Iran*, 28.

110. Schahgaldian, *The Clerical Establishment in Iran*, vii.

111. Jacob Weisberg, "Thanks for the Sanctions: Why do we keep using a policy that helps dictators?" *Slate Magazine*, 26 July 2006, http://www.slate.com/id/2147058/ (10 April 2008).

112. Weisberg, "Thanks for the Sanctions."

113. Weisberg, "Thanks for the Sanctions."

114. Ahmadi and Ahmadi, *Iranian Islam*, 179.

115. Katzman, *The Warriors of Islam*, 92.

116. Yossi Melman and Meir Javedanfar, *The Nuclear Sphinx of Tehran: Mahmoud Ahmadinejad and the State of Iran* (New York: Carroll and Graf Publishers, 2007), 30.

117. Melman and Javedanfar, *The Nuclear Sphinx of Tehran*, 31.

118. Melman and Javedanfar, *The Nuclear Sphinx of Tehran*, 31.

119. Melman and Javedanfar, *The Nuclear Sphinx of Tehran*, 30-31.

120. Timmerman, *Preachers of Hate*, 153.

121. A. M. Rosenthal, "Anniversaries of Murder," *New York Times*, 10 January 1987, Late Edition East Coast.

122. Shay, *The Axis of Evil*, 23.

123. Stern, *Terror in the Name of God*, 264-65.

124. Stern, *Terror in the Name of God*, 264-65.

125. Timmerman, *Preachers of Hate*, 130.

126. "Mullah admits Iran regime is threat and proud of it," *Iranian.ws*, 15 December 2006, http://www.iranian.ws/iran_news/publish/article_19545.shtml (16 December 2006).

127. "Mullah admits Iran regime is threat and proud of it."

128. Ahmed, *Islam Under Siege*, 3.

129. Ahmed, *Islam Under Siege*, 7.

130. Schahgaldian, *The Clerical Establishment in Iran*, ix.

131. Spencer, "Iran's Broken Moral Compass."

132. Melman and Javedanfar, *The Nuclear Sphinx of Tehran*, 30.

133. Taheri, "Who Are Iran's Revolutionary Guards?"

Chapter 7
Abu Ghraib: Torture Rationalized

In April 2004, the scandal went public. Photos of U.S. military police and inter-rogators abusing detainees at the Abu Ghraib prison in Iraq were broadcast around the world. As additional information leaked, the bigger picture came into focus. Members of the U.S. military had punched, kicked, and slapped detain-ees, stomped on their naked feet, forced them to pose naked in humiliating posi-tions, bullied them into homo-erotic contact with each other, threatened them with loaded guns and execution, sodomized them with chemical lights and broomsticks, and placed them on boxes with wires attached to their fingers, toes, and genitals, on threats of electric shock torture. Beyond its purely political im-plications, which included a precipitous drop in President George W. Bush's approval rating and a spike in anti-Americanism around the world, this news sparked a great deal of controversy about the definition of torture and when—if ever—it is justified.

However, the point of this chapter is neither to explain how terrible torture is nor to debate its value as a tool. It should be sufficient to say that many people believe that torture is acceptable in certain, very rare circumstances. Where that "line in the sand" exists is much harder to agree upon. Is it acceptable to torture one person who has been proven guilty of mass murder, beyond a reasonable doubt, if the torture will directly lead to information that will save an innocent person's life? What if it will directly save one hundred innocent lives? One thousand? Ten thousand?[1] Normally, peoples' answers to these questions de-pend upon their personal values. However, at Abu Ghraib, personal values were marginalized and the system's values became dominant. The following review will show how the U.S. military's strategies of recruitment, training, authoriza-tion, bureaucracy, isolation, and dehumanization transformed normal members of the military into abusive guards.

113

Recruitment

In this period of international conflict, war, and terrorism, the U.S. military enlists virtually anyone it can get to sign up. The military does have some basic requirements of sound psychological and physical health, fairly clean criminal records, and sufficient amounts of education. Pre-screening is designed to ensure that individuals with severe mental disorders or pathologies are not admitted, for example. In turn, such safeguards directly support this book's basic premise that most of the perpetrators of systematic violence are relatively ordinary people— they're not inherently flawed "bad apples" or sadists. But in any case, for the most part, the military is willing to take all types regardless of gender, age or ideology.

Nevertheless, the system's recruitment priorities do reflect the importance of getting new members who can be easily trained to perform violence on command. Men are the most common type of recruit—eighty percent of active army recruits are male.[2] Youth is also a key factor: the average marine recruit is nineteen years old, while the average army recruit is age twenty-one.[3] Though recruiters certainly sign up a lot of women, it is no coincidence that young men— who are the leaders in other aggressive endeavors, such as reckless driving and violent crime—are targeted as the best fit for violence on the battlefield. Because getting young men to enlist is such a priority, one army manual recommends a specific tactic to incite their adolescent machismo:

> This closing method works best with younger men. . . . When you find difficulty in closing, particularly when your prospect's interest seems to be waning, challenge his ego by suggesting that basic training may be too difficult for him and he might not be able to pass it. Then, if he accepts your challenge, you will be a giant step closer to getting him to enlist.[4]

Another army slogan reflects this same recruitment psychology in one bold dare: "Are you Army Strong?"[5] We can guess what the recruiter's natural follow-up is to the young man who verbally asserts his strength: "Then prove it!" As Charlie Savage reports, military recruiters "target certain schools and students for heavy recruitment, and then won't give up easily: Officers call the chosen students repeatedly, tracking their responses in a computer program the Army calls 'the Blueprint.'"[6] Beyond being contacted at schools, "Eligible students are hit with a blitz of mailings and home visits. Recruiters go hunting wherever teens from a targeted area hang out, following them to sporting events, shopping malls, and convenience stores."[7]

Having targeted young males, the military appeals to recruits on the basis of their shared values. Although some people mistakenly assume that most military recruits are poor, the majority actually come from middle class families.[8] Recruiters assume that this demographic is more likely to be interested in joining the military, more likely to have strong military traditions, and more likely to have the kind of persistent work ethic required to endure basic training without dropping out.

The military also targets people who share its warrior ideology, because they will be most easily shaped into violent tools of the system. The army defines this set of values in no uncertain terms:

> The Warrior Ethos forms the foundation for the American Soldier's spirit and total commitment to victory, in peace and war, always exemplifying ethical behavior and Army values.

> I will always place the mission first.
> I will never accept defeat.
> I will never quit.
> I will never leave a fallen comrade.

> The Army's continuing drive to be the best, to triumph over all adversity, and to remain focused on mission accomplishment does more than preserve the Army's institutional culture; it sustains the nation, and each individual Soldier.[9]

The rigid nature of this mentality is highlighted by the use of the words "always" and "never." Even though the army praises ethical behavior, such absolutes imply that the winning is always the ethical mission. As recruits should have been taught before Abu Ghraib, doing the ethical thing, like refusing to torture detainees, *requires* the willingness to make the mission secondary, accept temporary defeat, quit a given interrogation session, and leave comrades to fend for themselves until intelligence can be gained through humane means. However, these important distinctions are not marketed to recruits, who enlist with the moral certainty that the warrior way is true and right.

The army goes out of its way to help recruits embrace these warrior values. In the "Bound for Glory" section of its website, it describes "How the Army Relates to Football":

> Their absolute faith in themselves and their team makes the U.S. Army invariably persuasive in peace and invincible in war.

> Just as Soldiers put their mission first, football players need to put their mission first. Players must feel the same spirit as the American Soldier. When the team finds itself down by 20 points, it is easy to quit, but you must have the ability to use the spirit of the Warrior Ethos and overcome any and all adversities. When one of your comrades on the field needs support, you can use this spirit to help that player regain his. They must never accept defeat and never quit. The team counts on the spirit of each and every player.[10]

"Not good enough to play in professional football?—Well, the army's the next

best thing," recruiters seem to be subtly implying. If you pledge yourself to becoming a military warrior, you will make the U.S. "invincible in war," the military claims. But what if that aura of invincibility is shattered, as it was in Iraq?
How would the soldiers react? Perhaps they would become more aggressive and
unyielding—just like real warriors.

Training

The military did not specifically train its officers and guards to commit torture at
Abu Ghraib. The military police (MPs) were not even trained to serve as prison
guards, let alone trained in specific interrogation or coercive methods.[11] However, they did have an outdated military training manual that was "used as
CJTF-7's primary reference" at Abu Ghraib.[12] Perhaps the most dangerous section is cited below:

> FM 34-52 (1987) Chapter 3, Establish and Maintain Control. The interrogator
> should appear to be the one who controls all aspects of the interrogation to in-
> clude the lighting, heating, and configuration of the interrogation room, as well
> as the food, shelter, and clothing given to the source. The interrogator must al-
> ways be in control, he must act quickly and firmly. However, everything that he
> says and does must be within the limits of the Geneva and Hague Conventions,
> as well as the standards of conduct outlined in the UCMJ [Uniform Code of
> Military Justice].[13]

This section implies that the interrogator is supposed to appear as a virtual god
to the prisoner. It follows that the appearance of having control over the detainee's life or death would be useful, even if it was a contrived illusion. As
David L. Strauss explains, in interrogations, "Everything is designed to make it
clear that you are at the mercy of those whose job it is not to have any mercy."[14]
This section of the training manual's emphasis on obeying international conventions is important and cannot be dismissed. However, it could be intentionally
(or genuinely) misinterpreted to authorize abusive methods that help the interrogator maintain control, as long as they weren't blatant forms of torture prohibited under international law, like rape or mutilation.

Overall, however, the soldiers and guards at Abu Ghraib were not formally
trained to abuse detainees. That they did so anyway was in large part due to their
basic training experiences, which conditioned them to obediently follow orders
and use violence on command. As Staub explains, specific torture training
"might be unnecessary in groups with well-established hierarchical systems."[15]
This phenomenon has precedent: "the relatively sudden onset of large-scale torture in Argentina suggests that military personnel, who were the perpetrators,
did not need special training in obedience. Military training itself aims to pro-

duce obedience."[16] In the Argentinean case, the system's standard military training combined with situational factors to transform soldiers into willing torturers.
A similar combination of basic training lessons and contextual factors led U.S.
soldiers to abuse detainees at Abu Ghraib.

The U.S. military's basic training program itself conditions soldiers to use
brutal violence on command. The system attempts to wash away recruits' previous values so they can start fresh. As Ben Shalit explains, "The basic training
camp was designed to undermine all the past concepts and beliefs of the new
recruit, to undermine his civilian values, to change his self-concept—
subjugating him entirely to the military system."[17] This is all part of a calculated
effort to prepare soldiers to kill. As Grossman documents, even in battle, most
soldiers express "profound resistance to killing one's fellow man."[18] Historical
rates of non-firing show that in many early wars, including World War II, *over
seventy-five percent* of soldiers simply refused to fire at the enemy, even in open
combat when their lives were in great peril.[19] (These non-firers usually busied
themselves with supporting those who did fire, though some have admitted pre-
tending to fire at the enemy, while deliberately aiming over their heads). Once
militaries came to grips with this problem, they put an enormous amount of
time, money, and research into how to cut non-firing rates—how to transform
every soldier into a deadly killer. This led to the science of killing, whereby a
powerful program of psychological conditioning became a standard feature of
basic training. By Vietnam, the U.S. had so perfected its program that ninety-
five percent of soldiers consistently shot to kill.[20]

During basic training, recruits are desensitized to violence. Grossman highlights that the fundamental lesson the drill sergeant teaches "is that physical aggression is the essence of manhood and that violence is an effective and desirable solution for problems that the soldier will face on the battlefield."[21] But
although raising aggressive and violence-prone young soldiers is an important
first step, the military demands that recruits consider the ultimate violent act—
killing—as a normal part of the job. A U.S. sergeant and Vietnam veteran recounts that when he trained, "We'd run PT in the morning and every time your
foot hit the deck you'd have to chant 'kill, kill, kill, kill.' It was drilled into your
mind so much that it seemed like when it actually came down to it, it didn't
bother you, you know?"[22] Dyer also identifies desensitization as a prime feature
of U.S. military training since the Vietnam era:

> Most of the language used in Parris Island to describe the joys of killing people
> is bloodthirsty but meaningless hyperbole, and the recruits realize that even as
> they enjoy it. Nevertheless, it does help desensitize them to the suffering of an
> "enemy," and at the same time they are being indoctrinated in the most explicit
> fashion (as previous generations were not) with the notion that their purpose is
> not just to be brave or to fight well; it is to kill people.[23]

This "boot-camp deification of killing" is a fundamental part of training for one main reason: because it works.[24] Soldiers are more likely to kill when they have been psychologically prepared to do so, when they no longer hold the commandment "thou shalt not kill" sacred, and when they have really come to terms with the fact that their job (and job security) is based on their willingness to kill other human beings.

Basic training also exploits recruits' fears to get their undivided attention. Transparently, new recruits often try to disguise their fears about surviving upcoming missions by asking seemingly innocuous questions. As Sergeant First Class McKinley Parker reveals, "The most common question they ask is about Iraq—what's it like."[25] Parker further explains that he and his colleagues "drive home the point that they better pay attention to their training, because we were there and we know it's relevant."[26]

One lesson that is emphasized is the value of unity. According to the army's core values, which each recruit must memorize, soldiers must show loyalty, do their duty, and perform selfless service. Each is taught "Bear true faith and allegiance to the U.S. Constitution, the Army, your unit, and other Soldiers . . . by doing your share, you show your loyalty to your unit."[27] Furthermore, "Duty means being able to accomplish tasks as part of a team" and "The basic building block of selfless service is the commitment of each team member to go a little further, endure a little longer, and look a little closer to see how he or she can add to the effort."[28]

Beyond memorizing the army's core values, recruits learn the value of unity through training exercises. One example is the common challenge for them to make every single bunk in the bay in less than three minutes. As Sergeant First Class Joseph Gaskin explains, "That's an impossible task and an impossible time limit. But it builds teamwork. If you're that soldier, you feel real stress and you come together as a team with a bunch of complete strangers to accomplish the mission . . . everything is still based on teamwork."[29] There are many other exercises that emphasize that military culture is based on the "all for one and one for all" ethic, and that the unit will never leave a fallen comrade behind.

In addition, the system demands obedience from its members. As a U.S. drill sergeant told new recruits: "You will jump when I say 'frog' and when I tell you to s--- your only question will be 'What color.' IS THAT CLEAR?"[30] As Grossman observes, "the drill sergeant . . . teaches obedience. Throughout training the drill sergeant will not tolerate a single blow or a single shot executed without orders . . . [which] merits the harshest punishment."[31] During training, orders are designed to be very specific and very strict, so that recruits get used to full and total obedience, *even when their orders make no sense.* For instance, in 2005, the Air Force changed "its long-standing basic training policy about folding T-shirts and underwear into little 6-inch squares."[32] "Officials at Lackland estimate that eliminating the underwear folding classes and the folding time opens up 18 extra hours for weapons training."[33] The point here was that, even under the old policy, the eighteen hours spent folding underwear wasn't really about underwear. It was about shutting off the part of your brain that considers alternative actions, and instead following orders and doing exactly what you're told—no matter what.

When the Abu Ghraib prison came under fire from the raging insurgency, it was only natural that soldiers would fall back on their training lessons to try to survive. Thus, when suggestions for more severe interrogation methods came down the chain of command, the military intelligence officers (MIs) and MPs did what they were told. They did not rat on their comrades, and they tried to protect each other from the enemy by forcing detainees to provide information. This was all encouraged and promoted by the military system, and was rooted in their lessons from basic training.

Authorization

Political and military leaders throughout the system authorized the torture and abuse at Abu Ghraib. However, these directives were almost always indirect and vague. There is no evidence of leaders at any level telling their subordinates to "go torture those prisoners" or "beat them until they talk." Even those who appeared most in favor of torture were well aware of legal prohibitions against the practice, so they made a deliberate effort to ensure that there was no smoking gun that could be used against them at some future date. There was thus a constant disconnect between policy and practice—between leaders' public pronouncements about prioritizing human rights and their general approval of more aggressive methods for interrogation. As Zimbardo rightly asserts, this strategy "created the case for plausible deniability later on," since the system's leaders never gave specific orders for torture or abuse.[34]

The general authorization to treat Abu Ghraib detainees severely can be traced all the way back to Bush. As Seymour M. Hersh explains, "since the attacks of September 11th, President Bush and his top aides have seen themselves as engaged in a war against terrorism in which the old rules did not apply."[35] New rules and new techniques were needed. Critics such as John Gray claim that through its maneuverings, "the Bush administration deliberately created a lawless environment in which abuse could be practiced with impunity."[36] This may be an overstatement. What is clear, however, is that "Bush's aides knew he wanted them to take an aggressive approach."[37]

Bush had his underlings perform extensive reviews of the legal restrictions on torture, in search of ways to 'up the ante' without being criminally liable. For instance, the president's top legal advisor Alberto Gonzales and Justice Department official Jay Bybee counseled that Bush had the constitutional authority to rule that the Geneva Conventions do not apply to terrorists. They determined that "Any effort by Congress to regulate the interrogation of battlefield combat-

ants would violate the constitution's sole vesting of the commander-in-chief
authority in the president."[38] Furthermore, Bybee redefined the concept of torture itself: "Physical pain amounting to torture must be equivalent in intensity to
the pain accompanying serious physical injury, such as organ failure, impair-
ment of bodily function, or even death."[39] Beyond physical abuse, for a "cruel or
inhuman psychological technique to rise to the level of mental torture, the Justice Department argued, the psychological harm must last 'months or even
years.'"[40] These definitions authorized a lot of abusive acts as acceptable tools
for coercive interrogation.

Bush did not define precisely what techniques did and did not constitute torture, but having made it known that he favored an "aggressive approach," he left
a lot of room within the system for interrogators to decide for themselves. The
president based this edict on a fundamental transcendent authorization, emphasizing that these steps would protect the country. At the same time, he downplayed the violence implicit in such changes. Bush "felt very keenly that his
primary responsibility was to do everything within his power to keep the country
safe, and he was not concerned with appearances or politics or hiding behind
lower-level officials," a senior administration official explains.[41]

Other top government officials also provided general authorizations for torture. During a rare televised interview on September 16, 2001, Vice President
Dick Cheney sent a clear message about how terrorists should be fought:

> We also have to work, though, sort of the dark side, if you will. We've got to
> spend time in the shadows in the intelligence world. A lot of what needs to be
> done here will have to be done quietly, without any discussion, using sources
> and methods that are available to our intelligence agencies, if we're going to be
> successful. That's the world these folks operate in, and so it's going to be vital
> for us to use any means at our disposal, basically, to achieve our objective.[42]

Cheney essentially claimed that U.S. security was the top priority above all others—including human rights. He wanted the military system to be free to do
whatever it took to protect the country. As he said, he was willing to authorize
"dark"—that is, morally questionable—methods for intelligence gathering
which must be "done quietly" in order "to achieve our objective." In this transcendent authorization, Cheney made it clear that homeland security and the
defeat of terrorists worldwide were such crucial, noble goals that they would
justify any unspeakable violence used to achieve them.

As Hersh explains, secretary of defense Donald Rumsfeld similarly prioritized the ends over the means in his attempts to ensure a more hard line approach to the global war on terror:

> In the privacy of his office, Rumsfeld chafed over what he saw as the reluc-
> tance of senior Pentagon generals and admirals to act aggressively. By mid-
> 2002, he and his senior aides were exchanging secret memorandums on modi-

fying the culture of the military leaders and finding ways to encourage them "to take greater risks". . . . The Pentagon's impatience with military protocol extended to questions about the treatment of prisoners caught in the course of its military operations. Soon after 9/11, as the war on terror got under way, Donald Rumsfeld repeatedly made public his disdain for the Geneva conventions. Complaints about America's treatment of prisoners, Rumsfeld said in early 2002, amounted to "isolated pockets of international hyperventilation."[43]

Rumsfeld recognized that a more aggressive approach would put the system's leaders at risk of censure from the outside world, but he authorized it anyway. He sent secret memos because he recognized that much of what he wanted could not be spoken of publicly. This is another example of the gap between the official policies and the off-the-book procedures. Rumsfeld put pressure on military leaders to make progress by any means necessary, and this directive flowed down the chain of command and throughout the military system.

The transcendent authorizations for violence continued at Abu Ghraib. Zimbardo explains how as military officials "gave orders for abuse spoken from one side of the mouth, the official public statement from the other side of the mouth insisted that 'We do not condone prisoner abuse or anything but their humane treatment.'"[44] Within the system, the potential payoff from successful interrogations was emphasized by military leaders, who desired "operational intelligence on the enemy's identity, support systems, locations, leadership, intelligence sources, weapons and ammunition caches, and centers of gravity," along with information on missing Iraqi President Saddam Hussein and supposedly hidden weapons of mass destruction.[45] Meanwhile, the coercive methods needed to extract such information were deliberately discussed in ambiguous terms. For instance, Lieutenant General Ricardo Sanchez "issued several policy memos on treatment of prisoners in Iraq to put greater pressure on them to provide information on insurgent activities that could save the lives of American soldiers, then revised the memos in ways that left the rules vague."[46] This was not just some careless mistake. Sanchez purposefully left his orders on detainee treatment open to interpretation, while simultaneously being quite specific about the ultimate goal of intelligence extraction: saving American lives.

This type of transcendent authorization appears even more blatantly in an email a military intelligence captain at Abu Ghraib sent to his colleagues:

> The gloves are coming off gentlemen regarding these detainees; Col Boltz has made it clear that we want these individuals broken. Casualties are mounting and we need to start gathering info to help protect our fellow soldiers from any further attacks. I thank you for your hard work and your dedication. MI ALWAYS OUT FRONT![47]

This is a classic spin job. The MI captain uses the euphemism of someone removing his gloves to imply a more serious approach to interrogation, rather than discussing specifics tactics. Similarly, the point that the commanders "want these individuals broken" is also vague. The word "broken" could be interpreted literally, or it could just be a common figure of speech. This linguistic camouflage shields fellow soldiers from facing up to the brutal nature of torture, at least temporarily. At the same time, the MI captain frames the product of such methods as unequivocally positive. If a member of the system complained, he would be met with scorn and derision. "What, you don't want to reduce casualties?" "You don't want to protect your fellow soldiers?" "You don't value hard work and dedication?" "You're not proud to be a part of MI?" On the surface, there is not that much to object to in this email, which is why it is so effective in preparing soldiers for violence.

Transcendent authorizations much like this one characterized systematic indoctrination at Abu Ghraib. The Taguba report "made it clear that Army intelligence officers, CIA agents, private contractors, and OGAs 'actively requested that MP guards set physical and mental conditions for favorable interrogation of witnesses.'"[48] Again, on the surface, should any guard be *against* setting favorable conditions for interrogation? Of course not. However, the cruelty required to meet these goals was temporarily obscured from view.

Military leaders also used mundane authorizations to promote violence and the harsh treatment of detainees. There was a range of directives—mostly vague—which promoted a social climate where violence and intimidation became valued as the best way to get things done. According to the Fay report, "the abuse . . . was directed on an individual basis and never officially sanctioned or approved."[49] There was no official decree that said, "Let's torture." But as a lawyer for one of the soldiers facing criminal charges explains, "The story is not necessarily that it was a direct order. Everybody is far too subtle and smart for that. . . . Realistically, there is a description of an activity, a suggestion that it may be helpful and encouragement that this is exactly what we needed."[50]

Though the leaders at Abu Ghraib have tried to hide behind claims of confusion, misunderstanding, and ignorance, it is clear that the abuses were systematic—not isolated incidents. As a government investigation documents,

> MG Fay has found that from 25 July 2003 to 6 February 2004, twenty-seven 205 MI BDE Personnel allegedly requested, encouraged, condoned, or solicited Military Police (MP) personnel to abuse detainees and/or participated in detainee abuse and/or violated established interrogation procedures and applicable laws and regulations during interrogation operations at Abu Ghraib.[51]

The key phrase here is "requested, encouraged, condoned, or solicited." Technically, officers didn't "command" or "order" torture. Often they were purposefully vague, both to protect themselves and to strategically downplay the significance of the violence they authorized. As Baumeister describes, in general, violent perpetrators "play endless games with words, and one point of these games is to present the shocking and horrific as mundane and ordinary . . . most large-scale evils have involved some degree of concealment, and the manipulation of language is part of it."[52] In past cases, torturers have used terms such as "*tea party, dance, birthday party, the telephone, the submarine, the swallow,* [and] *the airplane*" to describe a range of ghastly abuses.[53]

The terms used at Abu Ghraib were less fanciful and creative. Perhaps this is because the guards really thought their abusive tactics were no big deal, and thus unworthy of emotional or linguistic distinction. Many orders for abuse implied that the guards should just use their aggressive common sense, and that this was not serious military violence, which must be meticulously planned and carried out with great precision. The language used in these authorizations was fittingly bland and mundane.

For example, the Ryder Report, one of the first to warn of abuses at the Iraqi prison, noted that "the MIs tried to enlist MPs to engage in activities that would 'prepare' detainees for interrogation."[54] Similarly, Private First Class Lynndie England reported that "MI Soldiers instructed them (MPs) to rough them up." Sergeant Theresa Adams admitted she may have told Corporal Charles Graner and Staff Sergeant Chip Fredrick to "soften up this detainee," as they claimed.[55] Other guards were told, "Loosen this guy up for us. Make sure he has a bad night. Make sure he gets the treatment."[56] Within the system, these mundane authorizations were assumed to be sufficient.

Overall, officers and guards were expected to be tough and do what was expected of them, even if it wasn't clearly defined. The system's social and professional climate was one that promoted intimidating violence as the clear solution to military obstacles.[57] Even when facing jail time for his participation in the Abu Ghraib torture, Sergeant Michael Smith refused to abandon the values he had been programmed to endorse. He insisted that "Soldiers are not supposed to be soft and cuddly."[58] While he may be right about what we expect from our soldiers, there is a big difference between being tough and abusing unarmed prisoners. But in any case, it's clear that his defensive statement reflects the hyper-aggressive military culture at Abu Ghraib, as it was authorized and designed from above.[59]

Bureaucracy

The U.S military bureaucracy played a critical role in enabling the torture and abuses at Abu Ghraib. As discussed in the previous section, this started with a range of authorizations, which were strategically vague regarding rules for interrogation but clear in tone: "Be more aggressive!"

Though the Bush administration initially tried to blame the Abu Ghraib scandal on a "few bad apples," it is clear that the overarching responsibility lies with the system itself. Pentagon reports point to "doctrinal confusion . . . a lack of doctrine . . . [and] systemic failures" as the causes for the torture, and label the illegal abuses "systemic" and "intentional."[60] The worst qualities of bureaucracies—decentralized leadership, inefficiency, and lack of communication—were exploited to foster a conveniently unclear work environment where new interrogation methods would emerge ad hoc. Adam Hochschild finds that in this sense, Abu Ghraib fits a common mold:

> military police officers at Abu Ghraib were encouraged to treat the prisoners so as to create "favorable conditions" for interrogations. What does this mean? Give the prisoners English lessons? New clothes? Come on. In any bureaucracy, orders or clearance to do something beyond the law always comes in code. For those in senior positions, deniability is vital.[61]

Despite pleading ignorance, the system's leaders were certainly aware of how new bureaucratic vagaries could be exploited.

The U.S. military leaders knew that interrogation is all about a battle of wills, based on using leverage to make the suspect tell you what you want to know. More leverage equals more information, and the greatest leverage has always been unbearable physical pain. Torturing suspects, or threatening to torture them, has been a central feature of interrogation lore, practice, and fiction since medieval times. More recently, the hit American television show *24*, which debuted some sixteen months before the U.S. invaded Iraq, seemingly features a scene where someone is tortured for information on a weekly basis. The risk of torture during interrogations is so well established that denials from the system's leaders are nearly impossible to believe. Based on her research, Lila Rajiva makes four astute conclusions about the true bureaucratic objectives for the Iraqi prison: (1) "Abu Ghraib is part of a deliberate policy," (2) "The policy is organized and secret," (3) "Abu Ghraib repeats systematic torture practices used by foreign militaries and intelligence services," and (4) "Abu Ghraib repeats systematic practices used by the CIA earlier and elsewhere."[62]

One main reason military leaders and soldiers felt safe to carry out this violent plan was because they were just small parts of such an enormous military bureaucracy. There were so many official and unofficial orders, directives, suggestions, memos, discussions, and debates about interrogation methods that people felt they could sink into the system, plead ignorance and expect to avoid reprimand if charges were ever brought. Given the context of war-torn Iraq, the orders and pressures from above, and the size of the system, the torture at Abu Ghraib was a predictable product. As Fareed Zakaria explains, "In a 2 million-person bureaucracy, such calculated ambiguities will inevitably lead to something like Abu Ghraib."[63]

In the post-scandal fallout, the Senate Armed Services Committee met to assign blame and hold military leaders responsible for the torture. They found the task exceedingly difficult—because of the large bureaucracy. As John Tierney puts it, "The senators were stymied . . . by the sheer complexity of figuring out who in the military bureaucracy was responsible for what. As the officers spewed military acronyms and a military lawyer tried explaining which rules applied to whom, the result was Washington's very own fog of war."[64] Minnesota Senator Mark Dayton expressed similar frustrations with the impenetrable bureaucracy:

> We've now had 15 of the highest-level officials involved in this entire operation, from the secretary of defense to the generals in command, and nobody knew that anything was amiss, no one approved anything amiss, nobody did anything amiss. We have a general acceptance of responsibility, but there's no one to blame, except for the people down at the very bottom of one prison.[65]

Again—this is by design. Without the protections of such a large bureaucracy, these officials would not have felt so comfortable implementing Bush's "aggressive approach" to interrogation, engaging the "dark side" tactics recommended by Cheney or taking the "greater risks" demanded by Rumsfeld. They wouldn't have been able to hide behind administrative misunderstandings and miscommunications.

Officers and soldiers throughout the system, including those at the very bottom, repeated these claims of ignorance. The MPs charged with the most egregious abuses claimed they received unclear directions about their roles and responsibilities at Abu Ghraib. However, this lack of clarity also served as a preconceived excuse for torture. As the Jones report documents, "under the guise of confusion or misinterpretation . . . some Soldiers may actually have intentionally violated approved interrogation techniques."[66] Some military personnel believed that they could disregard laws on human rights and get away with it, because they were just anonymous parts of a much bigger system and they were following orders from above. If there was blame to be placed, these MPs reasoned, surely it would not rest with them. After all, they were just doing their job—they had no role in determining military policy.

The fact that violence was already routine and expected within the military bureaucracy made it even easier to compel soldiers to commit torture at Abu Ghraib. The International Committee of the Red Cross reports that the torturous and abusive methods "being used by interrogators at Abu Ghraib 'appeared to be part of the standard operating procedures.'"[67] And as Guy B. Adams et al. wisely point out, the MP guards' "apparent willingness and comfort with taking photos and being photographed while abusing prisoners seems to reflect the 'normalcy' of the acts within the context."[68] If they felt that they had not been authorized to carry out such abuse, and if the violence registered a powerful guilty response for them, they probably wouldn't have taken the photos. The common mentality of these guards within the larger bureaucracy is typified by Specialist Sabrina Harman, who was asked about "the prisoner who was placed on a box with electric wires attached to his fingers, toes, and penis."[69] She explained that "'her job was to keep detainees awake' . . . and that it was the job of her and her colleagues 'to do things for MI and OGA . . . to get these people to talk.'"[70] Because the system had indoctrinated her so successfully, using violence seemed like just another routine bureaucratic procedure, and abusing detainees felt like just another part of the job.

The division of labor within the bureaucracy also made it easier for agents to accept and perform violence on command. Grossman uses the metaphor of a firing squad to explain how this works: "factors that enable killing on the battlefield can be seen in the diffusion of responsibility that exists in an execution by firing squad. . . . The leader gives the command and provides the demands of authority, but he does not have to actually kill. The firing squad provides conformity and absolution processes."[71] Similarly, the leaders at Abu Ghraib could avoid the full moral responsibility for torture because they did not personally carry it out. The guards who actually committed the abuses could rationalize that they were not fully responsible because they had not sanctioned the invasion of Iraq itself, captured the prisoners, or picked which ones needed "encouragement" to talk. The Jones report reveals that "At Abu Ghraib, the delineation of responsibilities seems to have been blurred when military police soldiers, untrained in interrogation operations, were used to enable interrogations."[72] Further complicating the picture was the fact that Abu Ghraib was the cross-jurisdictional domain of military intelligence, military reserves, OGAs, and some civilian contractors. Since it was often unclear who was professionally responsible for different aspects of the interrogation process, assigning the *moral responsibility* for such abuses was even less clear.

Institutional momentum further compelled soldiers to use violent interrogation methods at Abu Ghraib. As Hersh documents, "the pressure on soldiers to accede to requests from military intelligence was felt throughout the system."[73] Officers and soldiers found it easier to go with the flow than to try to fight the powerful bureaucracy authorizing the violent methods. Since most of their colleagues were not questioning orders, they did not question them either. As Sergeant Javal S. Davis explains, he just "assumed that if they were doing anything out of the ordinary or outside guidelines, someone would have said something."[74]

Even the guards or soldiers who were uncomfortable with the abusive methods mostly stayed quiet. They knew that public complaints would lead to backlash and trouble within the military bureaucracy. For example, Major General Antonio M. Taguba, whose report exposed many crimes at Abu Ghraib, faced significant criticism for his actions. As one military officer explains, "He's not regarded as a hero in some circles in the Pentagon. . . . He's the guy who blew the whistle, and the Army will pay the price for his integrity. The leadership does not like to have people make bad news public."[75] Taguba recognized the costs of following his conscience after he was forced to retire: "They always shoot the messenger. . . . To be accused of being overzealous and disloyal—that cuts deep into me."[76] Similarly, Sergeant Joe Darby, who sent a disc with photos of the torture at Abu Ghraib to a military investigator, was discharged from the army and faced scorn within his community. As his wife puts it, "People were, they were mean, saying he was a walking dead man, he was walking around with a bull's-eye on his head. It was scary."[77] Within the military bureaucracy, most soldiers chose to follow orders and do their jobs like everyone else. It's very risky to object and try to fight a system with such an impressive record of squashing troublemakers.

Isolation

The U.S. military system capitalized on the literal isolation of Abu Ghraib to compel guards to use violence on command. The Fay report notes that "there was a general feeling by both MP and MI personnel that Abu Ghraib was the forgotten outpost receiving little support from the Army."[78] Lacking sufficient military support to secure the area, guards felt increased pressure to get action-able intelligence from prisoners. Major General Geoffrey Miller recommended that "Army prisons be geared, first and foremost, to interrogations and the gath-ering of information needed for the war effort. . . . The military police on guard duty at the prisons should make support of military intelligence a priority."[79] Intelligence gathering became the main concern—rather than running the prison in a safe, organized, or humane way—specifically because Abu Ghraib was so isolated and vulnerable. In turn, this facilitated the extreme violence. As retired Army interrogator Specialist Anthony Lagouranis, who worked at Abu Ghraib and other facilities throughout Iraq, recounts, "Most of the abuses around Iraq are not photographed, and so they'll never get any outrage out of it . . . there's no one looking over your shoulder, so you can do anything you want."[80] Since Abu Ghraib was an isolated prison in a chaotic region, far removed from outsid-ers' eyes, soldiers felt they could use any means necessary to get intelligence to quell the dangerous insurgency surrounding them.

The U.S. military also ensured that Abu Ghraib was socially isolated from the rest of the world, so that new standards of conduct would be embraced. This emotional distance is commonly felt by soldiers who go abroad; Grossman re-veals that Vietnam veterans felt a notable "psychological and social isolation from home and society," even after the conflict had ended.[81] Within the military system, many peacetime values and assumptions no longer apply, and soldiers begin to feel like they are operating in an alternate universe. Leaders make this social distance very clear to their soldiers. As a U.S. drill sergeant told his young charges, "From this time on I will be your mother, your father, your sister, and your brother. I will be your best friend and your worst enemy. I will be there to wake you up in the morning, and I will be there to tuck you in at night."[82] Put another way: "You're not in Kansas, anymore."

This isolation allowed the military to establish a new moral order. At Abu Ghraib, Sergeant Davis and his fellow guards were constantly commended for the violent tactics they employed. "The MI staffs, to my understanding, have been giving Graner compliments . . . like 'Good job, they're breaking down real fast;' 'They answer every question;' 'They're giving out good information, finally;' and 'Keep up the good work'—stuff like that."[83] This praise showed the perpetrators that others within the system agreed on the morality of their tactics. It also provided the ultimate moral vindication: when it comes to extracting information from detainees—*torture works*. They were quick to believe this, even though such abusive tactics had to be kept secret from the rest of the world, from the American people, and from parents, spouses, and kids back home. As Lagouranis explained, within the military system in Iraq, "you really do feel like you're outside of normal society, you know? Your family, your friends, they're not there to see what's going on. . . . And you just feel so isolated, and morally isolated, that you felt like you could do whatever you want to this guy."[84] Again, the social and moral distance experienced at Abu Ghraib enabled the guards' systematic indoctrination and the violence that occurred as a result.

As part of the overall strategy, military leaders, officers, and soldiers were also isolated from others within the system. Hersh reports that after the Abu Ghraib scandal broke, a Pentagon official revealed that Rumsfeld's top associates and several high-ranking generals "had done their best to keep the issue quiet in the first months of the year."[85] "Secrecy and wishful thinking, the Pentagon official said, are defining characteristics of Rumsfeld's Pentagon, and shaped its response to the reports from Abu Ghraib."[86] This isolation and secrecy at the top levels of military command kept moral concerns from being openly discussed. Another one of Hersh's confidential sources supported this image of a system designed to protect top officials from knowing too much:

> Knowledge of the nature of the abuses—and especially the politically toxic photographs—had been severely, and unusually, restricted. "Everybody I've talked to said, 'We just didn't know'—not even in the J.C.S.," one well-informed former intelligence official told me, emphasizing that he was referring to senior officials with whom such allegations would normally be shared. "I haven't talked to anybody on the inside who knew—nowhere. It's got them scratching their heads." A senior Pentagon official said that many of the senior generals in the Army were similarly out of the loop on the Abu Ghraib allegations.[87]

Of course, these claims that "We just didn't know" could be cunning denials, if not bold-faced lies. However, if the officials wanted the benefits of making public denials, their identities would not have been kept confidential in Hersh's report. It's likely that there were deliberate efforts within the system to keep many generals and top officers away from the details of what was going on at Abu

Ghraib.

This strategy of isolating agents from one another was also apparent in the lower levels of the system. Many OGAs and MI officers at Abu Ghraib made sure they were unknown and safely unaccountable for the violence they both encouraged and carried out. As Hersh explains, they often wore "'sterile,' or unmarked uniforms or civilian clothes while on duty."[88] He adds that "The blurring of identities and organizations meant that it was impossible for the prisoners, or, significantly, the military policemen on duty, to know who was doing what to whom, and who had the authority to give orders."[89]

This anonymity made oversight and the rigid enforcement of rules much less likely—you could be working right next to someone, and have no idea who he or she was or what agency he or she worked for. This also added confusion about what different officers were allowed to do to detainees. As the Fay report indicates, "MI knew what MI could do and what MI couldn't do; but MI did not know what the MPs could or could not do in their activities. The same was true of MP ignorance of MI operational procedures."[90] Officers and guards were also kept from knowing the identities of certain ghost detainees, who were brought to Abu Ghraib by OGAs "without accounting for them, knowing their identities, or even the reason for their detention."[91]

For these men and women, it became easier *not* to know the details. Various members of the system didn't know exactly what was acceptable under international law, what had been authorized from above, who their peers were, why certain detainees had been captured, who the detainees were, what kind of intelligence they might hold, or what interrogation methods were being used to extract information. Without those details, it became much harder for anyone to be fully certain that something illegal and morally wrong was going on. This allowed the system to insulate its members from their own personal consciences.

When questions were raised about the legal, moral, and ethical nature of the interrogation methods at Abu Ghraib, they were quickly discouraged or rejected. Staff Sergeant Frederick reports that "One of the first things that I asked for as soon as I got there was regulations, operating procedures. . . . Usually they would tell me 'Just see what you can come up with, keep up the good work,' this is the way Military Intelligence wants it done."[92] Frederick also claims that if he continued to ask for specific directions and unambiguous orders about detainee treatment, "he would be scoffed at or reprimanded by higher-ups for complaining. Given the combat zone conditions, they told him, he would have to make do as best possible."[93]

Similarly, MP Reservist Ken Davis recounts a conversation he had with Corporal Graner, who was one of the most abusive guards at Abu Ghraib. This back-and-forth highlights how the system was designed to keep guards from fully engaging their moral reservations:

[Graner]: "I'm having to yell, and do other things to detainees that I feel are

morally and ethically wrong. What do you think I should do?"
I said, "Then don't do 'em."
And he goes, "I don't have a choice."
And I said, "What do you mean?"
He says, "Every time a bomb goes off outside the wire, or outside the fence,
they come in, and they tell me, that's another American losin' their life. And
unless you help us, their blood's on your hands as well."[94]

Rather than appeal to higher authorities or challenge the system, Graner felt like
his options were either (1) disobey orders and abandon endangered American
soldiers or (2) push moral concerns aside and do his job. Isolated from people
who would speak up against abusive interrogation methods, he chose the latter
option, and accepted the moral protection the system provided. Abu Ghraib was
geared to push members to carry out orders and do their duty, rather than weigh
the ethical implications of what they were doing. The implicit message was that
there wasn't enough time to worry about philosophical debates on human rights
and interrogation strategies, because if you stopped to think, you and your
friends would soon be dead.

Dehumanization

The military system dehumanizes its own members through a process known as
deindividuation. Soldiers lose some sense of their personal identities as they
increasingly become objectified tools of the organizations they serve. The more
they become immersed in their duties and part of a collective force, the more
likely they will follow orders and use immoral means to get the job done. As
Staub explains, "submerging oneself in a group makes it difficult to maintain
independent judgment of the group's conduct and exert a contrary influence.
Deindividuation, a disinhibition of the usual moral constraints on individual
action, is a likely consequence."[95] This is particularly common for large groups
of fighters and can yield particularly destructive results.

In the case of Abu Ghraib, deindividuation enabled torture and abuse. As
previously described, the personal identities of some officers were not only
blurred by their objectified roles in the large military bureaucracy and because
all soldiers wear similar uniforms, but by their strategic decision to wear "'sterile,' or unmarked uniforms or civilian clothes while on duty."[96] Keeping their
name and number secret was the first step in reducing their personal accountability for torture. Zimbardo, who saw deindividuation as a crucial enabler of
abuse in his Stanford Prison Experiment, also recognizes its ugly presence in the
torture at Abu Ghraib.[97]

Tellingly, Rumsfeld's reaction to the scandalous photos from Abu Ghraib
was that they portray "acts that can only be described as blatantly sadistic, cruel,

and inhuman."[98] He is wrong—these acts were not inhuman. In fact, abuses like those at Abu Ghraib and much worse have been carried out by relatively ordinary human beings for thousands of years—humans who chose to act immorally when facing dangerous situations and pressures from above. However, though the Abu Ghraib torturers were not inhuman, they *felt* less human because they were dehumanized by the system and conditioned to repress their personal thoughts, identities, and values.

The dehumanization of Abu Ghraib prisoners was much more blatant. This process served the military's goals, because it made it easier for guards to abuse and torture detainees without feeling like they were harming fellow human beings.

One dehumanization method was the decision to take clothes away from the prisoners. The Schlesinger report suggests that "The wearing of clothes is an inherently social practice, and therefore the stripping away of clothing may have had the unintended consequence of dehumanizing detainees in the eyes of those who interacted with them."[99] Though the report admits that "Dehumanization lowers moral and cultural barriers that usually preclude . . . the abusive treatment of others" and thus rightly sees this as a first step to abuse at Abu Ghraib, the assumption that this was an "unintended consequence," instead of strategic decision, is absurd.[100] The Fay report similarly documents that the forced nudity of prisoners "likely contributed to an escalating 'de-humanization' of the detainees and set the stage for additional and more severe abuses to occur."[101] Though the nakedness of detainees did emphasize their human anatomy, it also made them seem less like members of modern human civilization.

Other dehumanizing tactics were also employed at Abu Ghraib. One combined nudity with hooding. As Strauss explains, "Hooding victims dehumanizes them, making them anonymous and thing-like. They become just bodies. You can do anything you want to them."[102] In turn, Hersh suggests that the "photographing of prisoners, both in Afghanistan and in Iraq, seems to have been not random but, rather, part of the dehumanizing interrogation process," perhaps because it increased the notion that the detainees were powerless objects of scrutiny. One of the abused Abu Ghraib prisoners told interviewers that being photographed "added to his humiliation. He remembered how the camera flashed repeatedly as soldiers told him to masturbate and [they] beat him when he refused."[103] As Rajiva laments, "The diminishment of the victim to an object . . . is what makes the torture and terror of the warfare state ultimately pornographic."[104]

The military also endorsed the notion that the prisoners were mere animals. During the post-Abu Ghraib fallout, Brigadier General Janis Karpinski admitted that Major General Miller told her "You have to treat the prisoners like dogs."[105] He warned that if "they believe that they're any different than dogs, you have effectively lost control of your interrogation from the very start. . . . And it works. This is what we do down at Guantanamo Bay."[106] It is quite clear that this directive made its way down the chain of command. The Fay report reveals that "The detainees [of the naked human pyramid] were subsequently posed sexually, forced to masturbate, and 'ridden like animals.'"[107] Specifically, one detainee "described being made to bark like a dog, being forced to crawl on his stomach while MPs spit and urinated on him.'"[108] In another case, caught in the now infamous photo, Private First Class England is pictured "holding a leash which was wrapped around an unidentified detainee's neck."[109]

All of this was part of the system's strategy to dehumanize prisoners, so that military officers and guards would find it easier to endorse abuse and carry out torture on command, with hopes of an intelligence windfall to come. They didn't feel like they were abusing real human beings. Their violence was directed towards objects and creatures that seemed much less significant.

Conclusion

As of 2009, U.S. policy on detainee treatment remains unsettled. Leaders continue to be torn between the moral imperative to protect the nation and the moral costs of torture and abuse. To make things worse, the constantly changing terrorist threat has really raised the stakes. As Schlesinger writes, "The ability of terrorists and insurgents to blend into the civilian population further decreases their vulnerability to signal and imagery intelligence."[110] Thus, the nature of the enemy means that "human intelligence is absolutely necessary, not just to fill these gaps in information derived from other sources, but also to provide clues and leads for the other sources to exploit."[111]

The pressure to obtain actionable intelligence is likely here to stay—how the military system handles that pressure remains to be seen. The military has shown that it controls its members, for better or worse, and that it can steer their behavior in almost any direction. If the top leaders decide that humanitarianism and winning the war of ideas truly are top priorities, they can begin to make Abu Ghraib a distant memory from an extremely flawed era. On the other hand, the military's systematic indoctrination is so effective that many new recruits will continue to do whatever they are told—no matter how abusive, violent, or deadly those tasks may be.

Notes

1. These hypothetical "ticking time bomb" scenarios are often used to justify torture, but in reality things are rarely so black and white. In the real world, torture is often used as a fact-finding tool which sometimes yields valuable information but often

achieves nothing. Like any tool or tactic, its effectiveness depends on who uses it, when they use it, and how they use it.

2. Joe Burlas, "Army Recruit Statistics Improve Over 2001," *Military.com*, 6 April 2002, http://www.military.com/Resources/ResourceFileView/Army_Recruit.htm (10 April 2008).

3. Rod Powers, "Surviving Marine Corps Basic Training," *USMilitary.about.com*, http://usmilitary.about.com/od/marinejoin/a/marinebasic.htm (10 April 2008); Burlas, "Army Recruit Statistics Improve Over 2001."

4. Charlie Savage, "Military recruiters target schools strategically," *Boston Globe*, 29 November 2004, http://www.boston.com/news/nation/articles/2004/11/29/military_recruiters_pursue_target_schools_carefully/?page=full (25 July 2007).

5. "Army Reserve—Overview," *GoArmy.com*, http://www.goarmy.com/reserve/nps/index.jsp (26 July 2007).

6. Savage, "Military recruiters target schools strategically."

7. Savage, "Military recruiters target schools strategically."

8. Donna Miles, "Official Debunks Myths About Military Recruits," *Military Connections.com*, 5 December 2005, http://www.militaryconnections.com/news_story.cfm?textnewsid=1767 (10 April 2008).

9. "Bound for Glory—Warrior Ethos," *GoArmy.com*, http://www.goarmy.com/glory/warrior_ethos.jsp (26 July 2007).

10. "Bound for Glory—Warrior Ethos."

11. James R. Schlesinger et al., "Final Report of the Independent Panel to Review Department of Defense Operations," in *The Abu Ghraib Investigations*, ed. Steven Strasser (New York: Public Affairs LLC, 2004), 56.

12. George R. Fay, "AR 15-6 Investigation of the Abu Ghraib Detention Facility and 205th Military Intelligence Brigade," *Army.mil*, http://www4.army.mil/ocpa/reports/ar15-6/AR15-6.pdf (10 April 2008), 50. CJTF stands for Coalition Joint Task Force.

13. Fay, "AR 15-6 Investigation of the Abu Ghraib Detention Facility and 205th Military Intelligence Brigade," 50.

14. David L. Strauss, "Breakdown in the Gray Room: Recent Turns in the Image War," in *Abu Ghraib: The Politics of Torture*, ed. Meron Benvenisti (Berkeley, Calif.: North Atlantic Books, 2004), 88.

15. Staub, *The Roots of Evil*, 245.

16. Staub, *The Roots of Evil*, 245.

17. Grossman, *On Killing*, 317.

18. Grossman, *On Killing*, 250-51.

19. Grossman, *On Killing*, 250-51.

20. Grossman, *On Killing*, 250-51.

21. Grossman, *On Killing*, 319.

22. Grossman, *On Killing*, 251. PT stands for physical training.

23. Grossman, *On Killing*, 252.

24. Grossman, *On Killing*, 252.

25. Rod Powers, "Basic Training is Smarter, Not Softer," *USMilitary.about.com*, 9 September 2006, http://usmilitary.about.com/od/armyjoin/a/basicinterview_2.htm (10 April 2008).

26. Powers, "Basic Training is Smarter, Not Softer."

27. "Living the Army Values," *GoArmy.com*, http://www.goarmy.com/life/living_the_army_values.jsp (9 July 2007). Emphasis removed.

28. "Living the Army Values."

29. Powers, "Basic Training is Smarter, Not Softer."

30. Grossman, *On Killing*, 318.

31. Grossman, *On Killing*, 319.

32. Rod Powers, "Air Force Makes Significant Changes to Basic Training," *USMilitary.about.com*, 5 November 2005, http://usmilitary.about.com/od/airforcejoin/a/basic changes.htm?terms=basic+training (10 April 2008).

33. Powers, "Air Force Makes Significant Changes to Basic Training."

34. Zimbardo, *The Lucifer Effect*, 385.

35. Seymour M. Hersh, "Chain of Command: How the Department of Defense mishandled the disaster at Abu Ghraib," *New Yorker*, 17 May 2004, http://www.newyorker.com/archive/2004/05/17/040517fa_fact2 (10 April 2008).

36. John Gray, "Power and Vainglory," in *Abu Ghraib: The Politics of Torture*, ed. Meron Benvenisti (Berkeley, Calif.: North Atlantic Books, 2004), 50.

37. Mike Allen and Dana Priest, "Memo on Torture Draws Focus to Bush," *WashingtonPost.com*, 9 June 2004, http://www.washingtonpost.com/wp-dyn/articles/A26401-2004Jun8.html (10 April 2008).

38. "The Gonzales memos," *BBC News*, 6 January 2005, http://news.bbc.co.uk/2/hi/americas/4153479.stm (10 April 2008).

39. "The Gonzales memos."

40. Allen and Priest, "Memo on Torture Draws Focus to Bush."

41. Allen and Priest, "Memo on Torture Draws Focus to Bush."

42. Dan Froomkin, "Cheney's 'Dark Side' Is Showing," *WashingtonPost.com*, 7 November 2005. http://www.washingtonpost.com/wp-dyn/content/blog/2005/11/07/BL2005110700793_pf.html (10 April 2008).

43. Hersh, "Chain of Command."

44. Zimbardo, *The Lucifer Effect*, 385.

45. Anthony R. Jones, "AR 15-6 Investigation of the Abu Ghraib Prison and 205th Military Intelligence Brigade," *Army.mil*, http://www4.army.mil/ocpa/reports/ar15-6/AR15-6.pdf (10 April 2008), 17.

46. Craig R. Whitney, "Introduction," in *The Abu Ghraib Investigations*, ed. Steven Strasser (New York: Public Affairs LLC, 2004), xiii.

47. Mark Danner, *Torture and Truth: America, Abu Ghraib, and the War on Terror* (New York: The New York Review of Books, 2004), 33.

48. Zimbardo, *The Lucifer Effect*, 383. OGAs refers to other government agencies, a euphemism for the CIA and/or undercover CIA agents.

49. Fay, "AR 15-6 Investigation of the Abu Ghraib Detention Facility and 205th Military Intelligence Brigade," 41.

50. Danner, *Torture and Truth*, 20.

51. "Executive Summary—Investigation of Intelligence Activities At Abu Ghraib," *Army.mil*, http://www4.army.mil/ocpa/reports/ar15-6/AR15-6.pdf (3 September 2007), 4.

52. Baumeister, *Evil*, 316, 319.

53. Ibid, 316-17.

54. Zimbardo, *The Lucifer Effect*, 382.

55. Fay, "AR 15-6 Investigation of the Abu Ghraib Detention Facility and 205th Military Intelligence Brigade," 74.

56. Antonio M. Taguba, "Article 15-6 Investigation of the 800th Military Police Brigade," *NPR.org*, http://www.npr.org/iraq/2004/prison_abuse_report.pdf (3 September 2007), 19.

57. Fay, "AR 15-6 Investigation of the Abu Ghraib Detention Facility and 205th Military Intelligence Brigade," 105.

58. "Abu Ghraib Dog Handler Gets 6 Months," *CBSNews.com*, 22 March 2006, http://www.cbsnews.com/stories/2006/03/22/iraq/main1430842.shtml (10 April 2008).

59. The U.S. military's support for intimidating violence is perhaps most evident in its public endorsement and use of the "shock and awe" doctrine, which is designed to break the spirit and willpower of enemies through an overwhelming show of force. This strategy is also referred to as "rapid dominance." Typical warfare prioritizes the physical destruction of an enemy's armaments, infrastructure, and personnel. On the other hand, the shock and awe strategy is considered to be a tactic of psychological destruction. When implemented effectively, the enemy loses the will to fight back almost immediately. The U.S. military has repeatedly attempted to employ this tactic in recent large-scale military campaigns. In the March 2003 invasion of Iraq, the Iraqi army was crushed in less than three weeks, which likely increased the value of intimidating violence in the eyes of many members of the military.

60. Fareed Zakaria, "Pssst . . . Nobody Loves a Torturer; Ask any American soldier in Iraq when the general population really turned against the United States and he will say, 'Abu Ghraib,'" *Newsweek*, 14 November 2005, http://www.newsweek.com/id/51176 (10 April 2008); "Key excerpts from the Taguba report," *MSNBC.com*, 3 May 2004, http://www.msnbc.msn.com/id/4894033/ (10 April 2008).

61. Adam Hochschild, "What's in a Word? Torture," *New York Times*, 23 May 2004, Late Edition East Coast.

62. Lila Rajiva, *The Language of Empire: Abu Ghraib and the American Media* (New York: Monthly Review Press, 2005), 164-67.

63. Zakaria, "Pssst. . . . Nobody Loves a Torturer."

64. John Tierney, "Hot Seat Grows Lukewarm Under Capital's Fog of War," *New York Times*, 20 May 2004, Late Edition East Coast.

65. Tierney, "Hot Seat Grows Lukewarm Under Capital's Fog of War."

66. Jones, "AR 15-6 Investigation of the Abu Ghraib Prison and 205th Military Intelligence Brigade," 22.

67. Zimbardo, *The Lucifer Effect*, 416.

68. Guy B. Adams, Danny L. Balfour, and George E. Reed, "Abu Ghraib, Administrative Evil, and Moral Inversion: The Value of 'Putting Cruelty First,'" *Public Administration Review* 66 (2006): 680-93.

69. Danner, *Torture and Truth*, 8.

70. Danner, *Torture and Truth*, 8.

71. Grossman, *On Killing*, 191.

72. Jones, "AR 15-6 Investigation of the Abu Ghraib Prison and 205th Military Intelligence Brigade," 19.

73. Hersh, "Chain of Command."

74. Danner, *Torture and Truth*, 19.

75. Hersh, "Chain of Command."

76. Hersh, "Chain of Command."

77. "Prison Abuse Disclosure Puts Family in Danger," *ABCNews*.go.com, 16 August 2004, http://abcnews.go.com/GMA/story?id=127650&page=1&GMA=true (12 August 2006).

78. Fay, "AR 15-6 Investigation of the Abu Ghraib Detention Facility and 205th Military Intelligence Brigade," 79.

79. Hersh, "Chain of Command."

80. Zimbardo, *The Lucifer Effect*, 420.

81. Grossman, *On Killing*, 277.

82. Grossman, *On Killing*, 318. Emphasis removed.

83. Taguba, "Article 15-6 Investigation of the 800th Military Police Brigade," 19.

84. Zimbardo, *The Lucifer Effect*, 421-22.

85. Hersh, "Chain of Command."

86. Hersh, "Chain of Command."

87. Hersh, "Chain of Command."

88. Hersh, "Chain of Command."

89. Hersh, "Chain of Command."

90. Fay, "AR 15-6 Investigation of the Abu Ghraib Detention Facility and 205th Military Intelligence Brigade," 80.

91. "Key excerpts from the Taguba report."

92. Zimbardo, *The Lucifer Effect*, 346.

93. Zimbardo, *The Lucifer Effect*, 346-47.

94. Zimbardo, *The Lucifer Effect*, 362.

95. Staub, *The Roots of Evil*, 49-50.

96. Hersh, "Chain of Command."

97. Melissa Dittman, "What makes good people do bad things?" *APA Online*, 9 October 2004, http://www.apa.org/monitor/oct04/goodbad.html (10 April 2008).

98. Hersh, "Chain of Command."

99. Zimbardo, *The Lucifer Effect*, 402.

100. Zimbardo, *The Lucifer Effect*, 402.

101. Fay, "AR 15-6 Investigation of the Abu Ghraib Detention Facility and 205th Military Intelligence Brigade," 44.

102. Strauss, "Breakdown in the Gray Room," 88.

103. Hersh, "Chain of Command."

104. Rajiva, *The Language of Empire*, 100.

105. Zimbardo, *The Lucifer Effect*, 414.

106. Zimbardo, *The Lucifer Effect*, 414.

107. Fay, "AR 15-6 Investigation of the Abu Ghraib Detention Facility and 205th Military Intelligence Brigade," 112.

108. Fay, "AR 15-6 Investigation of the Abu Ghraib Detention Facility and 205th Military Intelligence Brigade," 108.

109. Fay, "AR 15-6 Investigation of the Abu Ghraib Detention Facility and 205th Military Intelligence Brigade," 111.

110. Schlesinger et al., "Final Report of the Independent Panel to Review Department of Defense Operations," 27-28.
111. Schlesinger et al., "Final Report of the Independent Panel to Review Department of Defense Operations," 27-28.

Chapter 8
Patterns of Violent Transformation: Comparative Analysis

Overall, the model of systematic indoctrination has proven itself both accurate and useful. In all four case studies—Nazi Germany, Al Qaeda, Iran, and Abu Ghraib—the specific strategies of recruitment, training, authorization, bureaucracy, isolation, and dehumanization transformed relatively normal people into violent tools of the system. The different systems' reliance on the same methods is not just a coincidence. Nor is it a matter of coordination—the U.S. military did not study Nazi Germany in search of best practices. There is one main reason for such an overlap of strategies and training techniques: they work. As violent leaders across different eras and different cultures have tried to perfect the science of killing, they have been drawn towards the same methods. Their success is rooted in the essentials of human nature—both people's strengths and their weaknesses—which explains the cross-cultural effectiveness of such strategies. Though the Milgram and Zimbardo experiments are not cross-cultural, they do provide powerful examples of similar strategies for violence in controlled environments. At the same time, their areas of disconnect—where the model's normal variables did not show up—help to explain why the violence in these experiments never reached truly tragic levels.

At this point, a comprehensive review of the book's findings would be redundant, considering that the details of each case have already been discussed in depth. However, it is worth reviewing some additional interesting parallels. Ultimately, the contrast between the experiments and the case studies, along with the similarities and differences between the case studies themselves, highlight some of the finer points of systematic indoctrination.

For starters, it is important to compare the violence in these cases. Table 8.1 shows the varied targets, levels of violence, and documented numbers of

Table 8.1. Characteristics of Violence by Case

	Targets for violence	Level of violence	Number of civilians and/or prisoners killed
Nazi Germany	civilians, prisoners & enemy soldiers	fatal	Over 20 million
Iran	civilians, prisoners & enemy soldiers	fatal	Over 5000
Al Qaeda	civilians, prisoners & enemy soldiers	fatal	Over 3500
Abu Ghraib	prisoners	severe physical & psychological abuse	1
Milgram experiment	civilians	appeared potentially fatal	0
Zimbardo experiment	mock prisoners	moderate physical & psychological abuse	0

civilians and prisoners killed. In the cases of Nazi Germany, Iran, and Al Qaeda, the systems' targets include active enemy soldiers. Since enemy soldiers carry weapons, pose a real threat, and are prepared for violent conflict, attacking them is not a crime. But even in the context of war, military and paramilitary groups must train and condition their members to ensure their willingness to kill. However, systematic indoctrination becomes even more vital when agents are ordered to attack civilians and prisoners. Violence against men, women, and children who cannot defend themselves is the most brutal type of aggression, for which we have the most deep-seated moral restraints. Nevertheless, the Nazi, Iranian, and Al Qaeda systems were able to compel agents to kill unarmed targets.

The fatality figures in Table 8.1 are conservative—if anything, they underestimate the extent of the bloodshed. The Nazis may have killed more than fifty million people, but we know at least twenty million were unarmed.[1] Iran executed hundreds of religious opponents in the early 1980s, over 4400 prisoners in the massacres of 1988, and has regularly and systematically murdered political opponents and media members since then.[2] Unfortunately, because the system is so isolated and well protected, good statistics are hard to come by. The estimate "over 5000" does not include nearly a thousand civilian deaths attributed to the terrorist group Hezbollah, which was established by Iran's Revolutionary Guard and is financed and supported by Iran to this day. Nor does it consider Iran's future killing potential, which could surge into the millions if the nation goes nuclear. By comparison, Al Qaeda has killed nearly 3500 innocents (2974 on 9/11), not including its insurgency-provoking strikes in Iraq or Afghanistan, where it has killed many thousands more.[3]

On the other hand, the violence employed at Abu Ghraib and in the Milgram and Zimbardo experiments was serious but much less deadly. In these cases, with the exception of one Abu Ghraib prisoner who was killed by mistake, at no point did the violence reach the fatal "point of no return" where the perpetrators *were certain* that their victims could not fully recover. Abusive members of the system could continue to deny the significance of the suffering they caused as temporary and no big deal—a moral luxury the Nazis, Iranian killers, and Al Qaeda terrorists did without. In the Milgram experiment, the subjects received mixed messages: they were reassured that the shocks were not dangerous, but the victim who screamed out in pain had complained of a heart condition and the panel with the shock switches said "Danger: Severe Shock" in big black letters. Ultimately, the Nazi, Iranian, and Al Qaeda cases clearly show the most successful systematic indoctrination and the most dramatic and deadly human transformations. We do not know how far the violent agents in the less severe cases would have gone, but we cannot assume that they would have indiscriminately killed for the system. As we continue to review some of the findings, we will uncover some key differences in systematic indoctrination across the cases that help explain these different levels of violence.

Overall, the analytical framework fits these systems' recruitment strategies quite well. As shown in Table 8.2, all of these systems targeted men as their ideal recruit, and only Milgram did not prioritize youth. However, the Nazi, Iranian, and Al Qaeda cases stand out as recruiting adolescent boys as young as ten, eleven, and twelve, while the U.S. military and Zimbardo did not enlist anyone younger than eighteen.[4] This distinction may be related to the respective degrees of indoctrination these systems required. The Nazis, Iran, and Al Qaeda needed their members to be so fully committed to the system that they would kill unarmed civilians on command. Though older agents can be compelled to commit these atrocities, they take to it with less enthusiasm and show a great deal of stress afterwards. Perhaps the type of total psychological transformation that makes this kind of killing seem easy is only possible with the youngest recruits.

When it comes to recruit ideology, all of the systems deliberately targeted those whose beliefs fit with the systems' goals, except in the psychological experiments. As it turned out, in the Stanford Prison Experiment, Zimbardo's volunteers actually held beliefs counter to the ideal guard mentality. During pre-screening, almost all of the volunteers identified with real prisoners more than they did with real prison guards. That they were successfully compelled to abuse the prisoners, despite their prior beliefs, shows the remarkable power of these methods.

As shown in Table 8.3, although the specifics varied, the basic training priorities were very similar across the cases. The biggest exception is the particularly cruel methods of desensitization found in the Nazi and Al Qaeda cases. In these systems, some agents killed dogs and other animals to become numbed to the use of violence. Animals are inherently innocent and without malice, so it is easy to see how this could prepare agents for a future of killing unarmed men, women, and children. As Albert Schweitzer wrote, "Anyone who has accustomed himself to regard the life of any living creature as worthless is in danger of arriving also at the idea of worthless human lives."[5] On a related note, though most serial killers are not ordinary people transformed by a violent system, but rather abnormal people who are pathologically impaired—it is worth noting that they too often show cruelty towards animals before engaging in more horrific crimes. This type of cruelty has a particularly powerful effect on young minds. As Margaret Mead explained, "One of the most dangerous things that can happen to a child is to kill or torture an animal and get away with it."[6] It seems likely that killing dogs and other animals had a similar desensitizing effect on young Nazi and Al Qaeda recruits. Apparently, there is something about cruelty towards animals that makes it the natural stepping-stone to extreme violence. In the Nazi case, some members of the SS were even pressured to kill Jewish babies in front of their mothers as a sign of toughness and moral fiber. Hopefully, that kind of horror is a thing of the past—it's not clear that even the most violent systems need to resort to such tactics to successfully desensitize their members.

Table 8.2. Recruits by Case

	Target recruit	Target ideology
Nazi Germany	age 10+, male	strong belief in Aryan glory and racial purity
Iran	age 12+, male	strong belief in extremist version of Shi'a Islam
Al Qaeda	age 11+, male	strong belief in extremist version of Sunni Islam
Abu Ghraib	age 18+, male	strong belief in American patriotism
Milgram experiment	age 20-50, male	N/A
Zimbardo experiment	age 18+, male	N/A

Table 8.3. Training by Case

	Trained to fear	Trained to obey	Desensitization
Nazi Germany	Bolshevik Russians and conspiratorial Jews with plans of world domination	taught "the leader is always right" & threatened with execution for disobedience	some strangled puppies, tortured prisoners, and/or killed babies in front of their mothers
Iran	The Great Satan (the U.S.) and the Little Satan (Israel), who corrupt the world, oppress Muslims and curse Allah	taught society depends on obedience & disobeying leaders = disobeying Allah	self-flagellation & self-mutilation, and violence against citizens to enforce Islamic laws
Al Qaeda	The United States: the "greedy, materialistic, dominant and arrogant infidel power," that is "evil in its essence"	taught to obey every order; often described by critics as following the "blind march to jihad"	some got weapons training killing dogs and other animals
Abu Ghraib	The Iraqi insurgency—especially its mortar attacks	taught to obey commanders fully, no matter how inane orders may seem	drill sergeant hostility, violent training songs, & practice firing guns at lifelike targets
Milgram experiment	N/A	N/A	N/A
Zimbardo experiment	The mock prisoners (but they learned this on the job)	N/A	learned that numbing their feelings made the job easier (but they learned this on the job)

In Table 8.4, we see the significance of authorizations by case. Transcendent authorizations were present in all six cases, but the goals varied dramatically. Interestingly, the Nazi, Iranian, and Al Qaeda cases all promoted similar goals, which emphasized pleasing an idealized leader as an end to itself, while romanticizing a quest to restore lost glory. Less dramatic or inspiring was the U.S. military's goal of securing Iraq, protecting its soldiers, and finding Saddam Hussein and weapons of mass destruction. Though members of the military cared about surviving and helping their comrades do the same, many lacked any passion for the nation's geopolitical aims. Very few, if any, idolized Bush as a godlike figure who must be pleased. Finally, while the potential for scientific progress was extremely exciting for Milgram and Zimbardo, this goal must have been far less stirring for the volunteer subjects in their studies.

When it comes to types of mundane authorizations, it is important to re-emphasize that specific authorizations for violence were not present in the Abu Ghraib case—which makes it fundamentally different from Nazi Germany, Al Qaeda, and Iran. When leaders give vague orders, their direct control over agents diminishes and it becomes harder for them to achieve specific goals. There is that old saying "If you want something done right, do it yourself." If you cannot or will not do it yourself, the next best thing is giving very specific, very clear orders to an obedient subordinate. Vague orders rank a distant third, and make it unlikely that the task will be completed in the way you want it done. Since being vague usually reduces the system's efficiency, we might assume that in violent systems, leaders would always want to give specific orders. However, sometimes they are intentionally and exclusively vague because they are afraid of being held accountable for giving specific commands. At Abu Ghraib, leaders needed to preserve their "plausible deniability," so they never specifically ordered torture or abuse. Instead, they told MPs to "take the gloves off" or to "soften up" or "prepare" detainees for interrogation. The result was a mess of improvisational abuse, rather than more efficient (and more horrific) systematic torture.

This is actually quite a good sign. The fact that the U.S. military felt it could not give specific orders for abuse indicates very real limits to its violent potential that did not exist in the other cases. By comparison, if the Nazi, Iranian, or Al Qaeda leaders feared the consequences of being specific, they would have given only vague authorizations for violence, and their systems' efficiency and effectiveness would have been dramatically reduced. Which means that far fewer people would have been tortured and killed.

As shown in Table 8.5, the significance of bureaucracy was also apparent across the cases and experiments. Naturally, the size and scope of the bureaucracies varied, ranging from large national government systems in Nazi Germany and Iran to local bureaucracies in the two experiments. It seems that in the larger bureaucracies, each individual agent felt more pressure to do his job because he was just a small cog in the huge machine, and thus was less likely to object.

Table 8.4. Authorizations by Case

	Goal of transcendent authorizations	Types of mundane authorizations	Values of the social climate
Nazi Germany	pleasing Hitler and achieving racial purity to restore the German empire	specific & vague	order, discipline and the strength to be ruthless
Iran	pleasing Allah, the Supreme Leader and Ahmadinejad by restoring the Islamic caliphate & instituting Sharia law	specific & vague	the divine mandate to fight oppressors to the death, and violence as a tool of justice & purification
Al Qaeda	pleasing Allah and bin Laden by defeating infidel oppressors and restoring Islamic glory	specific & vague	violence as the most effective weapon available and martyrdom as the highest honor
Abu Ghraib	gaining intelligence to secure Iraq, protect fellow soldiers, & find Saddam & WMDs	vague	military prowess, toughness, not being soft
Milgram experiment	advancing scientific progress	specific	temporary pain is no big deal
Zimbardo experiment	advancing scientific progress	vague	toughness, not being soft (as the prescribed role)

Table 8.5. Bureaucracies by Case

	Bureaucracy	Defined operating procedures became routine?	Labor divided between various agents
Nazi Germany	national government	yes	top leaders, mid-level executives, police and SS, prison doctors & camp guards
Iran	national government	yes	top leaders, security departments, IRGC, basij & the military
Al Qaeda	international organization	yes	top leaders, managers, intelligence teams, support teams & strike teams
Abu Ghraib	national department	yes, but procedures were unclear about detainee treatment	top leaders, commanders in Iraq, soldiers, MIs, OGAs, civilian contractors & MPs
Milgram experiment	local	yes	Milgram and, within the experiment, the scientist, teacher & learner
Zimbardo experiment	local	yes, but procedures were unclear about techniques	Stanford review board, Zimbardo & staff, real police officers, a real priest, friends & family, guards & prisoners

By contrast, in the Milgram experiment, where the bureaucracy was much smaller and institutional momentum was much less of a factor, the subjects showed the most resistance. While it was appalling that over sixty percent of Milgram's subjects were totally obedient as they delivered severe shocks, nearly forty percent refused to finish the experiment. Though we do not have exact statistics on the number of completely disobedient agents within the Nazi, Iranian, Al Qaeda, or Abu Ghraib systems, it is clear that they were much more rare. Instead of four out of ten who refused to complete their assignments, they may have had four out of a thousand. Like these systems, Zimbardo's experiment also had a larger bureaucracy than Milgram's, and even though some guards did their job with more passion than others, tellingly, no one refused to obey. An additional factor could have been the degree of the agents' commitment to the bureaucracy. Milgram's subjects were paid volunteers for a one hour experiment, while Zimbardo's were full-time employees for a two week stint, and most of the agents in the other cases were all serving their bureaucracies in full-time, professional capacities. Once agents are fully immersed in the bureaucracy, they are much less likely to act against it. In turn, the significance of division of labor as an enabler of violence was seen again and again across the cases—as long as individuals were not the sole contributors to pain and suffering, they felt less morally responsible for their cruel behavior.

Table 8.6 highlights the importance of isolation. Ultimately, it is much harder for a program of systematic indoctrination to be successful if the system is not isolated. Even in the Milgram experiment—which was the least isolated case—being separate from potential onlookers was deemed to be absolutely critical. Literal isolation was even more significant in the other cases, where agents were often far from home and fully immersed in their duties. Notably, both the Nazi and Iranian systems were marked by their total control over the media within their borders. Even though these systems had no power over foreign critics, who were free to say whatever they wanted, they did their best to keep their own citizens isolated from that discourse. The Nazis had a specific propaganda ministry that controlled the newspapers and the state-run radio, along with virtually all other types of media, including the arts. Iran has similarly shut down private newspapers, essentially leaving the government-run Islamic Republic News Agency as the country's sole news source. And in both the Nazi and Iranian cases, violence was used to intimidate internal critics and repress any information that contradicted the system's version of reality.

By comparison, Al Qaeda has worked its hardest to gain media control and provide its members with self-serving information, but as an international organization with members throughout the world, this is an extremely tough task. When recruits are brought to training camps, their isolation is complete and they only hear the information Al Qaeda provides, but when the agents re-enter society, their isolation is reduced. However, if their indoctrination has been successful, loyal agents isolate themselves and only consult Al Qaeda sources and

Table 8.6. Isolation by Case

	Literal isolation	Social/Moral isolation	Isolation within the system
Nazi Germany	isolated nation with total media control	Nazis rejected most outsiders after WWI failure and punitive Treaty of Versailles	need-to-know policy; officials grew afraid to ask for additional information
Iran	isolated nation with total media control	Iran rejected the UN and international values after the Islamic revolution; sanctions and criticism has led to further isolation	need-to-know policy; those not involved in security matters are prohibited
Al Qaeda	isolated training camps, far from home; partial media control	Al Qaeda rejected all international systems, agreements & values, including human rights, Geneva Conventions, etc.	need-to-know policy; recruits are not allowed to inform their parents about their missions
Abu Ghraib	isolated prison, far from home; limited media control	U.S. military rejected peacetime values; morality of effectiveness and survival took hold	need-to-know policy; abuses kept secret; some OGA/MI officers hid their identity
Milgram experiment	isolated laboratory	scientific ethics replaced normal values	N/A
Zimbardo experiment	isolated mock prison, but guards went home between shifts	prison ethics replaced normal values	N/A

websites for information. On the other hand, the U.S. military at Abu Ghraib was marked by its lack of control over the media, and in turn, its lack of isolation. Even though its location in Iraq was far from home, the military was still penetrated by the media, and the resulting front-page scandal was the major reason the prison abuses stopped. This is another good sign—the U.S. military's isolation is limited. With the media serving as public watchdog, the U.S. military has a partial safeguard against continued unethical violence that simply was not present in the Nazi, Iranian, or Al Qaeda cases.

Ultimately, systematic indoctrination both causes and uses dehumanization. It causes the dehumanization of its own members by stripping them of their individuality and personal values and compelling them to take limited, objectified roles within the system. Table 8.7 shows the different roles they took on in the various cases. Al Qaeda turned its suicide terrorists into virtual "weapons." They were no longer valued for any human capacity, other than their ability to die in the perfect place, at the perfect time, in order to strike the perfect blow. At Abu Ghraib, the MPs became glorified "attack dogs" that were used to scare detainees into providing information. Indeed, at times they actually used real attack dogs to perform exactly the same job. The advantage of the dehumanized guards, however, was that they were even more obedient than the dogs, and were able to devise more nuanced types of abuse and intimidation to attack the prisoners' minds. By contrast, the young men in Zimbardo's mock prison became "guard dogs"—guarding, not attacking and frightening the prisoners, was their primary task. However, abusing the prisoners became the best way for them to do their job—it helped them to guard the prisoners and prevent rebellion more effectively. In Milgram's experiment, the subjects became mere "scientific instruments." Their role was to read the learning test aloud and flick switches to deliver shocks, depending on the learner's answers. There was nothing human about the teaching they were doing—it was just reading from a predefined list. A tape recorder or a very basic computer program could have replaced them quite adequately. In Iran and Nazi Germany, different members of the violent systems took on different dehumanized roles: "weapons," "attack dogs," "guard dogs," "minefield clearers," and—in the Nazi case, "scientific instruments" engaged in eugenics and so-called race purification. Overall, the agents in all of these cases were expected to numb themselves, repress their consciences, give up control over their lives and jobs, and obediently follow orders to commit violence on command. And this made them feel less fully human.

Furthermore, in all four of the major case studies, there was clear evidence that the systems' leaders viewed the low-level agents as sacrificial pawns. This ethic was most pronounced in the Nazi, Iranian, and Al Qaeda systems. Hitler had his own people murdered on the "Night of Long Knives" because he wanted to increase his power and protect his authority from potential future challengers. Likewise, during the Iran-Iraq war, Khomeini sent tens of thousands of unarmed boys to their deaths as human waves surging across minefields. Similarly,

Table 8.7. Dehumanization by Case

	Agents take on dehumanized roles	Agents become sacrificial pawns	Dehumanizing labels for targets
Nazi Germany	agents = "weapons," "attack dogs," "guard dogs," "scientific instruments"	hundreds of Nazis murdered in the SA purge to consolidate power	cattle, lice, rats, other vermin
Iran	agents = "weapons," "attack dogs," "guard dogs," "minefield clearers"	tens of thousands die as human waves in Iran-Iraq war	satanic, demonic, tumorous cancers, blood-thirsty butchers, wild & brainless animals & wolves
Al Qaeda	agents = "weapons"	suicide terrorists sacrificed to increase precision of attacks	satanic, demonic, the enemies of God, a world of contaminants, pigs, dogs & mice
Abu Ghraib	agents = "attack dogs"	loyal MPs betrayed & prosecuted as "bad apples"	dogs & other animals
Milgram experiment	agents = "scientific instruments"	N/A	learner
Zimbardo experiment	agents = "guard dogs"	N/A	sheep living in cages & zombie-like creatures

bin Laden and his fellow Al Qaeda leaders clearly have had no qualms about pressuring their organization's members into suicide attacks. By contrast, even though the U.S. military recognizes that death is an inevitable part of war, it has not been nearly so quick to send soldiers to their deaths. However, after the Abu Ghraib scandal brought political and legal heat on the military, its leaders did betray the low-level agents accused of crimes. As part of the cover-up strategy, it portrayed them as "bad apples" who acted alone and out of personal sadism, rather than as the misguided but obedient employees they often were. This du-plicity led to what may have been overly severe criminal convictions and im-prisonment for some of the loyal MPs.

Beyond such sacrifices, in all of these contexts, the targets of violence were discussed in dehumanized terms. In the Milgram experiment, the label "learner" is not particularly negative, but it does help the person delivering the shocks think of his victim as an impersonal role, rather than as an individual with a name, feelings, and a family. The labels in all of the other cases were blatantly pejorative, and incorporated animal and demonic imagery.

Conclusion

This chapter has provided a side-by-side comparative analysis of Nazi Germany, Iran, Al Qaeda, Abu Ghraib, and the Milgram and Zimbardo experiments across the six key strategies of systematic indoctrination. As mentioned previously, systematic indoctrination has a psychological effect which is hard to measure: it increases agents' *willingness* to act violently, but their actual *use* of violence depends on many additional factors, including the system's resources, opportu-nities, and adversaries. Nevertheless, in these cases, there was a strong positive relationship between the degree of systematic indoctrination and the severity of violence against unarmed targets. Nazi Germany, Iran, and Al Qaeda fully im-plemented the strategies of recruitment, training, authorization, bureaucracy, isolation, and dehumanization. And their newly minted human killing machines slaughtered prisoners and civilians without mercy. At Abu Ghraib, the strategies were all employed, but with significantly less zeal. The military recruits were older, their shared ideology was less extreme, their desensitization training was less horrifying, their orders were never specific, and their isolation was less complete. Less fully transformed, the MP guards carried out severe physical abuse but never intentionally killed detainees. In the Milgram and Zimbardo experiments, systematic indoctrination was incomplete, and the resulting vio-lence was far less harsh. Thus, the contrasts between the cases—their structural similarities and differences—help to show the power of these violent methods.

Systematic indoctrination works, and the secret is out. But we *can* do some-thing about it.

Notes

1. Mann, *The Dark Side of Democracy*, 184.
2. "Ministers of Murder."
3. "Al Qaeda," *MIPT Terrorism Knowledge Base*, http://tkb.org/GroupCompari sonReport.jsp (19 January 2008).
4. Skeptics might point to Junior ROTC as a U.S. military recruitment program which targets adolescents, but since less than one percent of children participate in this program, and less than fifty percent of the participants even end up joining the military, the comparison to the Hitler Youth or Iranian Basij is quite limited.
5. "Bill Maher's PETA Ad," *PetaTV.com*, http://www.petatv.com/tvpopup/video. asp?video=bill_maher&Player=qt (14 January 2008).
6. "Cruelty and Neglect," *LA-SPCA.org*, http://www.la-spca.org/prevention/cruelty. htm (14 January 2008).

Chapter 9
Dismantling the Machines
and Restoring Humanity

Violent systems are not always bad. As Johnson is quick to point out, "Police, prison, and the military are necessary evils in an imperfect and often ugly world."[1]

Of course, people constantly disagree about when violence is necessary and when it is excessive. According to international law, the excuse "I was just following orders" is simply not valid and will not nullify criminal charges. But since the vast majority of orders are legal, it becomes hard to decipher the ones that are not. We often assume that people should have some instinctual barometer of what is right and wrong, but this notion is antiquated and unfounded. Sometimes what feels right is wrong and what feels wrong is right. Most people initially feel uncomfortable when they deal with violence, pain, suffering, and death. But over time, these instincts dull and they learn the virtue of repressing their feelings to get things done. The first time a rookie surgeon slices into a patient's chest, the act of violence may feel awkward, frightening, and wrong—but it is necessary. On the other hand, the most terrible violence has often been carried out by those who feel most righteous and certain at their core.

Since many people cannot simply trust their moral instinct, they often take cues from the systems around them on how to behave. However, even for violent systems, there is no universal moral code with the specificity to govern all situations. National and international law, religious doctrine, and The Golden Rule all offer some guidance, but many questions remain. The debate often surrounds notions of self defense. Most systems agree that violence is justified for protection, but they are often unclear about how immediate a threat must be to warrant it. Indeed, in the Nazi, Iranian, Al Qaeda, and Abu Ghraib cases, each system identified direct threats to its members' survival. As we now recognize,

155

these claims were often exaggerated for strategic purposes. But it is hard for ordinary people to know who and what to believe.

There is no miracle cure for this problem. As long as violent systems continue to indoctrinate their members with destructive ideas, they will continue to get destructive results. However, with sufficient political will, we may be able to limit the violent momentum in our own systems. When it comes to prisons, the police, and the military, Johnson sees hope in more recent, enlightened, and democratic "management perspectives [which] call for tapping an innate human desire to be effective and competent in one's work; to make things happen rather than be a pawn (even a loyal pawn)" and to have some control over the greater processes of the institution.[2] He also advocates "participatory management" policies that would give all members of a system some say in decisions about the use of violence, and encourage more autonomy and more personal reflection about moral dilemmas.

Increasing internal debate about violent measures is certainly a worthy goal, but it will not be easy to achieve. One challenge would be to implement these changes without crippling the systems' efficiency. For instance, the military could never function as anything close to a pure democracy—soldiers cannot be given a free choice to "pass the buck" on storming a hill or entering a particularly dangerous zone. There is also the risk that participatory management would lead to more violence, not less. Angered by the deaths of their comrades and fearing for their lives, the guards at Abu Ghraib may have voted for even more brutal torture techniques than they actually used. After all, there is a long history of mob violence where people have rushed to torture, lynch, and kill their enemies. Though giving more control to low-level agents could prove problematic, there are other ways we can attempt to reduce the risks of systematic indoctrination.

Abu Ghraib

Naturally, the U.S. military needs to preserve some necessary elements of its recruitment, training, and operating procedures. However, to avoid another Abu Ghraib-type scandal, it should consider changing some of its basic strategies of systematic indoctrination.

For one thing, soldiers and reservists might be less apt to act brutally if they were less isolated. As long as members of the media do not publish sensitive details on military strategy, they should be given greater access to military operations. The benefits of the media as an independent watchdog for bad behavior far outweigh the inconveniences of having them tag along. If the media had been given access to Abu Ghraib, the commanders would have been even more vague and limited in their authorizations for abuse, and the guards would have been much more reluctant to carry out their orders. Along these lines, the military's need-to-know policy should only apply to the most sensitive secrets. Too often secrecy is used solely to empower those who have information and to control those who lack it. In addition, isolation within the system should be reduced at all levels. This would mean more transparency at the top of the system—more responsibility for those in power and less plausible deniability. Military leaders knew the calls for aggressive action at Abu Ghraib were risky and borderline illegal, which is why they isolated themselves from the truth. With less isolation throughout the system, such excuses would no longer be acceptable and these practices would change. As Bruce Bueno de Mesquita et al. have found, "accountability appears to be the critical feature that makes full-fledged democracies respect human rights; limited accountability generally retards improvement in human rights."[3] As part of this change, the common practice of soldiers following orders with no knowledge of the bigger picture needs to be virtually eliminated.

In addition, we should reexamine the strategic dehumanization of targets. It may be that the modern soldier, who is better trained than ever before, no longer needs to devalue his enemy in order to be effective. The military should strive towards a future where its members are more like professional technicians than an angry, impassioned horde. Though their business is violent and the risks are great, future soldiers should not need to be fueled by hatred or fear in order to carry out their missions. While the image of soldiers as dispassionate and efficient killers is not pretty, this mentality could lead to fewer excesses than an overly emotional one.

Al Qaeda

Reducing Al Qaeda's deadly potential is a much more difficult challenge, but progress can be made. "The National Strategy for Combating Terrorism," which was published in February 2003, offered a sound four-pronged strategy:[4]

> We will *defeat* terrorist organizations of global reach through relentless action. We will *deny* terrorists the sponsorship, support, and sanctuary they need to survive. We will win the war of ideas and *diminish* the underlying conditions that promote the despair and the destructive visions of political change that lead people to embrace, rather than shun, terrorism. And throughout, we will use all the means at our disposal to *defend* against terrorist attacks on the United States, our citizens, and our interests around the world.[5]

These general objectives—to defeat, deny, diminish, and defend—may sound overly idealistic and politically triumphant, but they have been echoed by a number of scholars and government experts and still accurately describe the necessary components of a strong counterterrorism policy. Today, we can see

that the U.S. has successfully defeated many of Al Qaeda's leaders and operatives by killing and capturing them. And the post-9/11 defense of the American
homeland appears more effective, though we do not know whether this reflects a
change in our strategy or in Al Qaeda's choice of targets. On the other hand, Al
Qaeda's most influential leaders, bin Laden and Ayman al-Zawahiri, remain at
large, and the organization continues to find sanctuary and support in remote
areas around the globe. In addition, with anti-Americanism on the rise, the U.S.
has totally failed to win the war of ideas. The invasions of Afghanistan and Iraq,
the Abu Ghraib scandal, and several military mistakes that caused excessive
harm to civilians have made it easier for Al Qaeda to dehumanize Americans
and compel their agents to attack us. The U.S. has also been unable to defend its
own foreign interests against attack—particularly in Iraq. So a natural recommendation for combating terrorism is simply that the U.S. should stick to its
original plan, but execute it more effectively. It cannot afford to get sidetracked
on counterproductive missions or unnecessary battles.

Beyond such generalities, this book can offer some specific countermeasures to Al Qaeda's violent system. Systematic indoctrination is perhaps the
most important and the most fragile in this particular case, because a small psychological disruption can cause suicide terrorists to reconsider their impending
death. Even when things go according to plan, the risk of disobedience looms
ominously. A video of an Al Qaeda suicide attack against American forces in
Afghanistan shows this quite plainly. Despite Abu Muhammad Al-San'ani's
religious conviction, psychological indoctrination, desensitization, and weapons
training, his voice shakes and betrays him as he tries to convince himself that "I
feel a great calm," and again, seconds later, "I've never felt so calm in my life."[6]
Clearly he protests too much. As he drives towards the American convoy, he is
in radio contact with a team member, who urges him to speed up (lest he lose his
nerve) with a faltering stream of assurances:

> Did you see the Americans in front of you? Go on a little further, and you will
> see them in front of you. Abu Muhammad, there are Muslims behind you.
> Move a little faster, they are in front of you now. Place your trust in Allah, Mu-
> hammad. Remember Paradise, my brother, remember Paradise. Avenge your
> brothers' blood, Muhammad. Place your trust in Allah. I pray that Allah grants
> us an end like yours, Abu Muhammad. Did you see them?[7]

And then boom, the car explodes. This time it worked as planned, but by undermining some of Al Qaeda's strategies of systematic indoctrination, we can
potentially reduce the number of people who are willing to make the ultimate
sacrifice.

For instance, we have seen that as part of its authorizations for violence, Al
Qaeda glorifies pleasing bin Laden as a precious end unto itself. Attacks are
often carried out in his name, and his godlike stature, supposed connection to

Allah, and implied support of individual missions make it much easier for agents to disregard traditional moral values. For this reason, capturing, killing, or at least discrediting bin Laden should be a top priority.

Unfortunately, in recent years, many so-called experts have tried to diminish bin Laden's importance. In February 2007, the U.S. Army's General Peter J. Schoomaker expressed this view: "So we get him, and then what? . . . There's a temporary feeling of goodness, but in the long run, we may make him bigger than he is today. . . . We know he's not particularly effective. I'm not sure there's that great of a return."[8] Similarly, in January 2008, Pakistani President Pervez Musharraf acknowledged the importance of fighting Al Qaeda's agents, but stated that capturing bin Laden or al-Zawahiri "doesn't mean much."[9] Some base this claim on the assumption that bin Laden no longer runs the organization in a daily, hands-on fashion. Others suggest that killing bin Laden would just make him a martyr. Still others refer to Al Qaeda's decentralized structure, and contend that terrorist cells do not depend on their leaders, who are easily replaced. Proponents of this last perspective often cite the June 2006 killing of Abu Musab al-Zarqawi, Al Qaeda's leader in Iraq, and the minimal impact his death had on continued terrorist attacks in that country.

All of these points have some merit, and yet they overlook the symbolic importance bin Laden has as a living, breathing, U.S.-defying figure who inspires divine worship. As Riedel explains, at-large leaders like bin Laden "symbolize successful resistance to the United States and continue to attract new recruits. Settling for having them on the run or hiding in caves is not enough; it is a recipe for defeat, if not already an acknowledgment of failure."[10] As long as bin Laden evades capture, he can be seen as concrete evidence that Allah supports Al Qaeda in its mission against the U.S.. As the reasoning goes, without God's help, how else could one man evade the mighty U.S., which has put a $25 million dollar bounty on his head and pledged to take him "dead or alive?" Bin Laden has a supernatural status that puts him in a different category than other terrorist leaders, and he recognizes this. Abdel Bart Atwan noticed it when he interviewed the terrorist leader in the late 1990s: "So concerned was bin Laden about his image that he refused to have his voice taped during [the] interview. . . . [He] was afraid he might make some grammatical or theological mistakes which, if these were recorded, could tarnish his public image.[11] Even at this point, bin Laden was building his own form of papal infallibility, which grew dramatically on 9/11 and in the years that followed.

As a symbol, bin Laden will continue to be a major asset for Al Qaeda's systematic indoctrination of new recruits as long as he is not captured or killed. In fact, the worst thing might be for him to die of natural causes—as long as he lives, the U.S. has a chance of countering the powerful myths that surround him. But even if bin Laden is captured, tried, and executed, he may remain bold and defiant, as Saddam Hussein largely did. Furthermore, the ordeal would probably provoke hostage taking and demands for his release by Al Qaeda terrorists worldwide. Nevertheless, capturing him would still be much better than having him at large. However, the best scenario might be if he is killed by soldiers in a surprise attack, leaving a clearly identifiable corpse. It would be quick, degrading of his lofty image, and could shake Al Qaeda terrorists' confidence in their system and its goals.

Short of capturing or killing him, much more effort should be put into discrediting bin Laden as soon as possible. It is absurd that with as much mudslinging and dirty politics as goes on in America, thus far pretty much the only bad thing said about bin Laden is that he is the leader of a deadly terrorist organization. Because, of course, to members of Al Qaeda, that charge is a badge of honor—not something to be ashamed of. Characterizing bin Laden as violent does not discredit him to people who value violence, but it seems like it's the only thing we have considered trying. We should look at the traits that Al Qaeda detests and try to portray bin Laden in those terms. The U.S. needs him to suffer a "swift boat" scandal in the worst way. For example, he should be marketed as a traitor because Al Qaeda puts such a premium on loyalty. Indeed, there is evidence that at the very least, he abandoned his teacher and one of Al Qaeda's founding fathers: jihadist and radical Islamist Abdullah Azzam. There is even some evidence that he may have participated in or supported Azzam's 1989 assassination. This story is the kind of thing that everyone should know, the kind of black mark on bin Laden's character that could lead to some doubt about his virtues and those of the system.

But there is no need to stop there. Wherever there are questions about bin Laden's past behavior or his hypocrisy, they should be publicized. As America well knows, this kind of information spreads fast, regardless of its merits, and is easier to propagate than fight. Bin Laden has not been properly vetted—let's do it for him. Naturally, the stronger the evidence, the better. But trying to defame him for being violent is simply pointless: it's not Mother Teresa we're trying to convince. Ultimately, discrediting bin Laden would make him less useful as an authorization—and authorizer—for violence. We would see less of the idol worship that has surrounded him for the last eight years, and fewer attacks carried out in his name by agents who would happily die to do him proud. And in the event that bin Laden dies with his reputation intact, this strategy could still be employed posthumously.

At the same time that we're attempting to capture, kill, or discredit bin Laden, we should also consider negotiating with him or his terrorist followers. There is no reason we cannot pursue both paths simultaneously. The recommendation to negotiate is one that many Westerners find distasteful, but the refusal to at least consider its potential benefits would be rather shortsighted.

The fact is that negotiation may be able to weaken Al Qaeda's program of systematic indoctrination. Until now, the terrorist organization has been able to portray Muslims' options as rigid and unequivocal: fight or die. For its young male recruits, choosing the former has been a relatively easy decision. But if the

U.S. made a public offer to negotiate, it would introduce an important non-violent option into the cognitive mix. At the same time, by offering a few concessions, the U.S. and its allies would appear less inflexible and more reasonable, and thus become harder to demónize and dehumanize. Even if an agreement were not reached, the offer could provoke disagreements and disunity within the Al Qaeda system. Experienced negotiator Jan Egeland suggests that "there may come a time when cracks appear in Al Qaeda and negotiations can help split it further. . . . 'One likely scenario with Al Qaeda is that they will indeed become increasingly unpopular in the Muslim world and they will split.'"[12]

In addition, negotiations would reduce both Al Qaeda terrorists' isolation from the outside world and their isolation within the system. As recently as 2008, "Self-proclaimed al-Qaida supporters [have] appeared to be as much in the dark about the terror network's operations and intentions as Western analysts and intelligence agencies."[13] Islamic militant websites have been besieged by questions about why Al Qaeda has killed innocent people in Baghdad, Morocco, and Algeria, and whether the organization has a long-term strategy its supporters can buy into.[14] If the media published accounts of the negotiations or the basic bargaining terms, low-level agents would gain a greater understanding of their own system, why exactly they are being asked to forfeit their lives, and what the precise alternatives are to violence. It's certain that some operatives would remain fully committed to the system, but an increase in the discussion of options—a discourse that Al Qaeda has specifically attempted to repress among its members—would be almost inevitable.

Despite the risks to Al Qaeda, the terrorist organization would almost certainly agree to some sort of meeting. For one thing, hiding from this challenge would not fit with the extremists' honor-based value system. Bin Laden and his associates pride themselves on being daring, courageous, and never backing down, and they would not want Al Qaeda to appear afraid or intimidated by the prospect of open debate. Furthermore, al-Zawahiri has been priming himself for this type of opportunity, attempting to redefine himself as "a sophisticated leader rather than a mass murderer."[15] So this would appear to be a perfect chance for Al Qaeda to gain the exposure, prestige, and legitimacy it so desperately desires, by sitting down with world leaders at a negotiating table.

No doubt Al Qaeda leaders would hail the meeting as a huge victory and as confirmation of their righteous path. But ultimately, their gains would be very limited. The organization is already known worldwide and receives international media coverage for many of its public pronouncements. Some people fear that negotiating with terrorists is a terrible precedent that just invites more terrorism, but this is often not the case. Negotiation has worked in Northern Ireland with the IRA, as well as in several other cases. And again, even if the negotiations themselves failed, Al Qaeda's program of systematic indoctrination would be weakened. Their members would be less isolated and more aware of their non-violent options, debate would grow within the system, and it would become harder to fully demonize an enemy which has offered concessions and a potential path to peace. Because Al Qaeda's suicide terrorists are so vulnerable to hesitation and doubts, these countermeasures could end up saving many lives.

Beyond such specific recommendations, we need to finally jettison our self-comforting stereotypes about Al Qaeda. We can no longer dismiss the terrorist system as crazy and unpredictable. This book has shown that in many ways, Al Qaeda is run like a multinational corporation, with well-conceived strategies to manage its workforce. In addition, its employees behave like many other relatively normal people who are indoctrinated and conditioned to use violence on command: they do what they're told. This book has compared Al Qaeda's system to other systems that similarly promote violence, and has highlighted many of the strategies they have in common. However, there must be other characteristics common to national government systems, the military, prisons, police divisions, and certain industrial factories and corporations that are present in terrorist groups as well. The power of viewing terrorist groups through this lens is that you can see things you would not normally see, and ask questions you would not normally ask.

For instance, by looking at the forces and factors that cause corporations to fail, we might be able to arrange similar problems for Al Qaeda. We can increasingly try to use rational choice and game theory models to predict their corporate strategy. We can analyze the marketplace and try to pinpoint exactly what Al Qaeda is selling and in what quantities: brotherhood and the sense of community, romanticism and the chance for glory, escapism and thrill seeking, or optimism and newfound hope? Regardless of what Al Qaeda's prime cash crops prove to be, it is clear that the terrorist system need not have a market monopoly. We could go into business ourselves and offer alternative options to "consumers" at a lower price. For example, as part of positive reform movements, we could enlist restless young men for prestigious, daring, unifying, and courageous jobs in their regions. In these ways and more, if we move beyond old notions of terrorists as crazy, irrational lunatics and compare them to other workers who perform violence as part of their jobs, we may get a better sense of their collective psychology. And that could provide additional answers to the ultimate question—how do we stop them?

Iran

As dangerous as Al Qaeda is, it's Iran that may pose the greatest threat to world security since Nazi Germany. The comparison between these two violent systems has been made by a number of political leaders, including German Chancellor Angela Merkel, current Israeli Prime Minister Ehud Olmert, former Israeli Prime Minister Benjamin Netanyahu, Canadian Prime Minister Stephen Harper, and Australian Prime Minister John Howard.[16] Merkel, for instance, cited similarities between Ahmadinejad and Hitler before warning that the world cannot afford to underestimate Iran: "Looking back to German history in the early 1930s when National Socialism was on the rise, there were many outside Germany who said, "It's only rhetoric—don't get excited."[17] For its part, Iran has been defiant and inflammatory, with Ahmadinejad asking if the Jews are really human beings and demanding that "Israel must be wiped off the map."[18]

As this book has shown, the Nazi and Iranian systems have used strategies of recruitment, training, authorization, bureaucracy, isolation, and dehumanization in remarkably similar ways. Both have proven their ability to transform relatively normal people into obedient agents who will kill on command—and both have successfully done it on a national scale. At the very least, Iran has the *potential* to be the next Nazi Germany. It has the violent system, the time-tested program of systematic indoctrination, and the bureaucracy in place to mobilize the nation. It could certainly produce a Nazi-like workforce bent on religious war, genocide, and world domination. Iran also has a violent track record similar to the Nazis' early years, marked by the violent intimidation, persecution, and torture of religious minorities and political opponents and the deliberate murder of unarmed men, women, and children.

But it remains extremely hard to predict Iran's future behavior because we cannot gauge intent. Iran has the potential to be the next Nazi Germany, but does it have the *will*? Ultimately, we cannot read Khameini or Ahmadinejad's minds. The president's provocative statements could really just be rhetoric after all—we do not know. Many of Hitler's decisions, such as his invasion of Russia, his insistence on fighting on multiple fronts, and his refusal to surrender, were guided by ideology instead of logic. Are Iran's leaders also crazy, shortsighted, committed, or ambitious enough to act purely on ideological grounds? Are they willing to die for their cause like Hitler eventually did, or only willing to send others to their deaths? And who will succeed Khameini and Ahmadinejad, and how will they steer Iran in the future? Our best guesses must suffice.

To this point, there is no concrete evidence that either Khameini or Ahmadinejad is willing to go past the point of no return. Since the end of the Iran-Iraq war in the late 1980s, Iran's policy has combined religious extremism with a pragmatic strain of self-preservation.[19] As Shay explains, nowhere is this more clear than Iran's use of terrorism:

> where Iran believes it can act intensively and uncompromisingly to promote the concepts of the Islamic revolution, it aids radical Islamic organizations in terror acts and subversion aimed at ousting secular regimes and striking out at Western interests. . . . On the other hand, at spots where there is a fear Iranian subversion may be exposed, thus resulting in damage to Iranian interests, Iran adopts a more pragmatic policy.[20]

We have seen a good example of this over the past few years with Iran's training, financing, and arming of Iraqi insurgents. In order to avoid retribution—such as military counterstrikes from the U.S.—Iran has gone out of its way to disguise its support for the insurgency. This decision was practical, not ideological, and is typical of Iran's political strategy.

However, if Iran develops nuclear weapons its strategy may change. Like any smart fighter, Iran may be biding its time—waiting until it is strong enough to protect itself before pursuing its true ambitions. We know that Hitler had big dreams and extreme ideas well before he put them into action. He did not invade Poland in 1933—he waited until he thought Germany was too strong to be stopped. Iran's pragmatic past does not guarantee a similarly restrained future.

It is clear that Iran's violent capability, radical ideology, and alleged designs on nuclear weapons must be countered. Many experts believe that if the Iranian people were free to express themselves and truly influence the system, they would steer the country in a much more moderate and much less dangerous direction. Aslan, who was born in Iran and recently revisited his homeland, portrays young Iranians as primed for a more modern, globalized, and liberal society:

> This is the generation born after the revolution. They do not recall life under the Shah and are fed up with the anti-imperialist rhetoric of their elders. They were children during the Iran-Iraq War and have no experience of the horrible sacrifice Iranians were forced to make to keep the revolution alive. They couldn't care less about the revolution. They want what all teenagers want. They want what they see on their satellite stations . . . this generation will not put up with the clerical noose around their necks much longer.[21]

This reality stands in stark contrast to the oppressive, radical Islamic system. As Christopher Hitchens explains, "Iran is running on two timetables . . . the gradual but definite emergence of a democratization trend among the young and the middle class . . . [versus] the process by which a messianic regime lays hold of the means to manufacture apocalyptic weaponry."[22] By undermining Iran's program of systematic indoctrination, we can put great strains on the violent system and limit its control over the populace. This could simultaneously accelerate the democratization of Iranian society and decelerate the nation's arms race.

Practically, this may be hard to accomplish. Because Iranian leaders are notoriously suspicious of foreign attempts to "corrupt" the masses into rebellion or revolution, such efforts must be undertaken with great care. Since we do not have much access to Iran's violent system, available countermeasures are limited. It is hard to see how we could alter their strategies of recruitment, training, authorization, bureaucracy, or dehumanization.

However, since we have a great deal of control over their isolation, we should use this power much more effectively. Unfortunately, our current policy actually *helps* Iran's program of systematic indoctrination. In October 2007,

Bush outlined the basic principle of his administration's strategy: "My intent is to continue to rally the world, to send a focused signal to the Iranian government that we will continue to work to isolate you in the hopes that at some point somebody else shows up and says it's not worth the isolation."[23] He added that "The whole strategy is that, you know, at some point in time leaders or responsible folks inside of Iran may get tired of isolation and say, 'This isn't worth it.'"[24] This approach is nothing new—the U.S. and other world powers have been applying sanctions against Iran and attempting to isolate it for nearly thirty years. Though this strategy may have successfully hurt Iran's economy, even that much is unclear. A Congressional report released in December 2007 concluded that due to its "global trade ties and leading role in energy production," "Iran's overall trade with the world has grown since the U.S. imposed sanctions."[25] The sanctions have not even stopped Iran's arms race: "This trade included imports of weapons and nuclear technology."[26] Bueno de Mesquita, who famously predicted Khomeini's successors five years before they took power and now makes predictions for the CIA, insists that "The more aggressively the U.S. responds to Iran . . . the more likely it is that Iran will develop nuclear weapons."[27] If the U.S. continues its strategy of forced isolation, angry threats, and ineffective sanctions, it will accomplish very little and will provoke Iran further. While U.S. strategy has exacted a few political concessions over the years, the oil-rich nation has managed to survive. Meanwhile, the repressive regime has not budged. (Similarly, more than forty years of much more effective U.S. embargos have weakened Cuba's economy but done nothing to topple Fidel Castro's oppressive government.)

As this book has shown, increased isolation makes it *easier* for violent systems to indoctrinate their agents. Isolation allows the system to build its own world, removed and protected from outsiders. Milgram's and Zimbardo's experiments thrived because they were run in separate, controlled environments—away from distractions and outside influences. The U.S. is unintentionally giving Iran the space and power to establish its own controlled environment, where it has power over news, information, communication, and values to an extent most nations never could. In May 1933, *Time* magazine ran an editorial entitled "Isolation" which mocked Hitler for his extreme rhetoric and presumed his doom. It surmised that "What Handsome Adolf failed completely to realize was that the Anti-Semitism, the ranting speeches, the promises of ancient military glory that were winning him votes and power at home were isolating his country from the world and ruining her foreign trade."[28] But what *Time* magazine failed to realize was that this isolation was serving Hitler's goals. We now recognize that Germany's isolation enabled the Nazis' transformation of millions of normal people into violent members of their system. We cannot afford to make the same mistake with Iran.

The dramatic step of decreasing Iran's isolation and increasing its integration into the world community is the best chance for a non-military solution to its systematic indoctrination. In addition, reducing Iran's isolation would make it harder for the nation to run a secret nuclear weapon program. Given that "there is nothing the United States can do to prevent Iran from pursuing nuclear energy for civilian power generation," Bueno de Mesquita explains that "the international community needs to find out if there is a way to monitor civilian nuclear energy projects in Iran thoroughly enough to ensure that Iran is not developing weapons."[29] A less isolated Iran would have much more information flowing in *and out*, which would increase our intelligence returns and help IAEA inspectors get a more accurate assessment of Iran's weapons program.

The collapse of the Soviet Union provides compelling evidence that this strategy can work. In its final days, the Cold War superpower was certainly suffering economically, but that did not cause its fall. As award-winning British historian Archie Brown explains, "Many an inefficient state has been able to muddle through or 'muddle down' over decades. . . . This was not a case of economic and political crisis producing liberalization and democratization. Rather, it was liberalization and democratization that brought the regime to [its] crisis point."[30] Ultimately, it was the Cold War superpower's inability to keep its people isolated that spelled its doom. Brown explains further that it "was a different society . . . from what it had been at the time of Joseph Stalin's death just 32 years earlier . . . the general level of education had risen, millions more people had entered higher education, and there was greater (though still restricted) knowledge of the outside world."[31]

The people's increased knowledge of the outside world was the key chink in the Soviet Union's armor, because ultimately, it was *the failure of systematic indoctrination* that led to the violent system's collapse. In the summer of August 1991, hardliners declared a state of emergency, kidnapped liberal President Mikhail Gorbachev and called on the military to crush Boris Yeltsin and his liberal supporters to restore order. However, their oppressive agenda failed "under the sheer weight of public opposition—and because of the armed forces' reluctance to support the plotters. The hardliners would have had to kill many protesters to storm the White House and detain Yeltsin."[32] The deciding factor was the violent agents' *refusal to follow orders*. The Soviet Union's isolation had diminished, and external values and ideas had permeated the national system as never before. Increasingly cognizant of the outside world and their own moral options, the soldiers could no longer be certain that violence was justified. As Brown summarizes, this led to the best imaginable outcome: "Seldom, if ever, has a highly authoritarian political system, deploying military means sufficient to destroy life on earth, been dismantled so peacefully."[33]

Surely, this is the kind of success we should strive for in Iran. As Taheri documents, "Inside Iran, the IRGC . . . inspires a mixture of intense hatred and grudging admiration. While many Iranians see it as a monster protecting an evil regime, others believe that, when the crunch comes, it will side with the people against an increasingly repressive and unpopular regime."[34] It's this second possibility that offers our best chance for a peaceful solution in Iran. The evidence clearly shows that decreasing Iran's isolation and allowing outside values to permeate its violent system is our best hope for peace—for countering the systematic indoctrination that fuels the Basij and IRGC. We need to make sure that the oppressive Iranian regime goes out with a whimper—*not with a bang.*

Conclusion

There have been many scholarly efforts to explain human violence. Perhaps most compelling are the accounts that dare to face up to the devil that lurks inside ordinary people. These studies focus on people who are not plagued—nor excused—by developmental, psychological, or personality disorders. They focus on people who become part of a powerful, violent system that commands its agents to leap into action and attack its enemies. If these acts were crimes of passion, they might somehow be less horrible, but the systematic, bureaucratic, factory-styled production of violence makes them even more sickening. For instance, of all the Nazi atrocities, perhaps the most awful took place in their killing centers, which combined the best of man's practicality with the worst of his cruel potential. Hilberg makes this point quite plain:

> The killing centers worked quickly and efficiently. A man would step off a train in the morning, and in the evening his corpse was burned and his clothes were packed away for shipment to Germany. Such an operation was the product of a great deal of planning . . . upon closer examination the operations of the killing center resemble in several respects the complex mass production methods of a modern plant.[35]

As the preceding chapters have shown, it was not only violence that was produced by such modern methods—the human killing machines themselves came off the production line, carefully assembled, tested, and fine-tuned for loyalty and obedience to the system.

In *Blink: The Power of Thinking Without Thinking*, Malcolm Gladwell examines how the human brain "thin-slices"—how, in a split-second, it takes in a great wealth of information, discards the excess and focuses on a few key details to produce an intuitive response.[36] Sometimes these intuitive reactions contain powerful truths that we cannot articulate—other times they lead us astray. But more often than not, to 'he who knows what to look for,' less is more. For instance, in extended research projects, psychologist John Gottman and his staff have learned to predict which newly married couples will still be married after fifteen years and which will not—by watching them interact for just fifteen minutes.[37] He is ninety percent accurate. But if you do not know what to look for, you could watch them for fifteen straight days and still be unable to make reliable predictions. Similarly, expert selection committees evaluate musicians better when the musician plays from behind a black screen—when the committee cannot consider the musician's face, hair, body language, or personal charisma. In fact, some believe they could listen for just a few seconds this way and still make extremely accurate judgments about the caliber of the musician.[38]

The same type of thinking may be applied to analyses of systematic indoctrination and the promotion of violence. We confuse and distract ourselves when we examine too many variables. But by examining just six major strategies, this book has shown how we can thin-slice our way to a more user-friendly explanation for such atrocities—one that gives us better predictive and preventative powers. After all, most studies of mass violence should be designed to help us prevent future violence, future evils of a similar manner.

As previously discussed, Zimbardo and Milgram have shown us that ordinary people in violent systems can be compelled to do horrible things. Johnson has revealed that there are military institutions, prisons, police divisions, and industrial factories which have all—independently—developed similar practices to promote violence among their workers. Many other scholars have seen the same strategies applied across different cultures and different eras, but with the same horrific results. This book's model also fits the strategic production of violent workforces by the Nazis, Al Qaeda, Iran, and the U.S. military at Abu Ghraib.

As systems, organizations, and institutions continue to perfect their methods of indoctrination, the dangers will continue to grow. One day we may see agents recruited with incredible precision, sorted and selected by complex computer algorithms measuring thousands of factors to find the most malleable prospects. We may see virtual-reality training programs that desensitize recruits with unprecedented success and make killing an enemy seem like "just a game." We may see authorizations for violence that are increasingly based on classified information from above the average agents' security clearance level. "Trust us," they will be told, "Violence is justified this time." We may see increasingly impenetrable bureaucracies that succumb to institutional momentum and lack human operators with the power and oversight to slam on the brakes. "That's not in my job description," we'll hear, "You can't expect me to know what *he* was doing!" We may see increasingly isolated systems, where people communicate across hyperspace but are less likely to forge the personal connections that breed stability, community, and accountability. And we may see increasingly persuasive ways of differentiating between us and them, between the ingroup and the outgroup, between those who are part of the solution and those who can be blamed for the problem. But to keep this day from coming, we can use what we've learned here to disrupt and disable these strategies of systematic indoctrination.

Maybe it's just this simple: if you put certain normal people in the wrong place at the wrong time and deliberately indoctrinate them in the wrong way, they will do the wrong things. In practice, those people, places, times, and indoctrination methods rarely intersect on a large scale. When they do, it is not just a matter of bad winds or poor luck—look closely for a system with specific violent goals behind it all. If you see one, do what you can to fight its strategies of recruitment, training, authorization, bureaucracy, isolation, and dehumanization. Do what you can to inject more autonomy and personal reflection about moral dilemmas into the situation. And then pray it's not too late.

Notes

1. Johnson, "Institutions and the Promotion of Violence," 198.
2. Johnson, "Institutions and the Promotion of Violence," 200.
3. Bruce Bueno De Mesquita, et al., "Thinking Inside the Box: A Closer Look at Democracy and Human Rights," *International Studies Quarterly* 49 (2005): 439-58.
4. By comparison, the revised NSCT of 2006 appears to be a somewhat politically motivated, retroactive justification of the U.S. invasion of Iraq, and is thus less insightful and useful than the 2003 version.
5. "National Strategy for Combating Terrorism," *The White House*, http://www.whitehouse.gov/news/releases/2003/02/counter_terrorism/counter_terrorism_strategy.pdf (12 January 2008).
6. "An Al Qaeda Released Video of Attacks in Afghanistan."
7. "An Al Qaeda Released Video of Attacks in Afghanistan."
8. "General Plays Down Value Of Capturing Bin Laden," *WashingtonPost.com*, 24 February 2007, http://www.washingtonpost.com/wp-dyn/content/article/2007/02/23/AR2007022301799_pf.html (10 April 2008).
9. Associated Press, "Musharraf: Pakistan isn't hunting bin Laden," *MSNBC.com*, 22 January 2008, http://www.msnbc.msn.com/id/22791422/ (10 April 2008).
10. Riedel, "Al Qaeda Strikes Back," 35.
11. Fawaz A. Gerges, "The Osama Bin Laden I Know," *Foreign Policy* 156 (2006): 76-78.
12. Mark Trevelyan, "Talking to al Qaeda? Don't rule it out, some say," *Reuters.com*, 13 September 2007, http://www.reuters.com/article/newsOne/idUSL1183375220070913?sp=true (30 April 2008).
13. Paul Schemm, "Al-Qaida's No. 2 Defends Deadly Attacks," *FoxNews.com*, 3 April 2008, http://www.foxnews.com/wires/2008Apr03/0,4670,AskAlQaida,00.html (30 April 2008).
14. Schemm, "Al-Qaida's No. 2 Defends Deadly Attacks."
15. "Al Qaeda: We're open to questions," *CNN.com*, 19 December 2007, http://edition.cnn.com/2007/WORLD/meast/12/19/alqaeda.interview.ap/index.html (30 April 2008).
16. Peter Conradi, "Iran as bad as Nazis: Merkel," *Times Online*, 5 February 2006, http://www.timesonline.co.uk/article/0,,2089-2025730,00.html (10 April 2008); "Howard compares Iran to Nazi Germany," *The Sydney Morning Herald*, 20 May 2006, http://www.smh.com.au/news/world/howard-compares-iran-to-nazis/2006/05/20/11475

45561673.html (10 April 2008); Steven Stanek, "Olmert Compares Iran With Nazi Germany," *WashingtonPost.com*, 9 June 2004, http://www.washingtonpost.com/wp-dyn/content/article/2006/10/27/AR2006102700568.html (10 April 2008).

17. Conradi, "Iran as bad as Nazis."

18. "Iranian President Ahmadinejad asks: are Jews human beings?" *Iranian.ws*, 3 August 2006, http://www.iranian.ws/cgi-bin/iran_news/exec/view.cgi/15/17028 (10 April 2008); "Ahmadinejad: Wipe Israel off map," *AlJazeera.net*, 28 October 2005, http://english.aljazeera.net/English/archive/archive?ArchiveId=15816 (10 April 2008).

19. Shay, *The Axis of Evil*, 28.

20. Shay, *The Axis of Evil*, 28.

21. Aslan, "A weeklong journal of a writer in Iran—Entry 4."

22. Christopher Hitchens, "Dear Mr. President..." *World Affairs* 170 (2008): 9-13.

23. Sheryl G. Stolberg, "Nuclear-Armed Iran Risks World War, Bush Says," *New York Times*, 18 October 2007, http://www.nytimes.com/2007/10/18/washington/18prexy.html (10 April 2008).

24. Stolberg, "Nuclear-Armed Iran Risks World War, Bush Says."

25. "Iran Sanctions: Impact in Furthering U.S. Objectives Is Unclear and Should Be Reviewed," *GAO.gov*, December 2007, http://www.gao.gov/new.items/d0858.pdf (January 17, 2008).

26. "Iran Sanctions: Impact in Furthering U.S. Objectives Is Unclear and Should Be Reviewed."

27. Julie J. Rehmeyer, "Mathematical Fortune-Telling: How well can game theory solve business and political disputes?" *Science News Online*, 27 October 2007, http://www.sciencenews.org/articles/20071027/mathtrek.asp (10 April 2008).

28. "Isolation," *Time.com*, 22 May 1933, http://www.time.com/time/magazine/article/0,9171,745563-1,00.html (10 April 2008).

29. Rehmeyer, "Mathematical Fortune-Telling."

30. Archie Brown, "BBC History—Reform, Coup and Collapse: The End of the Soviet State," *BBC.co.uk*, 12 October 2001, http://www.bbc.co.uk/history/worldwars/coldwar/soviet_end_01.shtml (10 April 2008). British spellings changed for uniformity.

31. Brown, "BBC History—Reform, Coup and Collapse."

32. "Collapse of USSR: 10 years on," *BBC.co.uk*, http://news.bbc.co.uk/hi/english/static/in_depth/europe/2001/collapse_of_ussr/timelines/1991aug21.stm (10 April 2008).

33. Brown, "BBC History—Reform, Coup and Collapse."

34. Taheri, "Who Are Iran's Revolutionary Guards?"

35. Hilberg, *The Destruction of The European Jews*, 863.

36. Malcolm Gladwell, *Blink: The Power of Thinking Without Thinking* (New York: Little, Brown and Company, 2005), 252.

37. Gladwell, *Blink*, 21-22.

38. Gladwell, *Blink*, 250-54.

Bibliography

Abou El Fadl, Khaled. *Rebellion and Violence in Islamic Law*. Cambridge: Cambridge University Press, 2001.

"About IRNA: Guidelines." *Islamic Republic News Agency*. http://www.irna.ir /en/content/view/menu-240/id-24/ (15 January 2007).

"Abu Ghraib Dog Handler Gets 6 Months." *CBSNews.com*. 22 March 2006. http://www.cbsnews.com/stories/2006/03/22/iraq/main1430842.shtml (10 April 2008).

Adams, David. "Reality TV show recreates famed social study." *Nature* 417 (May 2002): 213.

Adams, Guy B., Danny L. Balfour, and George E. Reed. "Abu Ghraib, Administrative Evil, and Moral Inversion: The Value of 'Putting Cruelty First.'" *Public Administration Review* 66 (2006): 680-693.

Afshari, Reza. *Human Rights in Iran: The Abuse of Cultural Relativism*. Philadelphia: University of Pennsylvania Press, 2001.

Aghaie, Kamran S. *The Martyrs of Karbala: Shi'i Symbols and Rituals in Modern Iran*. Seattle: University of Washington Press, 2004.

Ahmadi, Nader and Fereshteh Ahmadi. *Iranian Islam: The Concept of the Individual*. London: Macmillan Press Ltd., 1998.

"Ahmadinejad: Wipe Israel off map." *AlJazeera.net*. 28 October 2005. http://english.aljazeera.net/English/Archive/Archive?ArchiveID=15816 (10 April 2008).

Ahmed, Akbar. *Islam Under Siege: Living Dangerously in a Post-Honor World*. Cambridge: Polity Press, 2003.

"Al Qaeda." *MIPT Terrorism Knowledge Base*. http://tkb.org/GroupComparison Report.jsp (19 January 2008).

"Al Qaeda: We're open to questions." *CNN.com*. 19 December 2007. http://edition .cnn.com/2007/WORLD/meast/12/19/alqaeda.interview.ap/index.html (30 April 2008).

Allen, Mike and Dana Priest. "Memo on Torture Draws Focus to Bush." *Washington-Post.com*, 9 June 2004. http://www.washingtonpost.com/wp-dyn/articles/A26401-2004Jun8.html (10 April 2008).

"An Al Qaeda Released Video of Attacks in Afghanistan." *MEMRITV.* 4 May 2006. http://www.memritv.org/clip/en/1131.htm (10 April 2008).

"'An eye for an eye—Iran hands out gruesome punishment.'" *IranFocus.com.* 27 September 2006. http://www.iranfocus.com/modules/news/article.php?storyid=8765 (10 April 2008).

"Army Reserve—Overview." *GoArmy.com.* http://www.goarmy.com/reserve/nps/index. jsp (26 July 2007).

Aronson, Shlomo. "Nazi Terrorism: The Complete Trap and the Final Solution." Pp. 169-185 in *The Morality of Terrorism*, edited by David C. Rapoport and Yonah Alexander. New York: Columbia University Press, 1989.

Aslan, Reza. "A weeklong journal of a writer in Iran—Entry 2." *Slate Magazine.* 8 September 2004. http://www.slate.com/id/2106317/entry/2106413/ (10 April 2008).

———. "A weeklong journal of a writer in Iran—Entry 3." *Slate Magazine.* 9 September 2004. http://www.slate.com/id/2106317/entry/2106465/ (10 April 2008).

———. "A weeklong journal of a writer in Iran—Entry 4." *Slate Magazine.* 10 September 2004. http://www.slate.com/id/2106317/entry/2106413/ (10 April 2008).

Associated Press. "Ahmadinejad warns Iran is ready for any possibility over nuclear row." *USATODAY.* 18 January 2007. http://www.usatoday.com/news/world/2007-01-18-iran_x.htm?csp=34 (18 January 2007).

———. "Musharraf: Pakistan isn't hunting bin Laden." *MSNBC.com.* 22 January 2008. http://www.msnbc.msn.com/id/22791422/ (10 April 2008).

Bartov, Omer. *Hitler's Army: Soldiers, Nazis, and War in the Third Reich.* New York: Oxford University Press, 1991.

Baumeister, Roy F. *Evil: Inside Human Cruelty and Violence.* New York: W. H. Freeman and Company, 1997.

Berg, Bruce L. *Qualitative Research Methods for the Social Sciences.* Boston: Allyn and Bacon, 2001.

Bergerson, Andrew S. *Ordinary Germans in Extraordinary Times: The Nazi Revolution in Hildesheim.* Bloomington, Ind: Indiana University Press, 2004.

Berkowitz, Leonard. *Aggression: Its Causes, Consequences, and Control.* Philadelphia: Temple University Press, 1993.

"Bill Maher's PETA Ad." *PetaTV.com.* http://www.petatv.com/tvpopup/video.asp? video=bill_maher&Player=qt (14 January 2008).

Boms, Nir T. and Elliot Chodoff. "Orwellian Censorship." *Washington Times*, 10 November 2006.

"Bound for Glory—Warrior Ethos." *GoArmy.com.* http://www.goarmy.com/glory/warrior_ethos.jsp (26 July 2007).

Braudy, Leo. *From Chivalry to Terrorism.* New York: Alfred A. Knopf, Inc., 2003.

Breckler, Steven J. "How Can the Science of Human Behavior Help Us Understand Abu Ghraib." *APA Online.* 10 June 2004. http://www.apa.org/ppo/issues/breckler604.html (6 February 2006).

Breitman, Richard. *The Architect of Genocide: Himmler and the Final Solution.* New York: Alfred A. Knopf, Inc., 1991.

Brown, Archie. "BBC History—Reform, Coup and Collapse: The End of the Soviet State." *BBC.co.uk.* 12 October 2001. http://www.bbc.co.uk/history/worldwars/coldwar/soviet_end_01.shtml (10 April 2008).

Browning, Christopher R..*Ordinary Men: Reserve Police Battalion 101 and the Final Solution in Poland.* New York: Harper-Collins Publishers, Inc., 1998.

Bueno de Mesquita, Bruce, et al. "Thinking Inside the Box: A Closer Look at Democracy and Human Rights." *International Studies Quarterly* 49 (2005): 439-458.

Bullough, Vern et al. *The Subordinated Sex.* Athens, Ga.: The University of Georgia Press, 1988.

Burger, Jerry. "Replicating Milgram." *APS Observer.* December 2007. http://www.psychologicalscience.org/observer/getArticle.cfm?id=2264 (10 August 2008).

Burlas, Joe. "Army Recruit Statistics Improve Over 2001." *Military.com,* 26 August 2002. http://www.military.com/Resources/ResourceFileView/Army_Recruit.htm (10 April 2008).

Byman, Daniel. *Deadly Connections: States that Sponsor Terrorism.* Cambridge: Cambridge University Press, 2005.

Cann, Rebecca and Constantine Danopoulous. "The military and politics in a theocratic state: Iran as case study." *Armed Forces and Society* 24 (Winter 1997): 269-289.

Caplan, Bryan. "Terrorism: The relevance of the rational choice model." *Public Choice,* (2006) 128: 91-107.

Carr, Caleb. *The Lessons of Terror.* New York: Random House, 2002.

Chasdi, Richard J. *Tapestry of Terror: A Portrait of Middle East Terrorism, 1994-1999.* Lanham, Md.: Lexington Books, 2002.

"Children Train with Weapons in Al Qaeda Film." *MEMRITV.* December 2005. http://www.memritv.org/clip/en/971.htm (10 April 2008).

Cloud, John. "Atta's Odyssey." *Time.com.* 30 September 2001. http://www.time.com/time/magazine/article/0,9171,1101011008-176917,00.html (10 April 2008).

"Collapse of USSR: 10 years on." *BBC.co.uk.* http://news.bbc.co.uk/hi/english/static/in_depth/europe/2001/collapse_of_ussr/timelines/1991aug21.stm (10 April 2008).

Conradi, Peter. "Iran as bad as Nazis: Merkel." *Times Online.* 5 February 2006. http://www.timesonline.co.uk/tol/news/world/article727156.ece (10 April 2008).

"Cruelty and Neglect." *LA-SPCA.org.* http://www.la-spca.org/prevention/cruelty.htm (14 January 2008).

Danner, Mark. *Torture and Truth: America, Abu Ghraib, and the War on Terror.* New York: The New York Review of Books, 2004.

"Data." *Start.Umd.edu.* http://www.start.umd.edu/data/ (31 March 2008).

Dittman, Melissa. "What makes good people do bad things?" *APA Online.* 9 October 2004. http://www.apa.org/monitor/oct04/goodbad.html (10 April 2008).

Dreifus, Claudia. "Finding Hope in Knowing the Universal Capacity for Evil." *New York Times.* 3 April 2007. http://www.nytimes.com/2007/04/03/science/03conv.html (10 April 2008).

Editor's Desk. "Talking to Iran." *The Christian Century,* 13 June 2006. http://www.christiancentury.org/article.lasso?id=2112 (12 December 2006).

Elshtain, Jean B. *Just War Against Terrorism.* New York: Basic Books, 2003.

Encyclopedia Britannica. *Iran: The Essential Guide to a Country on the Brink.* Hoboken, N.J.: John Wiley and Sons, Inc., 2006.

"Executive Summary—Investigation of Intelligence Activities At Abu Ghraib." *Army.mil.* http://www4.army.mil/ocpa/reports/ar15-6/AR15-6.pdf (3 September 2007).

Fay, George R. "AR 15-6 Investigation of the Abu Ghraib Detention Facility and 205th Military Intelligence Brigade." *Army.mil.* http://www4.army.mil/ocpa/reports/ar15-

6/AR15-6.pdf (10 April 2008).

Fletcher, George P. *Romantics at War: Glory and Guilt in the Age of Terrorism*. Princeton, N.J.: Princeton University Press, 2002.

Forest, James J.F. *The Making of a Terrorist: Recruitment, Training and Root Causes*, Vol. 1, *Recruitment*. Westport, Conn.: Praeger Security International, 2006.

"Former Bodyguard of Osama Bin Laden: I Love Him More Than I Love My Own Father." *MEMRITV*. 4 May 2007. http://www.memritv.org/clip/en/1462.htm (10 April 2008).

Froomkin, Dan. "Cheney's 'Dark Side' Is Showing." *WashingtonPost.com*. 7 November 2005. http://www.washingtonpost.com/wp-dyn/content/blog/2005/11/07/BL2005 110700793_pf.html (10 April 2008).

Gelston, Dan. "Temple's Chaney suspends self for game over 'goon' flap." *USATODAY*. 23 February 2005. http://www.usatoday.com/sports/college/mensbasketball/atlantic 10/2005-02-23-chaney-ban_x.htm (10 April 2008).

"General Plays Down Value Of Capturing Bin Laden." *WashingtonPost.com*. 24 February 2007. http://www.washingtonpost.com/wp-dyn/content/article/2007/02/23/AR 2007022301799_pf.html (10 April 2008).

Gerges, Fawaz A. "The Osama Bin Laden I Know." *Foreign Policy* 156 (2006): 76-78.

Ghiglieri, Michael P. *The Dark Side of Man: Tracing the Origins of Male Violence*. Reading, Mass.: Perseus Books, 1999.

Gladwell, Malcolm. *Blink: The Power of Thinking Without Thinking*. New York: Little, Brown and Company, 2005.

Glick, Peter. "Choice of Scapegoats." Pp. 244-261 in *On the Nature of Prejudice: Fifty Years after Allport*, edited by John F. Dovidio, Peter Glick, and Laurie Budman. Oxford: Blackwell Publishing Ltd., 2005.

Goldhagen, Daniel J. "The Road to Death," *The New Republic* 205, no. 19 (November 1991): 34-39.

Gonen, Jay Y. *The Roots of Nazi Psychology*. Lexington, Ky.: The University Press of Kentucky, 2000.

Gray, John. "Power and Vainglory." Pp. 47-55 in *Abu Ghraib: The Politics of Torture*, edited by Meron Benvenisti. Berkeley, Calif.: North Atlantic Books, 2004.

Grossman, Dave. *On Killing: The Psychological Cost of Learning to Kill in War and Society*. Boston: Little, Brown and Company, 1995.

Gruen, Madeleine. "Innovative Recruitment and Indoctrination Tactics by Extremists: Video Games, Hip-Hop, and the World Wide Web." Pp. 11-22 in *The Making of a Terrorist: Recruitment, Training and Root Causes*, Vol. 1, *Recruitment*, edited by James J. F. Forest. Westport, Conn: Praeger Security International, 2006.

Gunaratna, Rohan. *Inside Al Qaeda: Global Network of Terror*. New York: Columbia University Press, 2002.

Gunaratna, Rohan and Arabinda Acharya. "The Terrorist Training Camps of Al Qaeda." Pp. 172-193 in *The Making of a Terrorist: Recruitment, Training and Root Causes*, Vol. 2, *Training*, edited by James J. F. Forest. Westport, Conn.: Praeger Security International, 2006.

Hadid, Diaa. "Al-Qaida uses women as suicide attackers." *FoxNews.com*. 4 January 2008. http://www.foxnews.com/wires/2008Jan04/0,4670,IraqFemaleBombers,00.ht ml (10 April 2008).

Hersh, Seymour M. "Chain of Command: How the Department of Defense mishandled the disaster at Abu Ghraib." *New Yorker*. 17 May 2004. http://www.newyorker.

com/archive/2004/05/17/040517fa_fact2 (10 April 2008).

Hilberg, Raul. *The Destruction of The European Jews*. New York: Holmes and Meier Publishers, Inc., 1985.

Hitchens, Christopher. "Dear Mr. President . . . ," *World Affairs* 170 (2008): 9-13.

Hochschild, Adam. "What's in a Word? Torture." *New York Times*, 23 May 2004, Late Edition East Coast.

Hoffman, Bruce. *Inside Terrorism*. New York: Columbia University Press, 1998.

"Howard compares Iran to Nazi Germany." *Sydney Morning Herald*. 20 May 2006. http://www.smh.com.au/news/world/howard-compares-iran-to-nazis /2006/05/20/1147545561673.html (10 April 2008).

Hudson, Rex A. *Who Becomes a Terrorist and Why: The 1999 Government Report on Profiling Terrorists*. Guilford, Conn.: The Lyons Press, 2002.

"Iran: Alarming Increase in Executions." *HRW.org*. 27 February 2006. http://hrw.org/english/docs/2006/02/27/iran12724.htm (10 April 2008).

"Iran: Amnesty International appalled at the spiralling numbers of executions." *AmnestyUSA.org*, 5 September 2007. http://www.amnestyusa.org/document.php?lang=e&id=ENGMDE131102007 (10 April 2008).

"Iran: Human Rights Concerns." *AmnestyUSA.org*. http://www.amnestyusa.org/By_Country/Iran/page.do?id=1011172&n1=3&n2=30&n3=922 (18 January 2008).

"Iran Sanctions: Impact in Furthering U.S. Objectives Is Unclear and Should Be Reviewed." *GAO.gov*, December 2007. http://www.gao.gov/new.items/d0858.pdf (17 January 2008).

"Iran to review nuclear treaty protocol." *AlJazeera.net*. 30 September 2005. http://english.aljazeera.net/English/Archive/Archive?ArchiveID=15420 (10 April 2008).

"Iranian President Ahmadinejad asks: are Jews human beings?" *Iranian.ws*. 3 August 2006. http://www.iranian.ws/cgi-bin/iran_news/exec/view.cgi/15/17028 (10 April 2008).

"Iranians sought for Buenos Aires bomb." *BBC News*. 15 March 2007. http://news.bbc.co.uk/2/hi/americas/6454917.stm (12 July 2008).

"Isolation." *Time.com*. 22 May 1933. http://www.time.com/time/magazine/article/0,9171,745563-1,00.html (10 April 2008).

Johnson, Robert. *Death Work: A Study of the Modern Execution Process*. Belmont, Calif.: Wadsworth Publishing Company, 1998.

———. *Hard Time: Understanding and Reforming the Prison*. Belmont, Calif.: Wadsworth Publishing Company, 2002.

———. "Institutions and the Promotion of Violence." Pp. 181-204 in *Violent Transactions: The Limits of Personality*, edited by Anne Campbell and John J. Gibbs. Oxford: Basil Blackwell, 1986.

Jones, Anthony R. "AR 15-6 Investigation of the Abu Ghraib Prison and 205th Military Intelligence Brigade." *Army.mil*. http://www4.army.mil/ocpa/reports/ar15-6/AR15-6.pdf (10 April 2008).

Juhi, Bushra. "Iraqi Insurgents Claim Parliament Blast." *ABCNEWS.go.com*. 13 April 2007. http://abcnews.go.com/International/wireStory?id=3039023 (10 April 2008).

Karim, Ammar. "Sunni fighters take on Qaeda in Baghdad." *Yahoo! News*. 1 June 2007. http://news.yahoo.com/s/afp/20070601/wl_mideast_afp/iraq (14 June 2007).

Katz, Fred E. *Confronting Evil: Two Journeys*. New York: State University of New York Press, 2004.

Katzman, Kenneth. *The Warriors of Islam: Iran's Revolutionary Guard*. Boulder, Colo.:

Westview Press, 1993.

Kekes, John. *The Roots of Evil*. Ithaca, N.Y.: Cornell University, 2005.

Kenrick, Douglas T., Steven L. Neuberg, and Robert B. Cialdini. *Social Psychology: Unraveling the Mystery*. Boston: Allyn and Bacon, 1999.

"Key excerpts from the Taguba report." *MSNBC.com*. 3 May 2004. http://www.msnbc.msn.com/id/4894033 (10 April 2008).

Kruglanksi, Arie W. *The Psychology of Closed Mindedness*. New York: Psychology Press, 2004.

Kukis, Mark. "Ahmadinejad the Aggrandizer," *National Journal*. 22 April 2006.

Laqueur, Walter. *A History of Terrorism*. New Brunswick, N.J.: Transaction Publishers, 2001 (1977).

Leonnig, Carol D. "Iran Held Liable In Khobar Attack: Judge Orders $254 Million Payment." *WashingtonPost.com*. 23 December 2006. http://www.washingtonpost.com/wp-dyn/content/article/2006/12/22/AR2006122200455.html (7 July 2008).

"Living the Army Values." *GoArmy.com*. http://www.goarmy.com/life/living_the_army_values.jsp (9 July 2007).

Mann, Michael. *The Dark Side of Democracy: Explaining Ethnic Cleansing*. New York: Cambridge University Press, 2005.

———. *Fascists*. New York: Cambridge University Press, 2004.

Melman, Yossi and Meir Javedanfar. *The Nuclear Sphinx of Tehran: Mahmoud Ahmadinejad and the State of Iran*. New York: Carroll and Graf Publishers, 2007.

Meuschel, Sigrid. "The Institutional Frame: Totalitarianism, Extermination and the State." Pp. 109-124 in *The Lesser Evil: Moral Approaches to Genocide Practices*, edited by Helmut Dubiel and Gabriel Motkin. London: Routledge, 2004.

Miles, Donna. "Official Debunks Myths About Military Recruits." *MilitaryConnections.com*. 5 December 2005. http://www.militaryconnections.com/news_story.cfm?textnewsid=1767 (10 April 2008).

Milgram, Stanley. *Obedience to Authority: An Experimental View*. New York: Perennial Classics, 1974.

"Ministers of Murder: Iran's New Security Cabinet." *HRW.org*. http://hrw.org/backgrounder/mena/iran1205/2.htm#_Toc121896787 (8 January 2008).

"Mullah admits Iran regime is threat and proud of it." *Iranian.ws*. 15 December 2006. http://www.iranian.ws/iran_news/publish/article_19545.shtml (16 December 2006).

Nacos, Brigitte L. "Communication and Recruitment of Terrorists." Pp. 41-52 in *The Making of a Terrorist: Recruitment, Training and Root Causes*, Vol. 1, *Recruitment*, edited by James J. F. Forest. Westport, Conn.: Praeger Security International, 2006.

Naji, Kasra. *Ahmadinejad: The Secret History of Iran's Radical Leader*. Berkeley, Calif.: University of California Press, 2008.

"National Strategy for Combating Terrorism." *The White House*. http://www.whitehouse.gov/news/releases/2003/02/counter_terrorism/counter_terrorism_strategy.pdf (10 April 2008).

Netanyahu, Benjamin. *Fighting Terrorism: How Democracies Can Defeat Domestic and International Terrorists*. New York: Farrar Strauss Giroux, 1995.

"No clear winner in Iran poll trends." *AlJazeera.net*. 26 June 2005. http://english.aljazeera.net/English/Archive/Archive?ArchiveID=20208 (10 April 2008).

Pape, Robert A. *Dying to Win: The Strategic Logic of Suicide Terrorism*. New York: Random House, 2005.

Phares, Walid. *Future Jihad: Terrorist Strategies Against America.* New York: Palgrave Macmillan, 2005.

Post, Jerrold M. "When Hatred is Bred in the Bone: The Sociocultural Underpinnings of Terrorist Psychology." Pp. 13-33 in *The Making of a Terrorist: Recruitment, Training and Root Causes,* Vol. 2, *Training,* edited by James J. F. Forest. Westport, Conn.: Praeger Security International, 2006.

Powers, Rod. "Air Force Makes Significant Changes to Basic Training." *USMilitary.about.com.* 5 November 2005. http://usmilitary.about.com/od/airforcejoin/a/basicchanges.htm?terms=basic+training (10 April 2008).

——. "Basic Training is Smarter, Not Softer." *USMilitary.about.com.* 9 September 2006. http://usmilitary.about.com/od/armyjoin/a/basicinterview_2.htm (10 April 2008).

——. "Surviving Marine Corps Basic Training." *USMilitary.about.com.* http://usmilitary.about.com/od/marinejoin/a/marinebasic.htm (10 April 2008).

"Prison Abuse Disclosure Puts Family in Danger." *ABCNews.go.com.* 16 August 2004. http://abcnews.go.com/GMA/story?id=127650&page=1& GMA=true (12 August 2006).

"Prosecutor general considers promotion of security as gov't duty." *Islamic Republic News Agency.* 21 January 2007. http://www.irna.com/en/news/view/line-17/07 01210284165127.htm (24 January 2007).

Rabinovich, Abraham. "Weighing up the risks of a second Holocaust: Iran's bid for nuclear capability may force Israel to launch an attack." *South China Morning Post.* 17 December 2006.

Rajiva, Lila. *The Language of Empire: Abu Ghraib and the American Media.* New York: Monthly Review Press, 2005.

Rehmeyer, Julie J. "Mathematical Fortune-Telling: How well can game theory solve business and political disputes?" *Science News Online.* 27 October 2007. http://www.sciencenews.org/articles/20071027/mathtrek.asp (10 April 2008).

Riedel, Bruce. "Al Qaeda Strikes Back." *Foreign Affairs* 86 (2007): 26-31.

Rosen, Nir. "The Passion of Hussein." *Jerusalem Report.* 5 April 2004, 24.

Rosenthal, A. M. "Anniversaries of Murder." *New York Times.* 10 January 1987, Late Edition East Coast.

Savage, Charlie. "Military recruiters target schools strategically." *Boston Globe.* 29 November 2004. http://www.boston.com/news/nation/articles/2004/11/29/military_recruiters_pursue_target_schools_carefully/?page=full (25 July 2007).

Schahgaldian, Nikola B. *The Clerical Establishment in Iran.* Santa Monica, Calif.: The RAND Corporation, 1989.

Schemm, Paul. "Al-Qaida's No. 2 Defends Deadly Attacks." *FoxNews.com.* 3 April 2008. http://www.foxnews.com/wires/2008Apr03/0,4670,AskAlQaida,00.html (30 April 2008).

Schlesinger, James R. et al. "Final Report of the Independent Panel to Review Department of Defense Operations." Pp. 1-102 in *The Abu Ghraib Investigations,* edited by Steven Strasser. New York: Public Affairs LLC, 2004.

"Sean Tracey - Chicago White Sox - Player Card." *ESPN.com.* http://sports.espn.go.com/mlb/players/content?statsId=7793 (10 April 2008).

Shay, Shaul. *The Axis of Evil: Iran, Hizballah, and the Palestinian Terror.* New Brunswick, N.J.: Transaction Publishers, 2005.

Sick, Gary. "A Selective Partnership: Getting U.S.-Iranian Relations Right." *Foreign*

Affairs 85 (November/December 2006): 142-146.

Slackman, Michael. "Invoking Islam's Heritage, Iranians Chafe at 'Oppression' by the West." *New York Times*. 6 February 2006, Late Edition East Coast.

Snow, Robert L. *The Militia Threat: Terrorists Among Us*. New York: Plenum Trade, 1999.

Spencer, Robert. "Iran's Broken Moral Compass." *Human Events* 62 (6 March 2006): 15.

Stanek, Steven. "Olmert Compares Iran With Nazi Germany." *WashingtonPost.com*. 9 June 2004. http://www.washingtonpost.com/wp-dyn/content/article/2006/10/27/AR 2006102700568.html (10 April 2008).

Staub, Ervin. *The Roots of Evil: The Origins of Genocide and other Group Violence*. Cambridge: Cambridge University Press, 1989.

Stein, Ruth. "Evil as Love and as Liberation: The Mind of a Suicidal Religious Terrorist." Pp. 281-310 in *Hating in the First Person Plural*, edited by Donald Moss. New York: Other Press LLC, 2003.

Stern, Jessica. *Terror in the Name of God: Why Religious Militants Kill*. New York: Ecco, 2003.

Stolberg, Sheryl G. "Nuclear-Armed Iran Risks World War, Bush Says." *New York Times*. October 18, 2007. http://www.nytimes.com/2007/10/18/washington/18prexy.html (10 April 2008).

Strauss, David L. "Breakdown in the Gray Room: Recent Turns in the Image War." Pp. 87-101 in *Abu Ghraib: The Politics of Torture*, edited by Meron Benvenisti. Berkeley, Calif: North Atlantic Books, 2004.

Taguba, Antonio M. "Article 15-6 Investigation of the 800th Military Police Brigade." *NPR.org*. http://www.npr.org/iraq/2004/prison_abuse_report.pdf (3 September 20 07).

Taheri, Amir. "Who Are Iran's Revolutionary Guards?" *The Wall Street Journal*, November 15, 2007, Eastern Edition.

"Taliban Military Commander Mullah Dadallah: Bin Laden Planned the Baghram Base Attack on American VP Cheney." *MEMRITV*. 30 April 2007 http://www.memritv.org/clip/en/1437.htm (10 April 2008).

"The Attack Looms." *National Commision on Terrorist Attacks Upon the United States*. 26 August 2004. http://www.9-11commission.gov/report/911Report_Ch7.htm (1 July 2008).

"The Gonzales memos." *BBC News*. 6 January 2005. http://news.bbc.co.uk/2/hi/amer icas/4153479.stm (10 April 2008).

Theweleit, Klaus. *Male Fantasies*, Vol. 2, *Male Bodies: Psychoanalyzing the White Terror*. Minneapolis, Minn.: University of Minnesota Press, 1989.

Tierney, John. "Hot Seat Grows Lukewarm Under Capital's Fog of War." *The New York Times*. 20 May 2004, Late Edition East Coast.

Timmerman, Kenneth R. *Preachers of Hate: Islam and the War on America*. New York: Crown Forum, 2003.

Todorov, Tzvetan. "The Uses and Abuses of Comparison." Pp. 25-34 in *The Lesser Evil: Moral Approaches to Genocide Practices*, eds. Helmut Dubiel and Gabriel Motkin. London: Routledge, 2004.

"Top Lebanese Sunni Cleric Fathi Yakan: Bin Laden a Man After My Own Heart; I Am Not Sad Because of 9/11 and I Have Never Condemned this Attack." *MEMRITV*. 16 March 2007. http://www.memritv.org/clip/en/1408.htm (10 April 2008).

Trevelyan, Mark. "Talking to al Qaeda? Don't rule it out, some say." *Reuters.com*. 13

September 2007. http://www.reuters.com/article/newsOne/idUSL1183375220070 913?sp=true (30 April 2008).

Twain, Mark. *The Mysterious Stranger and Other Stories.* New York: Penguin Books USA Inc., 1980.

Victor, George. *Hitler: The Pathology of Evil.* Washington: Brassey's, Inc., 1998.

Waller, James. *Becoming Evil: How Ordinary People Commit Genocide and Mass Killing.* New York: Oxford University Press, 2002.

Weiner, Tim. "Killing machines prepare to do warfare's dirty work." *Sydney Morning Herald.* 19 February 2005. http://www.smh.com.au/news/Science/Killing-machines-prepare-to-do-warfares-dirty-work/2005/02/18/ 1108709439213.html (10 April 2008).

Weisberg, Jacob. "Thanks for the Sanctions: Why do we keep using a policy that helps dictators?" *Slate Magazine.* 26 July 2006. http://www.slate.com/id/2147058/ (10 April 2008).

Whitlock, Craig. "Al-Qaeda's Growing Online Offensive." *WashingtonPost.com.* 24 June 2008, http://www.washingtonpost.com/wp-dyn/content/article/2008/06/23/AR2008 062302135.html (7 August 2008).

Whitney, Craig R. "Introduction." Pp. vii-xxiv in *The Abu Ghraib Investigations,* edited by Steven Strasser. New York: Public Affairs LLC, 2004.Williams, Paul L. *Al Qaeda: Brotherhood of Terror.* Upper Saddle River, N.J.: Alpha Books and Pearson Education, Inc., 2002.

Woodward, Bob. *Bush at War.* New York: Simon & Schuster, 2002.

Wrangham, Richard and Dale Peterson. *Demonic Males: Apes and the Origins of Human Violence.* New York: Houghton Mifflin Company, 1996.

Zakaria, Fareed. "Pssst . . . Nobody Loves a Torturer; Ask any American soldier in Iraq when the general population really turned against the United States and he will say, 'Abu Ghraib.'" *Newsweek,* November 14, 2005. http://www.newsweek.com/id/ 51176 , (10 April 2008)

Zimbardo, Philip. *The Lucifer Effect: Understanding How Good People Turn Evil.* New York: Random House, 2007.

Zimbardo, Philip, Christina Maslach and Craig Haney. "Reflections on the Stanford Prison Experiment: Genesis, Transformations, Consequences." Pp. 193-237 in *Obedience to Authority: Current Perspectives on the Milgram Paradigm,* edited by Thomas Blass. Mahwah, N.J.: Lawrence Erlbaum Associates, Inc., 2000.

Index

Abu Ghraib, and authorization, 119-23; and bureaucracy, 123-27; and Bush, 113, 119-20, 123, 125, 145; and Cheney, 72, 120, 125; compared to other cases, 139-53, 155; and dehumanization, 130-32; general overview of, 9, 12, 113, 132; and Geneva Conventions, 116, 120-21; and isolation, 127-30; and recruitment, 114-16; and Rumsfeld, 120-21, 125, 128, 130; solutions to, 156-57; and training, 116-19

Afghanistan, and Al Qaeda, 68-69, 72, 75, 141; and Iran, 89; and the U.S., 106, 131, 158

Ahmadinejad, President Mahmoud, 8, 91, 96-97, 99, 100, 103, 105, 162-163

Allah, and Al Qaeda, 66, 70-73, 80, 158-59; and Iran, 93-97

Al Qaeda, and alleged coordination with Iran, 89-90; and authorization, 71-73; and bin Laden, 66-74, 76-77, 80, 153, 158-61; and bureaucracy, 74-76; compared to other cases, 139-53, 155; countermeasures against, 157-62; and dehumanization, 79-80; general overview of, 3, 8, 11, 65-66, 81, 107; and isolation, 76-79; and re-cruitment, 66-68; and training, 68-71; and al-Zawahiri, 69, 158-59, 161

The Al Qaeda Training Manual, 11, 69, 74, 78-79

Amnesty International, 88

animal abuse, 54, 70, 105, 143

anonymity 27, 43, 56, 98, 125, 129, 131

Argentina 6, 102, 117

Armenia 6

Ashura, 97, 100. *See also* Muharram rituals

assassination, 160; attempts against Bin Laden, 72, 158-59; Iranian use of 88, 90, 92, 99, 101, 103

Atta, Mohammed, 75, 81

Auschwitz concentration camp, 2

authorization, 3-4, 168; and Abu Ghraib, 119-23; and Al Qaeda, 71-73; and Iran, 95-98; and Milgram experiment, 32-33; and Nazi Germany, 54-56; and Stanford Prison Experiment, 39-41; strategy of, 20-22. *See also* countermeasures

Azzam, Abdullah, 160

basic training, 114-19

Basij, 11, 87-107, 167

Bin Laden, Osama, 66-74, 76-77, 80, 153, 158-61

About the Author

Adam Lankford is an Assistant Professor of Criminal Justice at the University of Alabama. He has also taught at Marymount University and the Corcoran College in Washington, D.C. From 2003 to 2008, he helped coordinate Senior Executive Anti-Terrorism Forums for high-ranking foreign military and security personnel in conjunction with the U.S. State Department's Anti-Terrorism Assistance program. He has studied a range of topics related to aggression, violence, counterterrorism and international security. He received his Ph.D. and M.S. in Justice, Law and Society from American University and his B.A. in English from Haverford College.

CPSIA information can be obtained at www.ICGtesting.com
Printed in the USA
LVOW041009221211

260673LV00001B/1/P